Sentimental
Confessions

Sentimental Confessions

SPIRITUAL NARRATIVES

OF NINETEENTH-CENTURY

AFRICAN AMERICAN WOMEN

Joycelyn Moody

THE UNIVERSITY OF GEORGIA PRESS

ATHENS AND LONDON

© 2001 by the University of Georgia Press
Athens, Georgia 30602
All rights reserved
Designed by Betty Palmer McDaniel
Set in 10 / 13 Caslon by G&S Typesetters
Printed and bound by Thomson-Shore, Inc.
The paper in this book meets the guidelines for
permanence and durability of the Committee on
Production Guidelines for Book Longevity of the
Council on Library Resources.

Printed in the United States of America
05   04   03   02   01   C   5   4   3   2   1

Library of Congress Cataloging-in-Publication Data
Moody, Joycelyn, 1957–
Sentimental confessions : spiritual narratives of nineteenth-
century African American women / Joycelyn Moody.
p.   cm.
Includes bibliographical references (p.) and index.
ISBN 0-8203-2236-9 (alk. paper)
1. Afro-American women authors—Religious life.
2. Afro-American women authors—Biography—History
and criticism.   3. Christian biography—United States—
History and criticism.   4. American literature—
19th century—History and criticism.   5. Sentimentalism in
literature.   6. Evangelicalism—United States—History—
19th century.   7. Nationalism—United States—History—
19th century.   I. Title.
BR 1690 .M59   2000
277.3′081′082—dc21   00-029925

British Library Cataloging-in-Publication Data available

For Patrick

CONTENTS

PREFACE

I felt at times that I must exercise in the ministry, but when I rose
upon my feet I felt ash[a]med, and so I went under a cloud for some
time, and endeavoured to keep silence;
but I could not quench the Spirit.

Memoir of Old Elizabeth, 1863

It is not enough simply to uncover the hidden facts, the obscure
names of black foremothers. [What we need is] the development of
an array of analytical frameworks that allow us to understand why
black women of all classes behave in certain ways,
and how they acquired agency.

DARLENE CLARK HINE, *Hine Sight*, 1994

In 1988 Oxford University Press published the thirty-volume Schomburg Library of Nineteenth-Century Black Women Writers. When I read the *Memoir of Old Elizabeth*, one of the library's volumes, my life changed and has not been the same since. Long an ardent reader of African American autobiography, I have often been completely dazzled by the religious and rhetorical power of Elizabeth's and other black women's spiritual autobiographies in the Schomburg series, so much so that I have often wanted to expose virtually everyone I encounter to these forgotten narratives. This book thus extends my mission: I hope it will propel early black holy women's stories into literary studies and, through them, recover a neglected chapter of American literary history and thereby reshape our understanding of nineteenth-century U.S. literature.

Christianity was abused during the slave trade by whites to control and dominate captured Africans. Albert Raboteau, a prominent scholar of black religion, has written that Europeans "claimed that the conversion of slaves to Christianity justified the enslavement of Africans" ("African Americans" 2). That is,

Europeans perverted both Christianity's concepts of charity and the Protestant teaching that Christians have a duty to convert the unsaved into rationales for exploiting blacks for labor. But the proponents of slavery did not count on Africans in turn using Christianity to interpret the bondage in which they found themselves. As religion historian Charles Long once said, "If we Black folk in America are Christians, then we're certainly unlike any other Christians I've met around here" (qtd. in Harding viii). In other words, blacks used "the language, symbols, and worldview of the Christian holy book" (Raboteau, "African Americans" 1) and its lessons to condemn false piety, particularly as it was used as a pretext for oppression, as well as to liberate themselves from such un-Christian and disempowering institutions as slavery.

Early black holy women autobiographers document their refusal to be silenced or to be silent. From describing their sacred visions of the resurrected Christ to detailing their secular protests against white supremacy, nineteenth-century African American women's life writing claims the right to reconstruct personal and national history from an unorthodox vantage point. Not even illiteracy could keep "certain" women—women both confident and conspicuous—from expressing the conviction that their lives were inherently important.[1] This book analyzes the autobiographies of six women: Maria Stewart, Jarena Lee, Zilpha Elaw, Nancy Prince, Mattie J. Jackson, and Julia Foote. It explores these authors' uses of Christian evangelicalism, literary sentimentalism, and African American nationalism for the articulation of their experiences as black holy women. Their appropriation of sanctioned popular literary designs demonstrates both their insights into diverse forms of oppression and their passionate determination to uncover the patriarchal posts that braced and abetted those oppressions.

While literacy itself, like the access to means by which narratives could and would be published, signifies a certain class distinction and social prominence above others less empowered, the women I focus upon in this book represent the lowest economic class in their society. They were poor. *None* of the women had any money; indeed, each makes it plain that a primary impetus for publishing her autobiography—perhaps the strongest motivation after religious proselytizing itself, except arguably in the case of Jackson—was to earn money for survival. Also, again with the exception of Jackson, they overtly state that they lived fundamentally on the charity and benevolence of others, even when they found it demeaning to do so. In addition, they survived by gathering contributions from worshippers, congregants, or philanthropists, by hiring themselves out as domestic servants, by indenturing their labor, and, in the case of the enslaved but righteous Jackson, by stealing from their enslavers.

Addressing the question of class distinctions in African American churches, Frances Smith Foster and Claudia May report that "African American writers have . . . noted connections between class formation and the nuances of Christianity." Foster and May observe that distinctions "between the churched and the unchurched mirrored class categories that were prevalent" elsewhere (155). Thus, blacks' participation in organized religion was as much about class mobility as the quest for literacy indisputably was. However, Stewart, Lee, Elaw, Prince, Jackson, and Foote, though aspiring to a quality of life greater than that they possessed at the time of their writing, do not advocate the acquisition of material wealth. As they critique the social and political forces that created and sustained their poverty, each also endorses an apostolic lifestyle that rejects worldly possessions, particularly as they would inhibit or compromise spiritual riches. Thus, in only one chapter of this book do I examine class issues as a primary category of scholarly analysis. In all chapters, of course, I focus upon class as an operative and significant factor in the lives of these women, and I have tried to attend to its relevance without losing focus on those issues the narratives themselves declare more prominent and pertinent.

In addition, *Sentimental Confessions* argues for an appreciation of the holy women's narratives *because*—not *although*—they are holy texts. Many scholars and archivists have effectively demonstrated that the Christianized autobiographies of early Africans and African Americans fulfilled a variety of political strategies. That valuable scholarship need not compel us to discount or disdain the import of the Christian discourse. I have written *Sentimental Confessions* because I am pained by the anti-spiritual context in which early black holy women's writings are generally read, when they are read at all. I am bothered by contemporary (feminist) scholars' compulsion to apologize for the Christian discourse in the autobiographies I examine. I am also disturbed by the sometimes implicit, sometimes explicit condemnation of black holy women's spiritual and religious discourse, as if this discourse were shameful. I believe that to overlook, to "read around" the spiritual dimensions present in these books is to neglect an essential and vital aspect of them. Readers can learn something from believers even without becoming converted if we so choose, and faith in the mystical need not be seen as an indication of imbecility. Many theorists have cogently shown that such thinking and such fears are white, western, and male in the worst senses of those terms. It is thinking of this sort that perpetuates the myth that black women cannot meaningfully contribute to American society. Any person who values literature should read spiritual texts *as* spiritual texts because we should not disparage or diminish the full complexity of any text. It is that simple.

This book recovers the voices of six women who knew that as poor black holy women they offered a unique perspective not only on their own lives, but on the state of the nation between 1835 and 1886 as well. My book transforms the ways we read issues of self-representation, national identity, and intercultural connections in nineteenth-century American literature. By focusing upon the earliest known book-length texts by African American women in chapters 1 and 2, I document early African American women's lamentation and exultation of their call by God in order to prick the nation's conscience.

Chapter 1 examines *Productions of Mrs. Maria W. Stewart* (1835) and chapter 2 focuses on the *Religious Experience and Journal of Mrs. Jarena Lee* (1836, 1849) and the *Memoirs of the Life, Religious Experience, Ministerial Travels, and Labours of Mrs. Zilpha Elaw* (1846) to show how Maria Stewart, Jarena Lee, and Zilpha Elaw, three northern black women, used the interlocking discourses of the American Revolution and the Second Great Awakening, along with the concept of *sympathy*, to argue for both the abolition of slavery and the autonomy of free black women. In addition, I illustrate how they inscribed the complex corporeality of the black woman's body to counter rampant stereotypes about black women's physicality. I concentrate on the luminous charisma and rhetorical power of these women who refused to be silent even when threatened with excommunication from their respective societies. Despite their religious ostracism from those who feared these women, their autobiographies constitute love tracts that espouse sacred doctrine to teach revolutionary redemption.

Chapter 3, a chronologically pivotal chapter, analyzes *A Narrative of the Life and Travels of Mrs. Nancy Prince* (1850–1860) as a spiritual autobiography that disdains sentimentalism. While each of the narratives examined in this book both deploys and derides sentimentalism, thus underscoring its limitations while coopting its efficacy, Prince's is the most dismissive of sentimental conventions. Her first edition, published coterminously with serialized installments of Harriet Beecher Stowe's *Uncle Tom's Cabin*, rejects rhetorical strategies that compel the representation of black inferiority. Prince seems especially determined to distinguish her *Narrative* from *Uncle Tom's Cabin*'s pathetic and bathetic depiction of African American women. Although Prince, a Baptist missionary, self-righteously asserts her distinction from other Americans from different religious, gender, ethnic, or class backgrounds, her double consciousness simultaneously draws her into the dominant culture. Her autobiography is the only one of those I address that does not attend to the black female body, except, significantly, as it is portrayed as under threat by nature, such as when the narrator travels on foot in the New England winter or sails through a tempest in the Atlantic Ocean. Her failure to inscribe the body, I suggest, is related to her class-consciousness, although she is as poor as, if not poorer than, the other women writers examined in this work. Furthermore, I briefly contrast Nancy Prince's *Narrative* with Mary Prince's *The History of Mary Prince, a West Indian Slave* to show that Nancy Prince's accounts of her journeys into the West Indies underscore the colonized/colonizer conflict readily apparent in her autobiography.

Autobiography scholars generally dismiss the *dictated* narratives of slave women like Mary Prince as extraneous or fraudulent. Influenced by Beverley's commentary on the *testimonio*, I analyze the discursive relationship between an amanuensis (or "editor") and a preliterate speaking subject in chapter 4 to disprove the critical assumption that conventional literacy is essential for rhetorical lucidity. Concentrating on the multivalent *Story of Mattie J. Jackson*, "Written and Arranged" by Dr. L. S. Thompson (1866), I read it first alongside Frederick Douglass's 1845 *Narrative* then contextualize it with other dictated slave narratives published during the Civil War or during the postbellum period. Jackson's is the only narrative that I have encountered in which the amanuensis overtly identifies herself as another black woman. While I generally attend to African American women autobiographers' appropriation of rhetorical strategies used by nineteenth-century European American women writers in illustrating the importance of Christianized domesticity to social reform, this chapter specifically addresses preliterate black women's reclamation of voice and textual authority to narrate their sacred and secular experiences.

In chapter 5, I assess Julia A. J. Foote's deployment of the figures of the holy child and the woman preacher for the promulgation of a sacred agenda in *A Brand Plucked from the Fire* (1879, 1886). Foote, the daughter of a former slave concubine, challenges readers' essentialist and stereotypical beliefs about African American women while at the same time she represents her own mother as alternately saved and depraved. Her postbellum spiritual narrative asserts a holiness theology to revise conventions of evangelicalism and sentimentalism and to explore issues that arise where blackness, femininity, and Christianity intersect.

Finally, in the conclusion I discuss the stereotype of the "good black church woman" and its impact on African American feminist scholars, particularly womanist theo-ethicists and literary historians who are themselves African American. In our contemporary sentimental critical judgment, we make no "sentimental confessions" about our fear of the prototype of the black church woman: we frequently (mis)read African American women's Christian zeal as sexual ecstasy. Or rather, we misread it as sexual *excess*—that is, as the lack of self-control and decorum that the academy conventionally, albeit inequitably, demands of its citizens. I briefly observe African and European influences in the literary tradition of religious ecstasy then discuss the representation of eroticized sacred possession in selections from the religious oral testimonies of former slaves in *God Struck Me Dead*. I close with an exploration of contemporary African American feminist scholars' ill-advised anxiety about an "excessive" display of emotion and religious enthusiasm and their unwarranted worry about the earnest piety of the six early black holy women whose lives are studied and celebrated throughout this book. With *Sentimental Confessions*, I mean to add a chapter to American literary history. In considering the authors I have chosen to focus upon, our understanding of the rich, complicated, and understudied relationships among literature, piety, and nationalism that were in play as the United States struggled to assume its place among the world's powers will be enriched.

ACKNOWLEDGMENTS

Chapter 3 was first published as "'But when they go into the West Indies, they forget God'" in *Women-Church: An Australian Journal of Feminist Studies in Religion* and in *Religion, Geography, Postcoloniality: Mapping Sacred Space across International Literatures* (ed. Jamie S. Scott, Rodopi BV, 2000).

My debts to those who have supported me in the process of preparing this manuscript are all outstanding. I cannot hope to identify and thank here all the persons who made this work possible, but there are some I can and do gratefully acknowledge. My deep thanks go to William L. Andrews for more than ten years of encouraging mentorship and faithful friendship. I am also unspeakably grateful to the three professional readers who regarded the finished manuscript with such care and enthusiasm; I cannot imagine having received three more conscientious or invaluable reports than those I received from Elizabeth Ammons, Sharon M. Harris, and Carla Peterson.

For their assistance with the three chapters here that developed from my dissertation research, I thank the members of my doctoral committee at the University of Kansas: Bill Andrews, Elizabeth Schultz, Janet Sharistanian, Arthur Drayton, and the much-missed Thomas O'Donnell.

I spent an unforgettable year (1996–97) at the Harvard University School of Divinity in the Women's Studies in Religion Program as a Research Fellow and Visiting Scholar. I will always be grateful for the generous and jovial support of Constance Buchanan, then the program's director, as well as that of the scholars whose critical attention to selected chapters sharpened my focus and thinking: Lindsey Harlan, Joan Taylor, and most especially Cynthia Scheinberg and Bonna Haberman. For also reading parts of the manuscript and offering indispensable advice, I thank my dear friend Barbara Neely and my sister-feminists at UW: Shelly Eversley, Priscilla Wald, and Shirley Yee.

Several institutions generously provided resources that made it possible for me to complete this project. The Departments of English at the University of Washington (since 1991) and at the Pennsylvania State University–University Park (summer 1996) have supported my research. A summer 1998 fellowship from the Institute for Ethnic Studies in the United States (uw) assisted me in the last stretch.

My graduate and undergraduate students at Penn State, Harvard's Div School, and especially uw have contributed to my work in countless ways.

I am grateful for excellent copyediting by Marlene Allen and thorough indexing by Andrea S. Harris.

On a more personal note, I humbly acknowledge the expert services and tender affection of D. Merilee Clunis, Sarah Halsey, and Pat Rathbone: thank you, good women. I wish that Mrs. Virginia Smith of Mobile, Alabama, had lived to catalog this book at the Toulminville Branch. I have too many generous, reassuring friends to name, but I lovingly single out Lorraine Martínez, my steady companion (and a dazzling computer wizard) especially during the last few weeks of work on this book. As always, my parents, George A. and Catherine E. Moody, and my brothers, Michael, Byron, and Clell, believed in me, and my sister, Traci, faithfully rallied me through to the end. I could not have completed this endeavor without Liz, Mike, or Shileen, whose profound respect for the project served as a constant source of inspiration: my vision of you reading it made all the difference. This study, finer moments and greater flaws, is dedicated to Patrick, beloved son.

Sympathy and Revolution

What did it avail her, that the walls of her lord were hung with splendor, and the dust trodden under foot in her native country, crouded [*sic*] his gates with sordid worshippers! The laws rendered her incapable of receiving property: and though she was a free moral agent, accountable for her own actions, yet never had she a moment at her own disposal! Fifty years her faithful hands have been compelled to ignoble servitude for the benefit of an Issac Royall, until, as if nations must be agitated, and the world convulsed, for the preservation of that freedom, which the Almighty Father intended for all the human race, the present war commenced.

BELINDA, "Petition of an African Slave, to the Legislature of Massachusetts," 1783

So exclaims a petition filed on February 14, 1783, in which an elderly African woman named Belinda appealed to the state legislature of Massachusetts for remuneration from the estate of slave master Colonel Issac Royall for involuntary yet "honest industry" she performed near Boston.[1] Although Belinda's brief legal document is a conventional official petition, not a traditional personal narrative, it serves as a crucial point of departure for this study of nineteenth-century African American women's spiritual autobiography. The petition is constructed as a biography; that is, the text narrates a brief linear account of the life of its subject, a person other than the author. In the American biographical tradition of Cotton Mather, creator of the encyclopedic *Magnalia Christi Americana: or, The Ecclesiastical History of New England* (1702), the petition implies the sacred worthiness—or "accountability"—of its subject. Alternatively, Belinda's petition may be read as a *dictated autobiography*, although it is constructed using the third person singular pronoun, because it encapsulates Belinda's life presumably as it was told to the transcriber of the text.[2] As such, Belinda's petition is a precursor of the six autobiographies that are studied in this book. While none of the six narratives is a formal legal document like Belinda's, each similarly petitions its hegemonic readership (of which the 1783 Massachusetts state legislature is a microcosmic analogue) to regard its poor, black, and formerly enslaved female subject as both "a free moral agent, accountable for her own actions" and as one due "that freedom, which the Almighty Father intended for all the human race."[3] Having made these specific assertions, the narratives further exhort their hegemonic readers to revise and to ameliorate the critical social condition of all African American women on the bases of the moral agency and divine intention defined in Belinda's supplication.

Belinda's petition also serves as a powerful predecessor to the nineteenth-century texts studied in this volume because it uses the same type of sentimentalism that is found in later African American women's writings. Belinda's interlocutor not only seeks to appeal to the legislators' reason and acumen to secure both autonomy and subsidy for the slave woman, but he or she also attempts to arouse the legislators' sympathy by delineating Belinda's experience from a perspective that emphasizes its pathos. Such a strategy is by definition sentimental. Furthermore, through the rhetoric of sentimentalism, the petitioner intimates that Belinda's situation is one that legislators should find intolerable and unethical—that is, one they would be unwilling to endure themselves; indeed, they had shown themselves unwilling to tolerate, among other things, the deprivation of their political freedom when they initiated "the present war" Belinda's petition refers to, that is, the Revolutionary War. Thus, the petition represents Belinda's predicament as grievous, unjust, and immoral—in short, as a challenge to the legislature's self-characterization as a body of nobility, sovereignty, and power great enough to recognize and to reform injustice.

Belinda and Eighteenth-Century African American Autobiography

The earliest known African American autobiography, the *Narrative of the Uncommon Sufferings and Surprizing Deliverance of Briton Hammon, a Negro Man,* was published in Boston in 1760. This "testimony of defilement," to borrow a phrase from Henry Louis Gates Jr., has spawned and shaped thousands of personal narratives, both dictated and self-authored, composed by blacks in America, such as slave autobiographies, spiritual and conversion narratives, picaresque travelogues, military memoirs, and various other life-writing subgenres. For many diverse reasons autobiography has consistently been the genre most often selected by African Americans for the creative expression of their life experiences and literary instincts; as William Andrews has written, "auto-biography has been recognized and celebrated since its inception as a powerful means of addressing and altering sociopolitical as well as cultural realities in the United States" (*African American Autobiography* 1). While black autobiography prevailed as a genre, several early black poets also overcame stupefying odds to see their verses published in the late eighteenth and early nineteenth centuries.[4] The first instances of African American fiction, however, did not appear until 1853—perhaps because of both the great capacity of the personal narrative to write the black person into being and because of blacks' hesitation to seem to validate the racist myth that they were inherently incapable of telling the truth.[5] Hammon's autobiography begins with a double-voiced disclaimer about his in-telligence and with an assertion that he will relate not falsehoods but "facts" about his life: "As my Capacities and Condition of Life are very low, it cannot be expected that I should make those Remarks on the Sufferings I have met with, or the kind Providence of a good GOD for my Preservation, as one in a higher Station; but shall leave that to the Reader as he goes along, and so I shall only relate Matters of Fact as they occur to my Mind—" (3). Although dis-claiming one's "Capacities and Conditions" was a common eighteenth-century literary convention, deployed to assert an author's modesty, Hammon's partic-ular disclaimer signifies (on) the constraints that slavery placed on his intellec-tual development and his class status.

Hammon's autobiography further illustrates that from the beginning African American autobiography engaged the religious and righteous rhetoric of its day. For although the majority of the fourteen pages of his narrative recount secular rather than sacred experiences, the tract ends with an extended state-ment of the former slave's "grateful Remembrance" of "Divine Goodness," just as it begins with a pledge to remark "the kind Providence of a good GOD." Not an evangelist, Hammon was simply a self-conscious adherent to the rhetorical modes of his day. While I claim Hammon's *Narrative* as a founding text in African American literary history, Vincent Carretta reads it as distinctly *Afro-British* and stresses in *Unchained Voices* that Hammon was one of several British blacks whose deployment of Christian rhetoric had more to do with freedom than with piety. Carretta argues, "Virtually all the [eighteenth-century] Afro-British publications in prose took the form of the spiritual autobiographies that trace the transition from pagan beliefs to the Christianity shared with the au-thors' [white] British readers. In each case, men and women escape from some type of physical captivity. . . . Even Green's *Life and Confession [of JOHNSON GREEN, Who is to Be Executed this Day* . . .] (Worcester, 1786), sensationalist though it is as a cautionary tale, is a spiritual autobiography" (9). In other words, the early prison confession, a subgenre that is perhaps intrinsically sentimental, also took the form of a Christian conversion narrative.

As a forefather of the black autobiographical paradigm, Hammon of necessity drew on the values of freedom and emancipation so central to the war between England and its New World colonies—and the Protestantism pervading both. For that Protestantism supported the emancipation of slaves.[6] It inspired so fervent a movement among blacks that "by 1706 the British colonies of the Carolinas, New Jersey, and New York all had declared conversion and baptism irrelevant to a slave's status" (Carretta 8). The implementation of these statutes implies that African Americans had used Christianity to argue and to agitate for their civil rights. The period after the Revolutionary War is, Carretta states, "known as the 'first emancipation'" (7), as indicated by texts like Belinda's petition and Benjamin Banneker's 1791 letter to Thomas Jefferson in which he asked the author of the Declaration of Independence to "acknowledge that it is the indispensable duty of those who maintain for themselves the rights of human nature, and who possess the obligations of Christianity, to extend their power and influence to the relief of every part of the human race from whatever burden or oppression they may unjustly labor under" (Carretta 319–20). The Christian discourse we read in the former slave's narrative, then, represents a cultural linguistics—indeed, a national aesthetics—more than a personal predisposition. As Sondra O'Neale has cogently argued about early American applications of Protestantism, "Ostensibly Christian and para-Christian institutions were not only the prime forces with which the white world defined the slave and exonerated slaveholding; white society's perspective of Christianity's logic and symbolism were the dominant informants of the semantic culture" (3).

That Christianity determined the discourse of early African American literature is further illustrated by the second instance of African American autobiography (and what we currently know to be the fifth "book" published by a black person in a western language), *A Narrative of the Most Remarkable Particulars in the Life of James Albert Ukasaw Gronniosaw, an African Prince, Written by Himself;* one of the earliest editions of the narrative was published in 1774 in Newport, Rhode Island. Gronniosaw worked first as a slave, then as a freedman on the estate of the Dutch Reformed minister Theodorus Jacobus Frelinghuysen (named in the autobiography as "Mr. Freelandhouse"); he gained literacy in Dutch by reading in translation such representative Puritan authors as John Bunyan, John Foxe, and Richard Baxter, whose works were provided to him by the Frelinghuysens.[7] These theologians would directly influence the black man's own literary endeavor. Indeed, Gronniosaw implies that he was motivated to write his story in part by the absence of blackness he noted in these narratives. He reconstructs his experience as an illiterate young slave confronted with a "silent" religious text (probably the Bible or a Protestant prayer book) that will not "speak" to him. As Gates has argued, the ex-slave elder resolved to compel the text to speak to him by writing a text of his own that would insinuate—"speak"—his blackness into the western literary tradition (135–36). The result is Gronniosaw's autobiography. In other words, the second known African American autobiography is modeled on the Puritan pilgrim narratives that occasioned his literacy; Gronniosaw structures his *Most Remarkable Particulars* using the same essential formula of sin, conversion, and renewal as he had read in, for instance, Bunyan's *Grace Abounding to the Chief of Sinners*. Given this fact, it stands to reason that Africans and African Americans who knew Gronniosaw's narrative and who were equally desirous of asserting the black self would follow the structural pattern of the earlier slave narrator.[8] Thus, the incipient black narrative tradition came to be characterized as much by Protestantism as by racial protest. Moreover, Gronniosaw clearly sought not only to emulate the literary form used by his Puritan predecessors but also to demonstrate that, though he was black (which for European exegetes connoted evil or, alternatively, vacuity), he too could develop a personal relationship with God. Gronniosaw's deployment of the conventions of the spiritual autobiography affirms his sagacity and humanity as well as his piety; his literary descendants perceived the advantage and followed suit.

Belinda's petition, submitted twelve years after the American publication of Gronniosaw's autobiography, likewise appropriates the Christian discourse of late-eighteenth-century America. Furthermore, the petition can be read as a spiritual narrative in that it summarizes Belinda's life from a halcyon prepubescence in northwest Africa, to her capture during religious worship, to a bewildering and crushing enslavement in the "New World." Representing its subject as a prayerful mourner, Belinda's narrative evinces the dual aspects of one particular spiritual autobiographical form, the confession. The spiritual confession is comprised of both the private speech act that is offered as evidence of the narrator's repentance from sin in the hope of sacred absolution and the public act that is submitted to the reader as evidence of the subject's contrition for his or her civil transgressions in the hope of social clemency. While Belinda's petition is neither a religious nor a legal confession, her text, which was probably dictated rather than self-authored, is virtually indistinguishable from a related autobiographical form, the *testimonio*. John Beverley characterizes the transcribed *testimonio* as concentrating on the intention more of the narrator than of the recorder, and thus it includes "an urgency to communicate, a problem of repression, poverty, subalternity, imprisonment, struggle for survival, implicated in the act of narration itself" (94). Unquestionably, Belinda's petition exhibits the *testimonio*'s exigency: as a poor black slave woman who at one time practiced a foreign, African religion, Belinda is forced by her class, race, caste, gender, and creed in post-Revolutionary America to adjure the state as if she were penitent or criminal. This same position was forced upon Belinda's literary descendants, among them the African American women whose spiritual autobiographies are examined in this work. Beverley notes that the *testimonio*'s urgency specifically results from a situation involving a speaker and her interlocutor; such is the case of both *The History of Mary Prince* (which I examine in chapter 4) and *The Story of Mattie J. Jackson* (discussed in chapter 5). Although not all of the six texts I study were dictated narratives or conventional confessions, the social and political status of all six authors required them to defend themselves as narrative agents even as they asserted their authorization by God to represent the divine. Consequently, each tacitly expresses an urgency that seems born of worry about the contract between texts and readers and between readers and authors. If all such contracts imply a set of power relations, the relations between these authors and their readers are not necessarily balanced. The tension permeating these autobiographies often emerges from the authors' suspicions about these imbalanced relationships and assumption of just such inequitable power relations. The "act of writing the black female self in the West," Nellie McKay has declared, "is the most political act of all" (94). The resistance to their humanity and subjectivity that nineteenth-century African American holy women confronted and documented validates this claim.

As I stated earlier, Belinda's suit for reparation takes the form of an autobiography, a reconstruction of her life begun on the paradisical "banks of the Rio de Valta" (Belinda 253), and thus illustrates and institutes the tradition of African American women's autobiography. Prior to Belinda, men like Hammon, Gronniosaw, and other Africans in the diaspora had realized the potential of the personal narrative to establish the black individual as an autonomous, rational self. They recognized the potential impact that life writing could have on their futures in the diaspora, for the genre required—or better, permitted—the negotiation of both black and white voices. Men and women of African descent shifted from oral traditions to western literary traditions and conventions, thus activating the written text to speak to and through them as literary subjects.[9] Indeed, because autobiography is, by definition, the assertion of an individual identity, it has always been an ideal means by which African Americans express their humanity. Moreover, early blacks wrote autobiographies "to engage in the search for political and psychological freedom for all black people," as Nellie McKay further demonstrates when she asserts that "the personal narrative became a historical site on which aesthetics, self-confirmation of humanity, citizenship, and the significance of racial politics shaped African-American literary expression" (74). Though it is a third-person narrative, Belinda's petition serves as an important precursor for African American women's self-representation.

Belinda's petition was filed in an era during which many blacks used the fledgling legal system to establish their collective right to the privileges of American citizenship. In doing so, they simultaneously forced whites to recognize their humanity, their various contributions to colonial society, and their capacity and desire for further social development. Sidney Kaplan and Emma N. Kaplan cite no fewer than five collective petitions made across New England between 1773 and 1774 alone, each in the spirit of Crispus Attucks's fiery slogan "Liberty or Death!" (11). Some of these other legal endeavors were led by groups of Revolutionary War patriots, who, having served and defended the colonies, now demanded privileges within the new nation.[10] In other words, petitions for manumission and/or civil rights were being filed by slaves and also by free blacks, the population of which was rising, especially in the North, where some towns implemented plans for the emancipation of slaves before 1800. Such appeals for human rights were one more rhetorical form in which African Americans claimed and asserted black selfhood.

Belinda and Eighteenth-Century American Sentimentalism

In a review of Claudia Tate's *Domestic Allegories of Political Desire*, I posed these questions: "Do sentimental, or domestic [texts], . . . form an unwarranted self-indulgence and distraction from the struggle for racial equality and political equity when constructed by nineteenth-century African American women? What are the rhetorical and political implications of an African American sentimentality? What justification, if any, exists for an African American female bourgeois Victorianism?" (242) Belinda's petition serves as an extraordinarily instructive starting point for answering these questions and for beginning this book because it deploys several of the tropes and characteristics associated with sentimentalism. Some characteristics of sentimental literature include the use of such figures of dejection, isolation, and transgression as children, orphans, slaves, unwed mothers, dissipated men, and the unregenerate dying; more than one pathetic trope may occur in a single character or persona. The use of literary sentimentalism by American authors enables them to generate in readers sympathy for or a psychic connection with a text's characters or cultural ideals; if they highly regard a character or ideal, readers will therefore desire to embody and evince them. This effect clearly depends on authors and readers sharing both a common Christian moral code and a common cultural aesthetic. Indeed, in her important study of sentimentalism and law, Laura Korobkin asserts that the very "success or failure of a sentimental text can be gauged by the intensity of response it elicits" (78). Each of the sentimental tropes used in Belinda's late-eighteenth-century petition has a particular literary resonance and "sentimental power," to borrow the title phrase of Jane Tompkins's acclaimed essay on *Uncle Tom's Cabin*.

In order to persuade the legislature to grant Belinda a share of the Royall estate, the petition had to manipulate its members into recognizing her plight—from an enslaved adolescence to an impoverished old age—as morally wrong. To achieve this effect, the author engages an established stock of sentimental tropes. The first is the use of the image of Belinda as a prepubescent child in the act of communion, "with each hand in that of a tender parent," worshipping "the great Orisha"; although this deity is not identical to the Christian God, Africans believed him to be the creator of "all things." While whites of the time generally would not have cared about (or believed in) the validity of Africans' religions, they would likely have been touched by the expression of a child's religious devotion in and of itself. (To be sure, sentimental pedagogy had expressly taught such readers to be so touched.) The depiction of the abduction of the pious girl amid "the tears, the sighs, and supplications" that "bursted from the tortured parental affection" is a second sentimental feature the author of the Belinda petition uses. In recounting the experience of being "ravished from the bosom of her country" and from her loving parents, the plaintiff singles out her father as especially affronted: "In vain she lifted her supplicating voice to an insulted father" (Belinda 253–55). Within a single decade after the emergence of Belinda's petition, American sentimentalism would become most concerned with women, particularly with motherhood (and its synecdochic "bosom"); the use of the word "ravished" in the petition evokes the idea of sexual violence and thus forecasts the later reverence of sentimental writers for chastity.[11] In addition, in the wake of a war fought in large part to declare the colonies' sovereignty, the author of this petition mourns the offense given to a *father* by threats to his offspring—that is, to his property, and by extension, to his sovereignty. One thinks especially of the outrage expressed by the Revolutionary-era father figure in Thomas Paine's *Common Sense* when his paternal power in the colonies, like his political power, is threatened by King George. Thus orphaned and enslaved, the subject quakes during the physical and psychic terrors of "the most excruciating torment" of the Middle Passage. On land, she is forced into "ignoble servitude" for more than fifty years, all the while denied her birthrights as a "free moral agent." Finally, as a decrepit mother of seventy, her retiring wishes are for "her more infirm daughter"—anticipating the turn toward at-risk mothers and dying daughters that American sentimentalism would take in the nineteenth century.

From the many different definitions of sentimentalism that have been generated by American literary critics since the initial experiments with the literary mode in the eighteenth century, it is difficult to isolate one that applies holistically to this project, which examines the applications of sentimentalism in the spiritual autobiographies of early African American holy women. Perhaps a useful definition is one recently formulated by Elizabeth Barnes, which contextualizes and revises the hyperbolic aspects of sentimentalism that have often offended and frustrated many literary scholars. Whereas many critics merely deprecate sentimental writers' apparent proclivity for "excess," Barnes explores the methodological and cultural incentives for sentimental conventions. In "Affecting Relations: Pedagogy, Patriarchy, and the Politics of Sympathy," Barnes characterizes "sentimental ideology" as "the cultural expression of the desire for union. Sentimentalism is a manifestation of the belief in or yearning for consonance—or even unity—of principle and purpose. Sympathy complements the work of sentiment: each can be defined as a set of registered impulses psychologically connecting an individual to things and people outside of him or her" (597). I would like to emphasize that this desired psychological connection originates in the sentimentalist's assumption that a code of Christian morality and theology is shared by the sentimental writer herself (or himself), the individuals whom she or he addresses, and the object or objective of "the work of sentiment." This definition granted, then the term *sentimental* applies to literature that paradoxically both assumes and seeks to bring about an emotional and moral alliance between reader and text (an alliance at once so mystical and material that critics generally read it as excessive), an intimacy that is rooted in common cultural assumptions about virtue and piety. For example, Harriet Beecher Stowe, an undisputed sentimentalist, deploys sentimental rhetoric in *Uncle Tom's Cabin* by referring to a specific set of cultural and rhetorical conventions designed to inspire readers to embrace her political causes (chief among them the abolition of slavery) by urging readers' vehement emotional union with or sympathy for the novel's characters and crises. In *Uncle Tom's Cabin* the most prevalent tropes of sentimentalism tend to aggregate around the image of the home and include slaves and slave atrocities, orphans and other estranged family members, persecuted Christians, infirm persons suffering one or more of a wide range of "social" and political dis-eases, concubines and other victims of sexual seductions, and, perhaps most important, the virtuous dead (especially women).

These elements of *Uncle Tom's Cabin* assume a "sentimental" aspect through the context in which Stowe places them. In fact, these same rhetorical features are used by numerous secessionists and slavery proponents no less ardently than they are used by abolitionists like Stowe. Such features are not inherently anti-slavery any more than they are intrinsically "emotional," even though they are deployed sentimentally to advocate an end to slavery. So rather than characterize some literary tropes and rhetorical features as fundamentally "sentimental," the term more precisely describes the common result that such features are engaged to effect. In this case, the purpose of sentimentality is to induce the *process* by which the reader's desire for psychic union with characters and tropes is aroused, particularly as these objects function as embodiments, or more precisely, representations, of some moral virtue, Christian concept, or cultural ideal that readers want to manifest or affirm in themselves. In other words, the distinction of sentimental literature is that it offers a reader evidence outside of herself that she has the capacity to form a deep emotional, ethical, or psychological alliance with another person or ideal. The more meticulously the sympathetic figure is depicted in a sentimental text (and the more exhaustively it is portrayed), the greater the author's concern is not with the character but with the reader and her response, for the ideological work of the sentimentalist is to assure us that we *can* and *do* feel culturally sanctioned and even socially prescribed emotions strongly.

One aspect of the early American sentimental tradition evolved from texts designed to propel readers to act subversively on passions these texts aroused in them.[12] Ironically, many early American texts that espoused sympathy and subversion and that borrowed from sentimental conventions to do so were produced almost exclusively by and for men. Yet, although there exists only the thinnest line between texts of "sensibility" and texts of "sentimentality," a great gulf has divided the respect granted to each since the turn of the eighteenth century. For example, Thomas Paine's acclaimed *Common Sense,* written and published in 1776, appropriates the discourse of domesticity to create a momentary blurring of the doctrinal lines figuratively separating men and women into different spheres. *Common Sense* calls British colonists in America to unify around a common cause, namely their economic independence from England. To rally the colonists' support, Paine sought to engender in his readers an inviolable emotional tie to the ideology of his treatise; by positing—that is, by constructing—the bond existing between his inscribed readers and their families, Paine equates the relationship between the king of England and the colonist in America with the relationship between the colonist and his family to suggest that these two connections were identical. For, as Winfried Fluck notes, "The family . . . was reconceptualized in the eighteenth century as the one social group which is held together by an emotional bond and thus entitles each of its members to a just share of solidarity and protection" (328).[13] Fluck's assertion is all the more compelling when one considers the family as unified by emotional (and genetic) links and as defined by the ancient Judeo-Christian concept of "God the Father." This concept serves as the basis for the notion that the father is the head of the family, thereby setting up the patriarchal hierarchy upon which families are constructed. Paine appeals ardently to his inscribed readers for two distinct types of sympathy: first, he pleads for their *compassion* for fellow colonists who suffered from the British invasion at Lexington and, second, for readers' protective *patriarchal devotion* to their own household and the persons within it. Both senses of sympathy are rooted in a historical, Judeo-Christian conceptualization of family. Paine writes:

> Hath your property been destroyed before your face? Are your wife and children destitute of a bed to lie on, or bread to live on? Have you lost a parent or child by their [British] hands. . . . if you have, and can still shake hands with the murderers, then are you unworthy the name of husband, father, friend, or lover, and whatever may be your rank or title in life, you have the heart of a coward, and the spirit of a sycophant. (qtd. in Barnes, *Affecting* 603)[14]

If we accept Barnes's definition of *sentimentalism* as "a manifestation of the belief in . . . consonance," then the paragraph above is sentimental. It incites united, collective resistance to Great Britain by appealing to Paine's readers' "common sense," that is, to sentiments presumably common to both the author and his readership. Paine metonymizes the nation-state with the symbol of a man's private home/household; his deployment of sentimentalism is further developed by means of the discourse of domesticity.[15]

Early American male authors' uses of sentimental and domestic ideologies were short-lived, however.[16] After the nation gained independence, most generally ceased to engage in a discourse that bespoke the obligation to protect one's family and to sever "relations" once filial affection was betrayed.[17] For this had been the case with the colonists and their "parent" country when England had tyrannically threatened colonial families' homes and property. Notably, in the passage from *Common Sense* cited above, Paine's rhetoric engages the impassioned resistance of the Old Testament rather than a New Testament theology of turn-the-other-cheek. The fervor of *Common Sense* was replaced after the war with a call for Christian humility and deference — of sorts. At the end of the eighteenth century, male authors' sentimentalism gave way to two ensuing trends: first, literature of civilization, then "anticivilization" literature. The former was defined by the trope of the "Man of Feeling," not coincidentally the title of a 1771 British novel by Henry Mackenzie, which, like its antithetical sequel *The Man of the World* (1773), intimated a particular sense of "civilization." Mackenzie's episodic first novel quite sentimentally follows the delicate orphan Harley from his pastoral home through a series of London adventures that reveal his unworldliness. In the end, however, Harley dies among his bucolic origins: though he loathes the world, he cannot live in his rural home. This ambiguously sentimental eighteenth-century British novel of manners gradually yielded another trope in America: the triumphant rugged individual, the American pioneer of the sort found in James Fenimore Cooper's 1823 Leatherstocking tale, *The Pioneers*. The figure of the American pioneer, as opposed to the Man of the World, connoted the idea of a disavowal of "civilization" — a disavowal that, ironically, was applicable only to white men of property, whose "civilized" status was undisputed.

The development of American sentimentalism turns significantly upon Mackenzie's fictional concerns and tropes and Cooper's corollary ones. In tracing the origins of American sentimental literature, one finds that the ideology of sentimentalism emerges from eighteenth-century national rhetoric. As Barnes contends in her analysis of *Common Sense*, "Revolutionary and post-Revolutionary concerns with the effects of sympathy, as it relates to both the novel and American socio-political structures, underscore the importance of relational methods and models in contributing to the liberal notion of individual authority" (*Affecting* 600). In other words, both novelists and political figures of the period relied on sentimental conventions, especially the effects garnered by engaging readers' sympathies, to rally citizens; both groups insisted that sympathy was intricately tied to individual authority and autonomy. However, late-eighteenth-century American commitment to both national and personal sovereignty provoked significant questions about the connection of sympathy to rights and about the conceivable consequences of sentimentalism. Is sympathy in fact a phenomenon characterized by psychic engagement with other persons? Could the construction of a sympathetic text inspire readers to share the passions of (fictional) others? Could a text so devised to elicit readers' "fellow-feeling" threaten individual rights and ultimately national security?

Such questions seem naturally to be at issue in the aftermath of a war fought (ostensibly) for freedom—as the initial success of Belinda's petition illustrates. Perhaps its realization that Belinda's personal autonomy had been compromised by her enslavement generated the Massachusetts legislature's decision in her favor. Within a year, however, she was obliged to return to court for a second hearing, this time with less success: instead of being awarded damages for life, she won them only for a single year. Yet this development, too, speaks to the anxiety wrought by sympathy as a literary phenomenon: the power of the text to sway a judiciary body apparently aroused not fellow feeling but a fear that the specific (and specifically) manipulative rhetorical strategy applied in Belinda's petition represented as great a hazard to national sovereignty as it stood to secure a former slavewoman's individual birthright. It is especially noteworthy that the *threat* of sentimentality was alone sufficient to deter some authors, almost all of them men, from engaging the subgenre. Perhaps they discovered—and feared—sentimentalism's capacity to empower all, that is, to assert the rights of "others."

A good deal of excellent feminist scholarship has focused on the disparagement of sentimentality, especially the aspersion of women's sentimental novels by male literary critics. Yet feminist scholars, like American male critics across the centuries who have responded to sentimentalism with antagonism, have largely overlooked the kinship of the political discourse of the Revolution and the American literature that derived from it.[18] These feminist scholars have analyzed male critics' objections and fears, but they have not consistently examined (the presumed threat to) personal autonomy as a source of the initial opposition to sentimentalism. Contemporary criticism has clouded a crucial aspect of the literature of the earlier period: whereas post-Revolutionary critics tended to regard sentimentalism and the sympathy it inspired as perilous to liberty, women writers of the day perceived sentimentalism as a moral cudgel they could use to beat back patriarchal obstructions to their individual and collective autonomy. In addition, many women writers saw the patriarchal Christianity of eighteenth-century America as an integral component of sentimentalism and developed a narrative strategy that espoused a covenant between authors and readers based on a tacit agreement about emotions and the range of right actions they incite.

The decline of sentimental and domestic discourses in (white) men's texts neither necessitated nor occasioned the absolute cessation of sentimental rhetoric by men or women in subsequent literature. It is true, however, that most nineteenth-century sentimental literature was produced by, for, and about (white) women, some authors endorsing, others impugning, the era's implementation of an age-old fallacious gyneolatry and its resultant relegation of women to the domestic sphere.[19] Among these authors, Susanna Rowson and Hannah Foster wrote the two best-selling novels in America for the first seventy years of American fiction. Rowson's *Charlotte Temple, A Tale of Truth* (1791) and Foster's *The Coquette, or . . . A Novel; Founded on Fact* (1797) continued to claim readers' avid attention until the mid-1800s. Consequently, Rowson and Foster determined the style, shape, ideology, and direction of the novel in America for over half a century. Both novelists told "true" stories that intrigued and captivated thousands of early American readers and that argued vehemently against patriarchal restrictions on women's proper behavior.[20] Therefore, American women writers have used the rhetoric of sentimentalism to assert a revised, gender-neutral theory of Christian benevolence almost since the nation's very beginning. Setting an example for subsequent writers, Rowson and Foster used the rhetoric of sentimentalism to subvert a code of conduct devised by white, middle-class men for their female counterparts. They effectively engaged a broad, extensive readership in a provocative redefinition of moral virtue and an impassioned critique of patriarchy (and its consequent evils, including such cognate oppressions as sexism and classism).

A principal critical charge leveled against sentimental literature has been that "the power of sympathy" is used as often to provoke readers to feelings of pathos for its own sake as it is used to agitate them into political action against the status quo. Therefore, according to the genre's detractors, because sentimental literature requires no great authorial skill to produce, and an author's audience is almost assuredly ingenuous enough to yield to its power, sentimental literature threatens to produce a society that is both unreasonable and irrational.[21] Indeed, in an essay published as recently as December 1996, philosophy professor Joseph Kupfer denounces sentimentality as "a deceptive, dangerous vice, not something to be brushed off as little more than a genteel foible," going so far as to warn his readers that "the distortion of and absorption in the self is dangerous for sentimental individuals and those with whom they interact" (560, 543). Unwittingly, Kupfer's condemnation of sentimentality as socially deleterious smacks of precisely the kind of hyperbole and hysteria that he attributes to the genre he rejects.

None of the major goals of white women's feminist sentimental fiction listed above pertain to Belinda's petition, however. Thus, the petition allows us to consider what happens when an *object* of sentimentality—a child, an orphan, an unwed mother, a dying daughter—becomes the narrating *subject* of sentimentality. Although the legal document applies several of the stock conventions of the later novels, it accentuates a radical shift in the rhetorical applications of sentimentalism in the eight years between Belinda's brief in 1783 and Rowson's novel in 1791.[22] Between these two publications, in 1789 William Hill Brown's antisentimental novel *The Power of Sympathy,* which expresses hegemony's profound fear of precisely that, the power of sympathy, appeared. Brown epitomizes early American writers who abandoned the discourse of sentimentalism because, for them, it imperiled an individual's ability to reason. He contended that sentimental conventions threatened readers' capacity to resist manipulation that would skew readers' judgment and would cause them to perform acts that could be injurious to the self or the state. European American men were generally suspicious of sentimentalism because they equated it with melodrama and believed it impeded reason (and ultimately, their rights as citizens); conversely, many European American women authors engaged sentimentalism to indict patriarchy for its impediments to women's equal rights. But unlike any other narrative before it, *Belinda* used sentimentalism to articulate African American women's predominant concern with the same fundamental issues of freedom and autonomy that had preoccupied the Founding Fathers, Revolutionary patriots, *and* the (white) women writing after them.

Belinda and
Nineteenth-Century African American Women Spiritual Autobiographers

Early uses of sentimentalism did not take only the literary form of the novel. Despite the tendency in literary scholarship to read sentimentalism as limited to fictional forms, in fact, some autobiographies may be rightly said to appropriate sentimental conventions. In fact, autobiography fictionalizes reality: the autobiographer mediates "real" experience through subjectivity, memory, and discourse into ordered verbal articulation; the autobiographical act, the reconstruction of any life necessitates the fictionalization of that life. However, one finds in studying the autobiographies of nineteenth-century African American women that the "fictions" of black personal narratives are rooted in the "facts" of the subjects' lives with a profound earnestness; then, as now, black people understood all too well the European American suspicion of their veracity. Conforming to the strategies of autobiographers like Briton Hammon as well as to those of such early black poets as Belinda's contemporary Phillis Wheatley, subsequent African American women transformed commonplace incidents from their private lives into the extraordinary subjects of their autobiographies.[23] They knew that the concept of "truth" in an autobiography, no matter how sentimentalized, has more to do with the meaning that an autobiographer infers from her life experiences and with the significance she ascribes to incidents in her life than with the "factual" details of her life.

The final clauses of Belinda's petition sentimentally state: "she prays that such allowance may be made her, out of the estate of colonel Royall, as will prevent her, and her more infirm daughter, from misery in the greatest extreme, and scatter comfort over the short and downward path of their lives: and she will ever pray" (255). The last word is obviously a pun, connoting both her *appeal* as well as her *piety*. By ending with the word "pray," the narrative circles back to its first image of Belinda's nuclear family at worship, and thereby reinforces the religious subtext of the secular document.[24] As Joanne Braxton explains, "'Belinda' records . . . the complete disruption of the narrator's emotional and spiritual life and the corresponding loss of her sense of place, both physical and metaphysical" (2). In this way Belinda's petition serves as a provocative precursor to later African American women's sacred and secular autobiographies, all of which "petition" the nation for the recognition of black women as "free moral agents" who are divinely granted but socially denied the opportunity to develop fully their intellectual and moral capabilities. (In contrast, of course, black women's menial skills were allowed to develop fully enough when in service to the economic and physical comfort of whites.) Belinda's petition, then, implies that slaveholders in particular and Massachusetts citizens in general—especially the landed white male gentry—are arrogant enough to usurp divine authority. This is obviously an audacious claim by a (former) slavewoman: when "Belinda" suggests that the ironically (or aptly!) named Royall had presumed to usurp, and thus execrate, divine authority by denying her birthright, she further implies that from him she in turn learned the audacity to make the presumption known to Royall's compeers. Moreover, the petitioner suggests that her observation is in concert with divine will whereas Royall's constitutes a violation of it. The theological inference further affirms that early black women perceived and seized the political dimensions and utility they could gain by writing and producing sacred literature. As autobiographers cum *theologians*, they could simultaneously pursue those political and social rights they were routinely denied as poor black devout women. Clearly, for black holy women both the personal and the *spiritual* are political.

The term *theologian* merits discussion, particularly since it may seem an odd designation to apply to six women, some of whom were only rudimentarily schooled and others denied schooling altogether. If theology denotes the analysis, application, or presentation of traditional doctrines of a religion or religious group, then Stewart, Lee, Elaw, Prince, Jackson, and Foote unquestionably produced theology. For their life stories not only investigate black women's interior spiritual lives and the centrality of Christianity to their individual identities, but each holy woman also theorizes on who and how God is. Each analyzes her own life for the application and fulfillment of Scripture, and each explicitly interprets the traditional Christian tenets that she endorses. Moreover, each woman's narrative exemplifies precisely the kind of theology recently described by theologian M. Shawn Copeland: "Womanist theology claims the experiences of Black women as proper and serious data for theological reflection. Its aim is to elucidate the differentiated range and interconnections of Black women's gender, racial-ethnic, cultural, religious, and social (i.e., political, economic, and technological) oppression" (111). The emphasis on the personal and secular that characterizes both early and modern black holy women's theology is mandated by many womanist theologians. In "The Sin of Servanthood and the Deliverance of Discipleship," Jacquelyn Grant decrees theological duty both private and social, asserting that "there must be a self-critical (evaluative) dimension to theology. In fact, theology must not only be reflection upon the lived realities of the faithful, but it must also be prophetic; that is, it must raise the critical and sometimes difficult questions that arise out of the various contradictions of life" (199). Especially striking is Grant's foregone conclusion that theology attends to experience, that it interrogates both self and others.

Although the spiritual autobiographies considered in this work do not constitute traditional or conventional Christian theology, collectively they nonetheless illustrate all aspects of theology.[25] Christian theological treatises offer, implicitly or explicitly, a definition of God. They posit that God is a mystery, and they strive to explicate the mystery of the Godhead. Although not consistently text-based, theology almost invariably entails interpretation of the Bible, usually in the process of exploring and explaining God. In addition, theology explores the science of divine things; it interrogates divinity and theorizes the "nature" and function of the divine. In as much as theology is a scholarly endeavor, frequently outside the traditional educational academy, it invokes its own tradition(s); that is, theologians typically engage, interrogate, resist, and endorse the texts of other theologians. Theologians sometimes appropriate the New Testament paradigm of the use of the epistolary to communicate—through dialogue, debate, or dialectic—with other (Christian) groups or theologians; the *Memoirs* of Zilpha Elaw, for example, are directed "To the Saints and faithful Brethren in Christ, who have honored my ministry with their attendance, in London and other localities in England" (51).

In that it is an other-directed enterprise, theology, especially as it was developed by women from Teresa de Avila to present female theologians, often combines the practical with the transcendent; thus, it not only explains the intersection of the divine and the mortal, but it also offers functional advice for the moral and spiritual improvement of human life. The final chapter of Julia Foote's *Autobiographical Sketch*, titled "How to Obtain Sanctification," is a case in point. Moreover, works of theology often theorize approaches to the discipline, thus sustaining the traditions that constitute the discipline. Finally, two interlocking aspects of theology are prophesying, as in the eschatological *Productions of Mrs. Maria W. Stewart*, and the recounting of visions, as in Jarena Lee's descriptions of the images infusing her dreams of a ministerial future.

Tacitly staked out in her petition to the state of Massachusetts, Belinda's theological and political claims also form the heart of her descendants' narratives. Nineteenth-century African American women autobiographers' polemic against injustice sometimes led, ironically, to greater transgressions against them. In particular, their religious devotion proved one more "flaw" for which they were oppressed, despite the fact that the most influential of them were writing during the Second Great Awakening of the 1830s and 1840s. During this period of concentrated evangelicalism, Christianity dominated virtually every social and cultural phenomenon. Like their European forefathers, American Christian patriarchs saw their leadership and personal deportment as divinely inspired, yet they often held others to a standard of piety and morality that they themselves decried in private and violated in public. And while they demanded, endorsed, and rewarded Christian behavior at will, they also determined that there could be *too much* goodness. While patriarchal church leaders called for women's assiduous religious devotion, they also at the same time insisted that some women's religious zeal led to fanaticism and therefore was detrimental to society. As Amy Lang and Susan Juster have demonstrated, during America's Great Awakenings evangelicalism was frequently equated with marginality, which in itself was often equated with femininity. At this time, the idea of the "feminine" was expanded to include "not only women but all those social groups that occupied the margins of colonial New England—the poor, transient, young, and unfree" (Juster 4). When the zealots were black, their fervor was regarded as proof not simply of all women's emotionality and hypersensitivity, but also of such allegedly innate African traits as irrationality, primitivism, docility, and credulity.[26] In *Primitive Passions* Marianna Torgovnick identifies in the West a "root connection between primitivism and religious traditions" that falls along a "double register . . . negatively—for example, as fear of the primitive or as a detour into violence; and positively—as admiration for the primitive, conceived to be the conduit of spiritual emotions" (7). The Western patriarchal mode of reconciling this conflict—and its associated phenomenon of ecstasy—has typically been intolerance and subjugation.

In spite of, indeed, because of the political, social, and religious oppression they faced, nineteenth-century African American women writers exploited many of the diverse literary genres and conventions available to them. Apparently vexed by and determined to discredit the pervasive myths about blacks' biology and (im)morality, including their veraciousness, these women's autobiographies appropriated a variety of narrative conventions, but they were emphatically *not* novels.[27] By insisting that their works were autobiographies, black women professed to tell the truth; with any lesser claim, they risked asserting the myth that blacks had a generic and a genetic predilection for fictionalization. Like black writers before them, they found autobiography the most effective means of unveiling and of protesting against the oppressed conditions of black women's lives.

Still, the autobiographical form was not without its singular problems and paradoxes for African American women. One of the most radical aspects of early African American autobiography, especially by women, is its intrinsic assumption that the life it reconstructs is exemplary, one worth telling about and reading about. During the nineteenth century, this assumption was forcefully flouted. Julia Watson and Sidonie Smith articulate the specific problems that autobiography poses for subjects that hold subordinate positions in societies in their introduction to *De/Colonizing the Subject:* "Despite their myriad differences, of place, time, histories, economies, cultural identifications, all 'I's are rational, agentive, unitary. Thus the 'I' becomes 'Man,' putatively a marker of the universal human subject whose essence remains outside the vagaries of history" (xvii). In this way, early black women's performance of the "master" discursive practice of autobiography entangled them in contradictory ideologies: the means they engaged to depict and resist their oppression stood to implicate them as both transgressive *and* transformative agents.

Despite the conflicts relative to property and subjectivity that the genre presents, the advantages of the autobiographical act for nineteenth-century black holy women outweighed its deterrents. They were unabashedly willing to confront the complexities of privilege in order to exploit autobiographical self-assertion and agency. Moreover, like Hammon and Belinda, the later narrators evidently realized that they could buttress their texts against white contempt and dismissal with discourses of sentimentalism and evangelicalism. With spiritual narratives that commingled Protestantism and sentimentalism, then, they maximized their opportunities to assert a counternarrative. This hybrid text contested the dominant misapprehensions of who they were, ironically by eschewing representations of the black body to insist on their likeness to the white body. Yet each autobiography unsurprisingly centers on the body since the oppressions they suffered were so fundamentally (and erroneously) based on the physical manifestation of the body and on the myths developed about the alleged differences between black bodies and white bodies and male bodies and female bodies. For all of that, their expression of fellow "feeling"—both emotion and tactility—yields a text that converts the material and secular into the spiritual and sacred.

I analyze African American women's spiritual autobiographies in particular because they espouse an exceptional theology that is rarely observed. Just as important, the texts express the women's Christian identity and their spiritual life as they believed they should live it, that is, on their own in accordance with their comprehension of divine will. It is no fortuity that the oldest extant prose texts by black women in America are *sacred* writings. To read African American holy women's writings without regard for their religious content is to misread them, even to distort them in search of significance—political, social, and cultural significance—that is actually ancillary to their theology and certainly inseparable from it. To misread in this way is to overlook the fact that these women's declarations of selfhood and birthrights are rooted in a context of Judeo-Christian hegemony. The narrators' very appropriation of Protestant discourse is itself theological: it functions as an avowal of their participation in the divine Judeo-Christian plan and thus forms a crucial argument for their complete humanity and their innate right to egalitarianism. More important, the narrators used evangelicalism to aver the magnitude of the power of the Christian God and of the breadth of the capacity for divine love.

Literary and cultural study of early African American narratives have insufficiently attended to their Christian discourse. Several factors might account for this, chief among them a modern academic elitism that rejects all religion as delusional and indefensible. Rooted in primordial instincts, religion and religious institutions have been associated in the academy with the irrational, with frenzy, and even with violence. Ultimately, when the patriarchal academy has regarded Christianity at all, it has belittled its emphasis on love and charity, perhaps because the academy feels Christianity makes us vulnerable to, as Torgovnick states, "uneasy, because unacknowledged, obsessions with male homosexuality, the working class, and women—and with the fragility and alienation of the modern human ego" (5). Another important reason is that scholars of black literary history and culture focus too cursorily and imperiously on protest literature. Moreover, scholars of African American "protest literature" use the term too narrowly to refer only to texts that advocate a frenzied, violent response to racism; as a result, other literary forms of resistance to white (male) supremacy are abnegated as irrelevant. As Sondra O'Neale has definitively shown, there has been a tendency among scholars of African American literature across the twentieth century to misread the religious rhetoric of early black writers and summarily to dismiss them as insignificant at best and as sycophantic at worst. Writing specifically about the first African American poet, Jupiter Hammon (unrelated to autobiographer Briton Hammon), O'Neale charges:

> Because modern critics make a distinction between religious art and the protest tradition when assessing formal aesthetic expression as opposed to indigenous folk creations, [Jupiter] Hammon's dual commitment to Christianity and freedom has been either undervalued or ignored. . . .
>
> Most current literary criticism of Jupiter Hammon's work reflects anachronistic thinking and ignores the racism pervasive in all aspects of a slave society, including the burgeoning publishing industry. (1, 3)

The critics whom O'Neale reproves emphatically underestimate the ubiquity and preponderance of Protestant discourses in eighteenth- and nineteenth-century America—and thus depreciate both their necessity and their authority. *Everyone*—despite their personal creed or lack thereof—engaged in Christian discourse during the Great Awakenings. Consequently, black women writers demonstrated the illegitimacy of their estrangement from hegemonic power with each Christian word they used. Frances Smith Foster describes the pervasiveness of the Christian conversion relation (to isolate only one expository form) in the American colonies thusly: "Believing there is no more praiseworthy quest than that for salvation, [Americans of all persuasions] had produced diaries, journals, testimonies, broadsides, pamphlets, and full-length books that chronicled the religious experiences and convictions . . . of Puritans, Calvinists, Quakers, and Methodists; of men, women, and children from all social classes and educational levels" (*Written* 59). In other words, virtually all texts were in some sense Christian texts.

Among Protestant doctrines, Wesleyan Methodism was most attractive to African Americans. The perpetuation of various Protestant discourses from the colonial era through the Second Great Awakening represents an exclusively American literary trend. The European colonization of America's eastern seaboard had been a Protestant enterprise; the original immigration was overtly a movement for the religious independence of the Puritans, Calvinists, and members of other Protestant denominations.[28] The early American Puritan requirement to describe one's individual experience with the divine, especially one's conversion, bears directly on the narratives examined in this book. The Puritans believed that an austere and impenetrable God "elected" certain persons to salvation; for them, the Puritan conversion relation expressly recounted how God had informed the Christian that she or he was among the elect. The Quakers, less interested in conversion and election, emphasized an individual and internal search for truth. Wesleyan Methodism constructed a more benevolent God and a more democratic means of redemption than Puritanism did, positing that salvation was achieved through Grace alone. The Methodist conversion relation, then, detailed how the Christian transformed her life from one of sin to one of sanctification.[29] Methodist theology, then, was one of personal transformation. To be sure, black Christians were drawn to the requirement that the conversion narrator, creed notwithstanding, should testify to God's intervention in the sinner's life, for they perceived it as a worthy rejoinder to the whites' theory that the Christian God did not esteem Africans as full—as opposed to "three-fifths"—human beings.

Enumerating some of the crucial differences between nineteenth-century spiritual narratives written in the United States by blacks and by whites is instructive.[30] One of the major features found in black spiritual narratives is the narrator's declaration of her or his racial identification (and in the case of African American women, gender specification); this often occurs in the very title of the narrative, as in the *Memoir of Old Elizabeth, a Coloured Woman*. While some scholars have suggested that this feature is superfluous, in fact from the outset it validates the idea that blacks, particularly black women, have a self to speak of. And, by contrast, it points to—and signifies on—the dominance of those who take for granted the hegemony of their unmarked sign of race and gender. Although epigraphs from the New Testament like the one found on the title page of Elizabeth's memoir are common, indeed formulaic, in spiritual narratives, the choice of Galatians 3.25 is especially trenchant: "There is neither Jew nor Greek, there is neither bond nor free, there is neither male nor female, for ye are all one in Christ Jesus." This Gospel verse subverts the spiritual narrative genre with its dual application to the black woman's religious position and her social status, and it nullifies the supposed supremacy of the genre's typical white (male) participant. Having identified herself as an African American (woman), the autobiographer often goes on, usually in a self-deprecating preface, to express the hope that her text will prove useful to others like herself. Thus she insinuates that a chief aim of the narrative is to speak directly to other African Americans (and also to nonblack women), to cultivate greater race (and/or gender) pride among them, and to encourage the delineation of their own life experiences in narrative form.[31] Apparently, white spiritual narrators felt the expression of such hope to be needless or inane. Nor did they develop another significant characteristic of African American spiritual narrative: authentication by prominent "others."[32] This feature elucidates the integral relationship of early African American spiritual autobiography to the (antebellum) slave narrative. Whites frequently penned prefaces or other textual apparati to endorse the veracity of a slave narrator's account of her or his life, and more fundamentally still, to verify that the slave author in fact existed and was not merely a white novelist's abolitionist device; hence, as James Olney has asserted, the profundity of the slave narrative's oft-repeated opening words, "I was born." With these words, both spiritual autobiographers and slave narrators tacitly argued for their textual and their social authority.

Black spiritual autobiographers and slave narrators also document the obstacles to their religious faith and practices erected by racism and the slaveocracy, whereas whites do not. For example, Sarah Douglass, a scientist, physician, teacher, essayist, and artist involved throughout her life in antiracist endeavors in Philadelphia, finally yielded to the beseeching of white Quaker abolitionist Sarah Grimké that she divulge particulars of the racism that she—and her mother a generation before her—had experienced while worshipping among the Friends. A letter Douglass wrote to Grimké in the early 1840s describes one of her experiences at Arch Street Meeting:

> I may say that there is a bench set apart at that meeting for our people, that my mother and myself were told to sit there, and that a [F]riend sat at either end of the bench to prevent white persons from sitting there. And even when a child my soul was made sad with hearing five or six times during the course of one meeting this language of remonstrance addressed to those who were willing to sit by us. "This bench is for the black people." "This bench is for the people of color." I have not been in Arch Street meeting for four years, but my mother goes once a week and frequently she has the whole bench to herself. (qtd. in Sterling 130)

Prior to this, at the end of the eighteenth century, the deleterious effects of racial prejudice and discrimination had so diminished the intensity of his religious fervor among whites at St. George's Methodist Church in Philadelphia that Richard Allen felt impelled to found the African Methodist Episcopal Church. The self-emancipated slave's ministerial narrative, *The Life, Experiment and Gospel Labours of the Rt. Reverend Richard Allen* (1833), is a historical account of the "persecutions" that white Wesleyans perpetrated against black Christians, not the least of which was Allen's own eviction from a "whites-only" church pew.

Like their eighteenth-century predecessors, the nineteenth-century autobiographies by Allen and by black holy women were shaped by the spiritual writings of John Bunyan, who, ironically, also influenced many of the white Protestants who discriminated against them. Bunyan's *Pilgrim's Progress* was an especially instrumental text for black spiritual autobiographers to follow, as it generally motivated them to describe the multifaceted quest they had undertaken. (Of course, Bunyan never had to worry that his readership would question his credibility.) Specifically, blacks found a trope for the Middle Passage and later for the "exodus" occasioned by the slave trade in Bunyan's description of the interior sacred journey from sin to the (metaphysical) state of salvation. This inner journey often coincides with a physical journey the narrative subject takes across geographical regions in order to arrive at a site where she or he can perform religious rituals with other converts without fear of being obstructed by oppressive forces.[33] This exemplar also informed the didacticism of blacks' appropriation of the genre: African American spiritual autobiography not only provided evidence that the convert was indeed saved (of especial import in the early American spiritual autobiography), but it also provided the reader with instructions on how to become sanctified. In some cases, like Julia Foote's Reconstruction narrative, which I discuss in chapter 6, the work also detailed how not to sin in the first place.

One of my goals in this book is to develop a theory of how to read the autobiographical writings of early black women. As Frances Smith Foster notes in opposition to Nina Baym's central argument about white women writers in *Woman's Fiction: A Guide to Novels by and about Women in America, 1820–1870*, "African American women writers could not assume a readership composed primarily or exclusively of women like themselves" (*Written* 83).[34] Nor could nineteenth-century black holy women assume that their readers would be mostly blacks—men or women. Their Du Boisian double consciousness meant that although they readily comprehended the "common sense" that white men and white women writers could both assume and sustain, they experienced the world in ways deeply different from these "others." To reach audiences of others both like *and* unlike themselves, they had to execute a double-voiced narrative technique. The success of this project attests to their ability to formulate and implement strategies in their own behalf. As rhetoricians and theologians, they skillfully mollified those readers who, dubious of their worth as autobiographical agents, distrusted them as narrative subjects; they appeased readers by "converting" the discourses of Protestant evangelicalism, literary sentimentalism, and (African) American nationalism into useful, useable rhetorical tools. Whereas those discourses in their conventional forms required the suppression or distortion of black holy women's actual life experiences, when revised to form an authentic African American women's spiritual autobiographical tradition they yielded a powerful means by which the authors could claim active subjectivity, narrative agency, and most significantly, divine ordination. More than their contemporary readers would have expected, perhaps more than their readers comprehended, nineteenth-century African American women's appropriation of the "sensational designs" of their day signifies their astute insight into the race, gender, ecclesiastic, and class oppressions they endured and their brave determination to unveil the patriarchal underpinnings that enabled those oppressions.[35] This book, then, becomes a "sentimental confession" of the ingenuity and intelligence of their autobiographical acts.

950966 72

ONE

(Im)Personal Complaints: Maria Stewart

My soul became filled with a holy indignation.
I complained.

MARIA W. STEWART

The theology of Maria Stewart is a theology of survival. Although the auto-biographical details that emerge in her writings would suggest that hers was a life greatly characterized by affliction, thus rendering her religious belief system akin to a theology of suffering like that described by contemporary theorist M. Shawn Copeland, Stewart nonetheless sought to embrace optimism and generate hope. Copeland defines the theology of suffering as reevaluative of "the cardinal virtues of patience, long-suffering, forbearance, love, faith, and hope . . . in light of Black women's experiences. Such reevaluation engages a hermeneutic of suspicion and a hermeneutic of resistance; but that reevaluation and reinterpretation must be rooted in a critical realism that rejects both naïve realism and idealism as adequate foundations for a theology of suffering" (122). These practices correspond to those that guided Stewart's life in the 1830s, for as an activist, speaker, and author in the jeremiadic tradition, Stewart was deeply critical of her era. Her public and private writings challenged the social and political hierarchies of her day by proclaiming God as determined to demolish those hierarchies and the immoral and profane institutions that devised and sustained them.

Before she ever took the platform in 1830 as the first American woman orator, Maria Miller Stewart had already protested against injustice: in 1827 she wrote to the editors of the first African American newspaper, *Freedom's Journal*, urging them not to exclude black women in their struggles for racial improvement. By the time she published the *Productions of Mrs. Maria W. Stewart* in

1835, she had acquired controversial renown as a radical abolitionist and an apostolic orator. However, the remarkable and provocative life that Stewart had led by the age of thirty-two is not the basis of the *Productions;* that text does not constitute the autobiography of the author as a young militant or evangelist. Given that an autobiography is a narrative of a person's life written by that person for complex purposes, chief among which is the author's desire to explicate and to evaluate her or his life, the actual achievements of Stewart's collection of political speeches and spiritual meditations conflict with the aims of conventional autobiography. For whereas autobiographers generally assume their lives to be in some way exemplary or representative and worthy of a readership, Stewart makes no such presumptions in her early compositions. Despite her use of personal detail in the writings that comprise the *Productions,* it was not until she revised her 1835 collection in 1879 to form *Meditations from the Pen of Mrs. Maria W. Stewart* that she set out to narrate a portion of her life. The earlier text draws frequently but reluctantly on Stewart's life; the author seems consciously to have resisted any impulses to reveal autobiographical details. Certainly, her use of the pseudonym "Mathilda" in her letter to the *Freedom's Journal's* editors (Hernton 60) illustrates the extent to which she repressed those impulses. In the end, however, Stewart shows a strong propensity toward personal narrative and self-disclosure.

The *Productions of Mrs. Maria W. Stewart,* first published by the Bostonian "Friends of Freedom and Virtue," contains an essay, a series of religious meditations and prayers, and four speeches. ("The Negro's Complaint," a hymn, is appended.) Stewart's postemancipation *Meditations* adds several supplemental documents to the complete *Productions.* Of Stewart's extant published writings, only two essays seem to adhere to a traditional definition of autobiography. To varying degrees, the 1831 essay "Religion and the Pure Principles of Morality" and the 1879 autobiographical sketch, titled "Sufferings During the War," recount the major events of the author's life more or less linearly and chronologically from the perspective of a constructed narrative self. None of Stewart's other extant texts exhibits a retrospectively autobiographical focus.

In these two essays, Christian evangelicalism, literary sentimentalism, and black nationalism converge specifically; these themes also surface throughout Stewart's writings generally. Until her later life, Stewart opted against writing "personal" narratives, apparently in the belief that her causes and the communities they influenced would be better served by a communal rather than an individualistic discourse. As one of the first (and grievously few) nineteenth-century African American women to whose writings we have access, Stewart elucidates the kinds of issues that concerned black women who both could and did take up the pen. As valuable as the petition of Belinda (discussed in the introduction) is to the history of African American women's literature, the uncertainty of its authorship affects its legacy. Stewart's texts, by contrast, are indisputably self-authored. Furthermore, their comprehensive reliance on the Scriptures not only validates Frey and Wood's contention that African Americans' conversion "to Protestant Christianity was a, perhaps the, defining moment in African American history" (xi), but it also demonstrates the centrality of religion to early African American women's experience. First printed in pamphlet form, "Religion and the Pure Principles of Morality" was excerpted in the October 8, 1831, issue of William Garrison's abolitionist newspaper, *The Liberator.* Though it is not a conventional personal narrative, this essay features Stewart's autobiographical declaration of existence: "I was born in Hartford, Connecticut, in 1803" (3). Such a statement typically signifies the beginning of a personal narrative, but the paragraph in which this one appears exhausts the autobiographical properties of "Religion and the Pure Principles." In "I Was Born: Slave Narratives, Their Status as Autobiography and as Literature," James Olney identifies the formal and thematic characteristics of early African American autobiography. He notes that "the simple, existential claim: 'I exist,'" cast as "I was born," forms the first three words of virtually every African American narrative (155). Contrary to these early black autobiographies, Stewart's inscription of her being appears in the second, not the first, paragraph of her essay, and, moreover, belongs not to the narrative proper, but actually forms part of the essay's separate introduction. This positioning suggests that Stewart does not intend the tract to be an autobiography but rather she inserts only enough autobiographical details into the essay for it to be sufficient to establish her narrative credibility.

Interestingly, Stewart's postemancipation volume, *Meditations from the Pen,* does evince some of the traits of early African American autobiography. Extratextual literary paraphernalia cited by Olney as characteristic of nineteenth-century black autobiography—namely, authenticating documents and the titular tag "Written by Herself" (Olney 152)—prominently appear in Stewart's 1879 edition. Unlike the supporting apparati (generally inscribed by white men to confirm the black person's existence and integrity) that usually prefaced the antebellum narrative of an African American, the "Letters and Commendations" that introduce Stewart's *Meditations* do not function as authentication. Stewart did not need verification of her life story, even though many of her postbellum readers would not actually have heard any of the speeches she had delivered in Boston nearly half a century before. Instead, the letters—written by three black ministers, the Reverends Alexander Crummell, William B. Jefferson, and Henry Bailey, and two well-known whites, Amos Hunt and William L. Garrison—document Stewart's achievements as a mature educator. Further distinguishing Stewart's 1879 text is Louise Hatton's brief commendatory "Biographical Sketch" of Stewart. These various documents, placed before the narrative "Sufferings During the War," which is in turn placed significantly before the contents of the 1835 *Productions*, suggest that Stewart thought of the enlarged edition of her collected works as autobiographical. In this way, Stewart at age seventy-six revises the genre of her earlier work: although she did not initially inscribe the *Productions* as autobiography, she reprinted it fully within the contents of the *Meditations*, which explicitly narrates her story.

Taken together, Stewart's complete works comprise the form of spiritual autobiography identified as the black jeremiad, after the Hebrew prophet Jeremiah who warned Israel that it would be destroyed for deserting its covenant with God. In *Black Messiahs and Uncle Toms*, Wilson J. Moses uses "the term 'jeremiad' to describe the constant warnings issued by blacks to whites, concerning the judgment that was to come for the sin of slavery" (30–31). Corruption and covenant, indignation and urgency, religion and reform characterize the black jeremiad. Like the jeremiads of seventeenth-century American Puritans, African American jeremiads are by definition a sentimental form since they rely on moral suasion, deep feeling, and a shared sense of social justice. They also optimistically postulate "an errand into the wilderness" to fulfill God's will and the Manifest Destiny of His chosen people, that is, African Americans. For, as David Howard-Pitney asserts in *The Afro-American Jeremiad*, "the dominant black American jeremiad tradition conceives of blacks as a chosen people within a chosen people" such that the fates of white and black Americans, "while distinct, are also inextricably entwined" (15). African American jeremiahs blend the discourses of black nationalism and Christianity to prophesy, in the first person, the annihilation of racists and negrophobes. As she or he condemns race-based oppression, the black jeremiah expressly deplores the social, moral, and spiritual condition of African Americans.

In neither the prophetic nor the plaintive mode do jeremiahs narrate their own lives. The jeremiad differs from the spiritual confession in that the former generally lacks the introversion and introspection of the latter. While the jeremiad sharply critiques a society and a culture and provokes specific groups into self-scrutiny and social change, a confession, on the other hand, contemplatively turns such matters inward: passion is to the jeremiad as placidity is to the confession. While the traditional spiritual autobiography counsels conversion to Christianity by chronologically narrating an exemplary life, the jeremiad foments social equity by expressing disdain for the present and hope for the future. Like traditional spiritual narratives, however, jeremiads are didactic and formulaic. Bristling with discontent, they demand the ideological and ecclesiastical conversion of a mass of people from sinners, slavers, and oppressors to righteous, just, Christian folk.

Yet Stewart's early jeremiads strain at the seams both to divulge the author's life circumstances and to establish her Christian faith. In this way her texts are not clear-cut jeremiads. In fact, Stewart's gender complicates labeling her a jeremiah, for the black jeremiah, like the earlier American Puritan jeremiah, confidently assumes the power of the patriarch. Though she is austere, Stewart does not write or speak with absolute patriarchal authority. In discussing the imperious rhetoric deployed by Ida B. Wells, the late-nineteenth-century African American journalist who campaigned against lynch laws and Jim Crow segregation, Howard-Pitney explains that "the stern jeremiah figure peering down disapprovingly at the people and harshly denouncing their conduct continued to be considered a singularly male public role and image" (85). The gendered limitations restricting Wells and her crusade in the Victorian 1890s were already firmly erected when Stewart dared to ascend the lecture platform in the 1830s. Perhaps because both activists risked—and received—censure for being "unladylike," the aggressive, inflammatory tone of the jeremiad permeates their writing, as Howard-Pitney concludes about Wells's writing, only "somewhat haphazardly and irregularly" (82). The cultural prescriptions/proscriptions of true women as demure, compassionate, and soft-spoken fully spanned the nineteenth century (and still persist even today) and were patently incompatible with the fire-and-brimstone stridence of the jeremiad.

Nineteenth-century audiences had access to Stewart's jeremiads in two forms: public performances and published documents. The lectures she performed attest especially to her conviction and valor. For she subjects herself to hostile objectification and a violent gaze as she denounces her era's doubt and faithlessness while proclaiming her own clairvoyance and clarity. In *Elegant Jeremiahs*, George P. Landow distinguishes between Victorian sages and modern sages thusly: "Although Victorian sages frequently open lectures, essays, or books with a pose of humility, they quickly assert their superiority over the audience. Modern sages, in contrast, may inform their readers specifically about personal weakness and also enter into intimate details of health and behavior" (35).

Stewart, while neither Victorian nor modern, shows affinities with both kinds of the "elegant jeremiah" that Landow describes. Like the Victorians, Stewart claims divinely sanctioned authority over her listening and reading audience immediately after asserting her "feebleness" and inadequacies: "I am sensible of my ignorance; but such knowledge as God has given to me, I impart to you" (6). And, like the moderns, she occasionally alludes to her private life, then self-effacingly retreats into public discourse, as if suddenly aware of the taboo against black women speaking in a public space before mixed-race and dual-gender spectators. This paradoxical posing is itself gendered. On the one hand, Stewart's claims of moral superiority are supported by her womanness (though she is black), for patriarchy anxiously alleged that true women naturally embodied Christian virtue. And though she is not an actual mother, at thirty-two (the ideal age for the republican mother and the age at which she first published the *Productions*), she figures as one ideally suited and responsible for the correct rearing of the young, impressible members of the nation's populace. For the republican mother, as Linda Kerber defines her, was "forthright and practical, impervious to fashion and frivolity," and dedicated to raising "her children to be decent and public-spirited citizens, and thus by her private decisions strengthen[ing] the civic order in which she lived" (*Intellectual History* 211, 121). On the other hand, Stewart's professions of humility conform to the code of conduct requiring women to be deferential, retiring, self-abnegating, and altruistic. In an important and scathing assessment of the roles permitted women in the early republic, Julia Stern explores not only republican motherhood, but also republican "daughterhood" and "wifehood" (roles that the widowed Stewart did not truly fit into by 1835) as "three socially sanctioned roles [through which] patriarchy annexes political agency for its own purposes and reroutes it inside the family, enabling middle-class white women in post-Revolutionary America to take up public identities at no cost to a conservative social agenda" (96). Thus, Stewart, black, female, proud, and public, rhetorically exploits the ideology of true womanhood and the forces that would restrict her were it not for the forces' conflicting race, class, and gender codes.

Moreover, Stewart brilliantly reconciles the doctrine of separate gender spheres. The rhetoric of her early jeremiads brings moral suasion together with unflinching rebuke. In *Home Fronts,* Lora Romero has astutely observed a "bilingualism" in Stewart's *Productions;* that is, "the conjunction in her writing of both vocabularies of nationalism: the language of life and the language of death" (68). In other words, by merging the discourse of nurturance associated with women and the discourse of aggression associated with men, Stewart subverts the oppositionality of white and black, male and female, public marketplace and private home that dominated American thought and letters in the wake of the Revolution. Romero goes on to argue, "The domestic woman could and did leave the home, but she could not do so if she abandoned the claim of her moral difference from men. Stewart repeatedly and flagrantly risks that moral difference by placing sword, shield, and helmet on the woman warrior" (68–69). While Romero's analysis offers exceptionally valuable insights, its ultimate contention that Stewart's "bilingualism threatens the ground of powerlessness on which social housekeeping rests" (69) needs qualification. The hegemonic devaluation of African American women meant that their "social housekeeping," a term Romero borrows from Eileen Boris, did not rest on (the premise of) their powerlessness. As I explore later in this chapter, Stewart does not claim to be morally different from *all* men nor different to the same degree. Certainly, using the rhetoric of sentimentalism she does assert, as Romero notes, that women are morally superior to men, but the black nationalism of the *Productions* argues as well for the moral superiority of blacks over whites. Though even they too come under the jeremiah's scrutinizing eye, African American women unquestionably emerge as the most Christian—and therefore the most powerful—beings in the new nation. Uncorrupted by the marketplace, they are more pious and more pure than men; untainted by racism and slavery, they are more chaste and more righteous than white women. Stewart, like her holy women descendants, perceives the anomalous and sanctified position that black women (can) occupy and anticipates former slave Harriet Jacobs's call for a new measure of African American women's virtue, a revised standard by which to assess black women's chastity and charity. Furthermore, the immasculinization of African American women that Romero attributes to Stewart more precisely derives from a society that persistently denied/denies black women's capacity for virtue and blacks' capacity for reason. Stewart's placement of the "sword, shield, and helmet on the [black] woman warrior"— that is, her appeal to African American women to work for black spiritual, social, and political improvement—must be read in the context of her Christian devotion. Because the *Productions*—both the separate volume in 1835 and the latter section of the 1879 *Meditations*—is a collection of sacred jeremiads, it clarifies Stewart's double-voiced nationalism, her "bilingualism," as Christian morality and radical militarism. Both discourses suppress the personal: the one as a performance of humility and charity, the other as a performance for the good of the nation.

"Religion and the Pure Principles of Morality"

The introduction to "Religion and the Pure Principles of Morality" asserts a common nineteenth-century disclaimer. The essayist expresses hope that her "friends will not scrutinize these pages with too severe an eye," for she has written not "to display elegance or taste," but "in order to arouse you to exertion, and to enforce upon your minds the great necessity of turning your attention to knowledge and improvement" (3).[1] From the beginning, then, Stewart identifies a major jeremiadic goal, that is, to provoke those trapped with her in "our wretched and degraded situation" to revolt. The second paragraph, only two sentences long, autobiographically enumerates the milestones of Stewart's twenty-eight-year-long life, ending with an allusion to her religious conversion:

> I was born in Hartford, Connecticut, in 1803; was left an orphan at five years of age; was bound out in a clergyman's family; had the seeds of piety and virtue early sown in my mind; but was deprived of the advantages of education, though my soul thirsted for knowledge. Left them at 15 years of age; attended Sabbath Schools until I was 20; in 1826, was married to James W. Steward [*sic*]; was left a widow in 1829; was, as I humbly hope and trust, brought to the knowledge of the truth, as it is in Jesus, in 1830; in 1831, made a public profession of my faith in Christ. (3–4)

This succinct paragraph prefacing Stewart's first jeremiad elucidates the sentimentality of the genre. The shock value of the jeremiad is designed to evoke in readers the psycho-social responses that sentimental literature ideally elicits: first, the intense emotions (i.e., anguish, devastation, anger, hope, and so on), then the corollary physical sensations of sympathy (viz., sighs, tears, swoons, and swells), and finally, the specific political actions to effect ideological and social change (e.g., munificence, crusade, legislation, the vote). Although the jeremiah estranges himself—or, much more rarely, *herself*—from those whom he or she addresses and castigates, both the jeremiah and the sentimental writer assume that readers and writers are bound by a common code of Christian morality and charity. Stewart's autobiographical statement at the outset of "Religion and the Pure Principles" highlights fundamental events of the author's life, encoding them in sentimental terms. As Harriet Wilson would do at mid-century in *Our Nig*, Stewart anticipates the "sensibility" of a readership who will feel and feel for the pathos of her young life: as an orphaned child (through parental desertion rather than death, as she implies in the passive construction

"was left"), as an obligatorily indentured servant, as a bright girl "deprived of . . .
education," and as a childless widow by age twenty-six, after only three years of
marriage.

This sequence of tragedies occurring so early in her life is rhetorically balanced by a series of happenstances and characteristics that render the narrator
yet more pathetic but also endearing, and, to a degree, admirable as well. First,
she is "bound out in a clergyman's family." Stewart's statement thus propels
her into the domestic sphere, in spite of her orphaned status. Implicit in this
clause is the sacred salvation she would receive as part of living with a clergyman
in addition to her secular rescue in the domain of the family, the home. Moreover, her tacit allusion to the home conjures up the image of the minister's wife,
who, in turn, recalls the figure of republican motherhood, two sentimental
tropes of goodness, charity, and nurturing nationalism. Until this point, Stewart does not mention race—unless we are to understand "bound out" as signifying (on) the abject conditions of voluntary servitude blacks faced in early
nineteenth-century America. However, another passive construction she uses
("was deprived of the advantages of education") insinuates that, contrary to the
"seeds of piety" that were "sown in [her] mind," race and gender prejudice prohibited her intellectual development even "though [her] soul thirsted for
knowledge." Stewart's declaration of her intellectual precociousness calls for her
readers to admire her early desire for education as much as it requires them to
condemn the white family's disregard for her fine mind. Since Stewart's readers
were generally New England whites like the clergyman and his family, she
seems subtly to reassure readers that had *they* taken her in, they surely would
not have deprived her so. Or, to put it another way, the assertion charges white
readers with the responsibility of fostering African American educational opportunities, especially when they are faced with evidence of intellectual curiosity and capability in an African American child like herself. Similarly, her pursuit of knowledge in the Sabbath Schools implicitly reassures readers that their
own ability to read is both a virtue and a privilege and that their very reading
of Stewart's book substantiates their capacity for pity and for affective fellow
feeling and its redeeming influence. The final clause, testifying to the narrator's
religious conversion and her continued good faith, draws a cloak of both sanctity and civility (hardly disseverable at the time) around the author and her
reader. Having intimated her confidence that all of her readers are Christian,
and therefore "saved" in the spiritual, cultural, and political senses of the word,
Stewart can turn in the succeeding paragraph to a familiar rant found in jeremiads: "All the nations of the earth are crying out for Liberty and Equality.

Away, away with tyranny and oppression!" (4) Then she asserts that while European Americans' "highest aim is to excel in political, moral and religious improvement . . . very few among them . . . bestow one thought upon the benighted sons and daughters of Africa" (12). In the introduction to "Religion and the Pure Principles," however, she strategically lures readers toward the transcendent state of sympathy.

Although the essay's first paragraph does not mention religion or conversion, the second paragraph introduces the narrator as a woman whose entire life has involved hardship, sorrow, racial discrimination, and religious perseverance. Stewart's express intention to incite her diverse readers to personal and political reform in the first paragraph and her declaration of Christian faith in the second one converge in a series of statements about the need for blacks to pursue liberty and resist oppression. Apparently, her resumé serves to assure readers of her qualifications as an informed and faithful critic of their culture.

At the end of the introduction to "Religion and the Pure Principles of Morality," Stewart eulogizes her deceased mentor, David Walker, as "noble, fearless, and undaunted" (5). She continues to allude to him throughout her essay in terms that verify their shared visions and that reveal her self-conscious deployment of jeremiadic conventions. A classic early nineteenth-century black jeremiad, Walker's 1829 *Appeal to the Coloured Citizens of the World* champions the use of armed force in the fight against American slavery and racism in unexpurgated and incendiary terms. Similarly, Stewart's essay, addressed explicitly to "MY RESPECTED FRIENDS" (5), pleads primarily with "the benighted sons and daughters of Africa" (12). However, as Paul Goodman has shown, Walker's *Appeal* "was more than a cry of conscience. For all its impassioned rhetoric, prophetic denunciations of white cant and injustice, and apocalyptic predictions, the *Appeal* advanced a complex, cogent argument with an immediate political purpose: to persuade blacks to struggle with whites to abandon colonization for racial equality" (28). This he did by singling out whites like Thomas Jefferson and Henry Clay to show that many "great Americans" were antiblack and by ridiculing the hypocrisy of Christian sects as much as he did by directing his gravest assertions to blacks. Like Walker, Stewart also addresses God and European Americans as well as blacks. Perhaps Walker's influence on her is clearest in the passages where she deftly fuses the Holy Scriptures with the United States Constitution to arouse blacks' passion and pride, as when she exclaims: "He hath crowned you with glory and honor; hath made you but a little lower than the angels; and according to the Constitution of these United States, he hath made all men free and equal" (5). At the beginning of her essay, then, Stewart, like Walker before her, appropriates the impassioned discourse of major national documents to dismantle post-Revolutionary racism, especially as it was manifested in the form of slavery.

Stewart apparently opted to write a jeremiad rather than a confession in part because she thought African Americans would be better served by grim prophecies than by her story. Its autobiographical introduction aside, "Religion and the Pure Principles" suggests that autobiography is superfluous among a people whose spiritual and political salvation is their highest priority. Thus, the design of Stewart's first essay is to argue that the myths African Americans most need to debunk are the racial myths obstructing their political and spiritual development. Like other black jeremiads, "Religion and the Pure Principles of Morality" calls on northerners to take swift, assiduous action against racism and slavery: "Show forth your powers of mind," Stewart commands her readers, and: "let us promote ourselves and improve our own talents" (4, 12). She denies advocating violence in the pursuit of racial independence when she exclaims, "Far be it from me to recommend to you, either to kill, burn, or destroy" (4). Yet the effect of her disavowal of violence is to urge it simply by recognizing it. In this way, she revises her mentor's rhetorical stance, perhaps to avoid the charges of sedition that were leveled against David Walker's *Appeal* and that ultimately led to his mysterious death. More overtly, Stewart encourages African Americans to "sheath [their] swords, and calm [their] angry passions" (20), and to replace their lethal arms with "the weapons of prayer" (21).

Stewart exhibits fierce racial pride throughout "Religion and the Pure Principles of Morality." Even though she addresses multiple audiences in the essay, directing her rantings to first one group then another, she most explicitly writes to African Americans. She is sometimes their spiritual peer, "a dying mortal" speaking to "other dying mortals" (6); more often she writes from the distance of a self-made pariah. Unlike such traditional spiritual autobiographers as Jarena Lee, whose *Life and Religious Journal* appeared only one year after the *Productions*, Stewart does not claim to have been called by God to preach to others—except insofar as she believed it the duty of every Christian to broadcast the Gospel: she says, "*[W]ere I called upon*, I would willingly sacrifice my life for the cause of God and my brethren" (4, italics added). As Landow asserts, "the style, tone, and general presentation of the sage derive from the fact that [her] voice resides at the periphery; it is . . . an eccentric voice, one off center" (23); thus, Stewart's jeremiadic alienation from her readers parallels the marginality of other visionaries. In her words, "I have neither kindred nor friends.

I stand alone in your midst, exposed to the fiery darts of the devil, and to the assaults of wicked men" (21).

Like Jeremiah in Lamentations, Stewart moans in poetry: "O that my head were waters, and mine eyes a fountain of tears, that I might weep day and night, for the transgressions of the daughters of my people" (5). Outside the sphere of domesticity herself as seer, writer, and orator, she eludes conventional nineteenth-century notions of ideal femininity. The isolating effects of the role of the jeremiah enable her to exempt herself from the cultivation of true woman values. Yet her interpretation of African American women's current grievous condition is based on the idealized figure of the true *white* woman. She warns black women—whom she identifies as workers, sinners, maidens, wives, mothers, homemakers, and other servants—that the burden of racial uplift lies with them. Calling for "the maiden who will blush at vulgarity" (7), Stewart urgently links black women's power to transform African American cultural and political values to the cult of true womanhood's proverbial "piety, purity, submissiveness, and domesticity": "Did the daughters of our land possess a delicacy of manners, combined with gentleness and dignity; did their pure minds hold vice in abhorrence and contempt, did they frown when their ears were polluted with its vile accents, would not their influence become powerful?" (7). Interestingly, this sentence juxtaposes affected qualities (of "delicacy of manners" and frown—or consternation—at the "vile accents" of vulgarity) with intrinsic qualities (of "gentleness and dignity" as well as "pure minds"). Although the assertion is formulated as a conditional statement, it nonetheless posits that African American women always already possess "pure minds" and that the effect of the cultivation of the stated virtues would inarguably increase black women's power, presumably over forces—human and thus social—that currently restrict their political maturation. And while she urges them to "strive to excel in good housewifery" (16), she also bitterly laments African American women's neglected intellectual development because of compulsory domestic work: "How long shall the fair daughters of Africa be compelled to bury their minds and talents beneath a load of iron pots and kettles?" (16).

In succeeding sentences Stewart also associates piety with liberty and the cultivation of traditional white women's values with the improvement of black women's social and spiritual condition: "Their souls would become fired with a holy zeal for freedom's cause . . . Knowledge would begin to flow, and the chains of slavery and ignorance would melt like wax before the flames" (7). Moreover, Stewart implores African American mothers to educate young blacks by interweaving self-determination with moral instruction. Education, like the construction imagery of the essay's subtitle ("the Sure Foundation on Which We Must Build") forms a leitmotif in "Religion and the Pure Principles of Morality." She warns black mothers that they "must create in the minds of [their] little girls and boys a thirst for knowledge, the love of virtue, the abhorrence of vice, and the cultivation of a pure heart" (13). Some of her advice in this regard is extraordinarily practical and specific, as when she counsels daughters of Africa, "Let every female heart become united, and let us raise a fund ourselves; and at the end of one year and a half, we might be able to lay the corner-stone for the building of a High School, that the higher branches of knowledge might be enjoyed by us" (16). Thus, Stewart appropriates and repeats the key terms of sentimental and Revolutionary rhetoric.

Widowed early in her marriage, Stewart never bore her own children; hence, she risked being dismissed by parents for instructing them without having personal experience as a mother. To compensate, Stewart exhorts from the margins in self-effacing terms. Her freedom from domestic duties provided Stewart with the time and latitude to speak with some impunity on the responsibilities of women who filled more traditional roles. From the beginning of "Religion and the Pure Principles," she confesses, "I feel almost unable to address you; almost incompetent to perform the task" (5), and says, "I am but a feeble instrument. I am but as one particle of the small dust of the earth" (7). Prophesying that other sages will follow her, she professes her inferiority to her successors: "After I am dead, perhaps before, God will surely raise up those who will more powerfully and eloquently plead the cause of virtue and the pure principles of morality than I am able to do" (7).

Her own death fascinates Stewart, who declares that if she could but see African Americans choosing chastity and piety over sin and affliction, "then could I say, now, Lord, let thine unworthy handmaiden depart in peace, for I have seen the desire of mine eyes, and am satisfied" (10).[2] Imagining and inscribing herself as deceased is one way she repeatedly dramatizes her insignificance and tacitly coaxes readers to grieve not for the individual loss her demise would signify, but the desperate condition of the nation as her jeremiads depict it. Thus, death functions metaphorically and pedagogically for Stewart: mourners can be taught to feel sympathy, "and weeping over the dead can serve as preparation for a vital religious experience" (White 103). A staple of sentimental literature, ritualized death is a major trope for traumatic loss, transcendent love, and divine reunion. As Isabelle White bluntly states, "Death scenes sold novels in mid-nineteenth-century America" (99). The seduction novel, another cautionary genre popular in Stewart's day, narrates the death of a fallen woman and thereby preaches women's strict adherence to a Christian code of chastity and morality. High infant mortality rates and higher numbers of women dying during childbirth also account for the preponderance of death scenes in early nineteenth-century sentimental literature. Moreover, as Harriet Beecher Stowe would exploit in the deaths of Little Eva and Uncle Tom at mid-century, fictionalized death scenes soldered the rhetoric of sentimentality to the rhetoric of Christianity by linking dying innocents/innocence to the martyred Christ. Stewart herself was intimately familiar with death since she was both an orphan and a widow. And, as a jeremiah, she draws upon the human fear of death— especially violent and torturous death at the hands of an angry God—to arouse her readers' urgency about their souls and the state of the nation.

In the midst of her powerful testimony, Stewart invokes the sentimentalized figure of the sacred child to proclaim herself blessed:

I, even I, who am but a child, inexperienced to many of you, am a living witness to testify unto you this day, that I have seen the wicked in great power, spreading himself like a green bay tree, and lo, he passed away; yea, I diligently sought him, but he could not be found; and it is God alone that has inspired my heart to feel for Afric's woes. (20)

This rhetorical presentation of herself as *naïf* recurs in other instances where Stewart castigates the racism of her white readers and the idleness of her black readers. This passage also illustrates her tendency to refer to her own life but stop short of elaborating upon it, neglecting to explicate the "moral" of her story. The jeremiad form permits Stewart to abbreviate portions of her story that a more conventional autobiographical form would require her to substantiate.

In order to project her prophetic voice outside and above society synchronously, Stewart had to be perceived by readers as both extraneous and essential. She depreciates herself by describing her isolation and consequent vulnerability. At the end of the essay, she skillfully positions herself both within and outside her audience. The essay's final statement, however, reaffirms her faith in God's approbation of her mission, and obliquely her faith in her readers, on whom racial equity and enlightenment ultimately depend: "For I am fully persuaded, that he will bring me off conqueror, yea, more than conqueror" (22).

In the final analysis, "Religion and the Pure Principles of Morality," its autobiographical introduction notwithstanding, is more of a jeremiad than a confession or conversion narrative, for it divulges very little of its author's spiritual life. Instead, it primarily proclaims a nation's potential for transcendence and evolution from the Christian hypocrisy associated with its slaveholding practices and prophesies certain doom if this potential remains unfulfilled. The essay makes an important contribution to the tradition of black American women's (spiritual) autobiography, however, through its introduction, which signifies Stewart's interest in black nationalism and the conversion narrative and her familiarity with each. (Indeed, the essay adumbrates the spiritual dimensions found in later works by African Americans such as Frederick Douglass, Harriet Wilson, and later black writers. It also attests to how Stewart intermingled the particular tropes she developed with those she borrowed from early American Puritan writers like John Winthrop, Thomas Shephard, and their literary descendants, most notably Benjamin Franklin.) The introduction preceding "Religion and the Pure Principles of Morality" serves as an overture to the whole of the *Productions* (1835), for no other word from the author appears between the essay and the title page. Therefore, when Stewart commences her address to her "respected friends," she has already justified herself and her jeremiad. In the 1879 *Meditations*, however, "Religion and the Pure Principles" falls after "Sufferings During the War," the last of the prefatory documents; by introducing the earlier essay with elements of the conversion narrative, the jeremiadic "Religion and the Pure Principles" is recast in 1879 into autobiographical relief.

"Meditations"

In the same way that "Religion and the Pure Principles of Morality" avoids autobiographical detail, Stewart's fourteen meditations and seven intermittent prayers allude to elements of her life but abstain from developing them. Stewart's "Meditations," first published as a separate religious pamphlet in 1832, is an extraordinarily personal and self-conscious collection of reflections and prayers that demonstrate the author's private anguish as prophet and penitent.

Modeled on the book of Lamentations, written by the prophet Jeremiah, the "Meditations" is full of pathos, pain, and self-deprecation. It begins, like "Religion and the Pure Principles of Morality," with a brief introduction in which the narrator acknowledges her unworthiness. This introduction offers incipient autobiographical information. The second paragraph indicates the level of Stewart's self-erasure because she denotes herself in the third person in it: "The author has . . . basked in the sunshine of prosperity; and . . . she has drunk deep in the cup of sorrow" (23). She does not clarify either her prosperity or her sorrow. The next paragraph recalls her recent grief, but the statement, "It is now

one year since Christ first spoke peace to my troubled soul" (24), is not qualified
by either details of her past distress or by descriptions of her present peace. This
autobiographical reticence Stewart exhibits in the introduction to the "Meditations" is reinforced by the terse, fragmented structure of the whole section.

Although Stewart uses the first person singular more often in the "Meditations," it shares the focus of "Religion and the Pure Principles of Morality" on
the private and public, on domesticity, and on nationalism. As she struggles to
"become a humble instrument in the hands of God" (24), she remains devoted
to liberation and antislavery movements. The "Meditations" is more classically
spiritual than its predecessor, yet it also reflects Stewart's domestic concerns; for
example, she writes that "the chains of slavery and ignorance will never burst,
and morality and virtue will never flourish, till pure and holy examples are set
at home" (24). In other words, even Stewart's private sacred meditations take
on the conventions of the jeremiad, emphasizing her commitment to her cause
and her community. "Home" signifies both the African American society of the
North and the nascent nation as readily as it does an individual domicile; thus,
she reiterates the connections between private/domestic and public/political.
Stewart's choice of genre reveals her worry that a personal narrative delineating
the means by which she developed her own spiritual and political convictions
would be either insufficient or inappropriate to encourage others to set pure and
holy examples at "home."

The "Meditations" is also like "Religion and the Pure Principles of Morality"
because it, too, is addressed to "my respected friends." Lest there be any question that her friends are African Americans, Stewart explicitly names "all the
benighted sons and daughters of Africa" as her primary subjects (30, 37). She
also names her own church's congregation in her prayers and appeals, frequently
referring throughout the "Meditations" to "the church to which I belong," "our
pastor," and "my church and pastor." The most melancholic prayers are for herself, though. In these she effaces herself by or because of her "deep sense of guilt
and unworthiness" (30), her "plainness of speech" (39), her "poor and needy"
state as both orphan and widow (49), and her wretchedness as a "poor unworthy worm" (50). Generally, she declares herself "sick and full of diseases"
(36) in most of her meditations and even revives the fascination with death she
displays in her earlier essay. Like the sermons and contemplations of John
Donne (whose writings Stewart might well have known), images of physical
and spiritual death recur in Stewart's "Meditations." In the significantly num-
bered "Meditation X," she grieves over the premature death of her husband,
who died unconverted, "with no God to look to! Heart-rending scene!" (41). In

this meditation, Stewart appropriates both conversion and sentimental narrative conventions, for as Virginia Brereton has observed, "Death usually played a prominent role in the conversion story, for the manner of one's passing was considered the sign and seal of a genuine conversion and a holy life" (9). So pervasive was this trope that, as Brereton further asserts, regardless of the form of the conversion narrative, converts who were dying women were considered "more beautiful the closer they approached the end" (9). Stewart's complex "Meditations" deploys this convention.

The "Meditations," composed when Maria Stewart was a spirited twenty-nine years old, leaves readers feeling exhausted and voyeuristic at the end. Its cadences rise and fall with her tempestuous and private emotions. "Meditation IV," for example, depicts her melancholic mood swings within a few lines: "Why art thou cast down, O my soul, and why art thou disquieted within me? Hope thou in God; for I shall yet praise him. . . . Lord, thou hast chastened me sore; but though thou hast caused me to fall, thou hast not utterly taken from me thy loving kindness; but thou has dealt in tender mercy and compassion with me" (28–29).

The feeling that one is peering too closely into Stewart's heart, however, derives partly from the limited exposure she allows into it. Stewart, like Emily Dickinson, selects her own society, "Then—shuts the Door—." For example, in "Meditation IV" she also states, "Have just returned from church-meeting. Did not perceive that Christian spirit of fellowship which ought to exist" (28–29). But instead of exploring the real causes of her discontent with the congregation, as she might have done in a spiritual autobiography, she ruminates using a scriptural allusion: "Is there an Achan among us, O God . . . or is there a Jonah among us, who has refused to obey thy will?" (29). Later in the same paragraph, she writes, "Have met with an earthly disappointment. Am somewhat disheartened" (29). But rather than explicate her defeat or analyze her discouragement, she again discounts the force and validity of her emotions by juxtaposing them against a biblical quotation. In this particular instance, her detachment is rhetorically punctuated by a discursive dash in the text. That is, a literal empty space separates Stewart's "disheartened" self from the Scripture she affixes to it: "—Naked came I forth from my mother's womb" (29). Instead of seeming to extend the autobiographical comment, however, the dash underscores her abrupt shift in subject. Thus, Stewart assiduously resists constructing a narrative self and avoids any protracted personal narration or revelation.

Although Stewart's first two publications impart much about Maria W. Stewart, neé Miller, as a poor orphan cum brave orator, they divulge few of the circumstances of her daily life, as might a diary, or the specific details of her religious transformation, as would a conversion narrative. And unlike a conventional spiritual autobiography, "Meditations" recounts or analyzes events of the author's life. Stewart subverts every instance of private discourse. Through her construction of a self that avoids retrospection, however, the narrator emerges as pious, passionate, valiant, and brilliant. "Religion and the Pure Principles of Morality" and "Meditations" further proclaim Stewart's anxiety about the condition and the future of blacks in America. As a writer who was an activist and an abolitionist, she clearly hoped to radicalize whites and blacks. Moreover, as a freeborn northern African American, she appeals in particular to free(d) African Americans, whose plight she considers "but little better than that" of slaves (52), to involve themselves in the antislavery crusade and to determine their own moral and social uplift. The advancement of such radical theses attests to Stewart's piety, courage, and tenacity. Walker's unsolved murder in 1830 provided her an example of the possible fates of "subversives" like herself. Trusting in God's protection, she risked physical assault to speak to promiscuous audiences beginning in 1832, even though she reports that by 1831 she had begun to be harassed as a woman writer "exposed to the . . . assaults of wicked men" (21). Stewart's jeremiadic *Productions* encompass various "personal" literary forms—the essay, the lamentation, and the lecture—and endow her literary heirs with the license to appropriate these forms, to select different ones, or to transcend the limits Stewart imposed upon herself by reconstructing their own experiences as autobiographies.

Four Public Addresses

The protofeminist lectures Stewart gave during the two and a half years after she published the "Meditations," beginning in the spring of 1832 with her "Address, Delivered Before the Afric-American Intelligence Society, of Boston" and ending with her "Farewell Address to Her Friends in the City of Boston" on September 21, 1834, are also jeremiads. As such these orations are characterized by indignation and warning. First, she charges free blacks with indolence. One of her most vituperative speeches, the "Lecture, Delivered at the Franklin Hall" on September 21, 1832, opens with a demand: "Why sit ye here and die?" (51). Placing the burden of black productivity on black shoulders, she argues that "were the American free people of color to turn their attention more assiduously to moral worth and intellectual improvement . . . prejudice would gradually diminish, and whites would be compelled to say, unloose those fetters!" (52). The Franklin Hall lecture also condemns European Americans for avarice and injustice. Furthermore, Stewart interrogates her "fairer sisters, whose hands are never soiled" by asking, "And why are not our forms as delicate, and our constitutions as slender, as yours?" (52–53). Later, at the African Masonic Hall in 1833, she compares America to the biblical Babylon and denounces whites for having "made the Africans drunk with the wine of fornication" (71). As she condemns white privilege and acknowledges that "there is no [equal] opportunity for the sons of Africa" (66), Stewart also reproves blacks for "bear[ing] the yoke of oppression" (63) and for failing to rise to distinction. At the same time that she exclaims, "Cast your eyes about, look as far as you can see; all, all is owned by the lordly white, except here and there a lowly dwelling [for] the man of color, midst deprivations, fraud and opposition" (67), she also urges African Americans "to follow the example of the whites" (68).

Besides illuminating ambivalent feelings about race relations, Stewart's lectures also speak about the persecutions she endured on the platform because of her gender. Without providing specific details about her experiences, they elucidate not only her detractors' reprehensible abuses, but also her salient response to Christ's call, "'Who shall go forward, and take off the reproach that is cast upon the people of color? Shall it be a woman?'" (51). Stewart replies to this summons by saying, "I believe that God has fired my soul with a holy zeal for his cause" (59). Her lectures include numerous references to her being rejected as a woman by church patriarchy and lay people of both races. She is compelled repeatedly to declare in a characteristic military trope, "I have enlisted in the holy warfare . . . the Lord's battle I mean to fight, until my voice expire in death" (59). Her "Farewell Address" draws on biblical and contemporary sources to claim her right to a public persona. In it, she cites the examples of brave women from the Bible and even corrects Paul's condemnation of women's public speaking. However, the decorum and credibility that is a feature of sentimental literature as well as her personal proclivities require Stewart to efface herself. The *Productions* thus demonstrates her belief that, as God's foot soldier, she must balance humility with temerity to advocate His cause.

"Sufferings During the War"

Stewart's "Farewell Address," which summarizes her activities in Boston and justifies her emigration to New York, indulges only briefly and randomly in personal detail. The final text in *The Productions* (save a reprint of "The Negro's Complaint"), the address is dated "New York, April 14, 1834"; no additional lectures appear in *Meditations from the Pen of Mrs. Maria W. Stewart.* Apparently, Stewart ceased lecturing once she left Boston in 1833. Upon receiving her long overdue widow's pension in 1879, Stewart immediately arranged for the publication of a second, revised edition of her 1835 volume.[3] The supplemental apparati of the *Meditations* indicate that though she operated small private schools between 1835 and 1879, Stewart was effectively silenced by rejection, despair, and destitution. The brief preface to the 1879 text asserts that the *Productions* "was suppressed for forty-six years" (87).[4] With this passive construction, Stewart reinforces the self-abnegating quality of the preface, which studiously effaces its author by referring to her in the third person rather than the first. Moreover, echoing the Christian discourse of her earlier "Meditations," she names herself in the preface's final clause as "the unworthy author." Most important, the 1879 preface establishes the importance of the documents that reconstruct Stewart's life as a Christian widow. While five of the preface's seven sentences refer overtly to Christianity or God, none mentions the African American race, gender or racial discrimination, antebellum abolitionism, or even postemancipation racial uplift rhetoric. Rather, she overtly declares a desire to convert readers to Christianity as the impetus for her second publication. In addition, the several allusions to the narrator's "standing as a woman and a Christian in poverty's dark shade" (87) suggest that the seventy-six-year-old Stewart hopes the revised text will relieve her persistent financial difficulties. By highlighting her own impoverished yet pious life and her late husband's war service in the *Meditations,* the 1879 preface transforms the nature and significance of her *Productions.* By adding a personal memoir to the second edition, Stewart transforms a collection of religious and political writings into a spiritual autobiography.

Yet Stewart's is an odd specimen of the spiritual autobiography genre. The traditional spiritual autobiographies of Jarena Lee and Zilpha Elaw, whose conventional conversion narratives were written in the 1840s, reconstruct the ministers' lives expressly to call readers to Christ and salvation. But Stewart's 1879 spiritual autobiography does not augment the sparse details found in her sacred writings of 1835. Although it maintains the passivity, self-erasure, and repudiation of the personal that characterize the *Productions,* the *Meditations*'s major addendum, a personal memoir titled "Sufferings During the War," is strikingly self-absorbed. Its distinctive tone is neither fiery like the *Productions* generally nor sentimental like specific parts of "Religion and the Pure Principles" and the "Meditations." In the end, however, it is not surprising that "Sufferings During the War" does not galvanize its readership toward progressive and dramatic social change or that its sentimentalism does not inspire benevolence. The sharp difference between the 1835 and the 1879 texts parallels the vast distinctions that occurred between Harriet Jacobs's *antebellum* slave narrative, which was published in 1861, and the *postbellum* autobiography written by former slavewoman Elizabeth Keckley, which was published in 1868. The two texts were published a mere seven years apart but the gaping divide caused by the devastating Civil War is evident in their respective works. Similarly, one finds remarkable disparities between the first (1845) and last (1892) autobiographies penned by Frederick Douglass. In the wake of emancipation, Stewart joins other (African) Americans in the celebration of black progress, if not exactly black power. As Garrison's letter, included among her appendices, exults, "Through what marvelous changes and experiences we have since [the abolitionist period] passed! How many rights and privileges are now accorded to the colored people at the North that were then everywhere denied them!" (Richardson 89).

Rather than reinforcing the national rejoicing, however, Stewart's evasion and passivity in 1879 undoubtedly emanate from the consequences of her early activism. Being cast first out of Boston, then Brooklyn and Long Island, and falling on hard times in Baltimore and Washington, D.C., her rejection of the rhetorical strategies that had taken her to both prominence and notoriety makes sense. Given that the outcome of her militant stance and strident discourse had been destitution and a kind of excommunication from the abolitionist community in Boston, no wonder that she would opt for a radically divergent strategy in a new narrative. But whereas her rejection of the personal in the 1830s at once asserted a collective racial identity and a unique divinely granted authority, Stewart's subversion of the personal in later life seems only ameliorative, reactionary, and finally pathetic. *None* of the ideological movements she represented in the *Productions* appears in the new texts of the *Meditations*. Stewart constructed the *Productions* during an era that radiated with challenges to the racial status quo, an era that produced Walker's audacious *Appeal* and the infamous insurrections led by Nat Turner, Gabriel Prosser, and Denmark Vesey. But Reconstruction occasioned in blacks a very different sensibility; African Americans were determined to confirm that they were ready to receive their full civil rights, largely by attempting to conform to narrow definitions of propriety, temperance, and morality. Thus, the latter-day Stewart appears not to be visionary, but regressive instead. Her use of the words "Mrs.," "Widow," and "Matron" in the title of her revised edition (*Meditations from the Pen of Mrs. Maria W. Stewart, Widow of the late James W. Stewart, Now Matron of the Freedman's Hospital*) hollowly reiterates her status as an elderly matriarch, thricely relating her claims to honor and homage. Stewart's innovative use of specific sentimental tropes in the *Meditations* subverts the personal even more than her deployment of the jeremiad in the *Productions* does. Despite an apparently repressed desire to tell her life, as illustrated so vividly in "Religion and the Pure Principles of Morality," even Stewart's expressly autobiographical sketch effaces her. The longest of her extant writings, the rhetoric of "Sufferings During the War" differs radically from that of Stewart's other texts. Yet like the other works, it exposes her anxiety about self-representation since its very title obscures her both as agent and as subject.

According to Marilyn Richardson, to whom we are indebted for her dazzling recovery of Stewart's forsaken texts, "Sufferings" demonstrates Stewart's interest in experimental narrativization. Richardson describes the sketch as a "curiously hybrid document" inspired by the novel and the theater (82). Its mid–Civil War and postbellum temporal settings, Richardson continues, allow Stewart to use the war as "an epic framework" for her memoir (83). Indisputably, Stewart appropriates nineteenth-century fictional and theatrical conventions, drawing especially on sentimental novels to create "cliff-hanging moments of uncertainty, cruel misunderstandings which compromise the heroine's reputation, a sense of bleak despair set on Christmas Eve, and, of course, prayers answered in the fullness of time" (Richardson 82). Richardson also reads Stewart's "deliberate disruption of the chronological sequence of the events she recounts" (82) as evidence of Stewart's use of the conventions of nineteenth-century fiction.

"Sufferings During the War" details Stewart's experiences in the Washington, D.C.–Baltimore area between 1852, the year she left New York, and 1879, the year she published the *Meditations,* just months before her death that December. The most striking characteristic of the sketch is its chronological discontinuity. She begins by obliquely pinpointing the temporal setting: "It was on a beautiful Sunday morning in the month of ———, in the year of ———, between the hours of 10 and 11 o'clock" (98). The realistic details Stewart provides make plain her allusion to the Baltimore riots of April 1861, however. After an extended dialogue between the narrator and "a young lady"—a narrativized dialogue in direct discourse—the narrator digresses to explain how she "wended [her] way to Baltimore in 1852" (98). Chapter 2 starts out with her living in Baltimore during the Civil War, but later digresses to locate her in Washington from 1861 to 1863. This digression, marked by the literal space between consecutive paragraphs in the text, begins with the sentence, "But to return to my trip to Washington" (102), and runs through the end of the chapter. Chapter 3 begins similarly, asserting, "But to return to the Christmas tree" (103). The first sentence of chapter 4 reads, "But to my new house" (105), after a second substantial digression in the third chapter. To complicate the memoir further, Stewart randomly shifts from first to third person, effacing the narrator as "Mrs. Stewart," or as "our heroine," or with greater detachment as "your heroine." In addition, several vignettes end with the melodramatic summation, "The curtain falls thus and ends the scene" (102).

The five chapters recount Stewart's midlife poverty, her struggle to secure a teaching position and steady pupils in the war-ravished South, and her central role in postbellum religious denominational disputes. "Sufferings" manages to convey this in spite of its convoluted chronology. Chapter 2 explains that "Mrs. Stewart" experienced great difficulty sustaining herself primarily because, as an Episcopalian, she belonged to a sect of Christians "unpopular with the Government and [who] were going to have nothing to do with the colored school" (101). The text further reports, in passive constructions, the means by which "our heroine" gained relief: "So, in despair, after much persuasion, [Stewart and a woman friend] went together to see Dr. Hall; were kindly received; the tale of woe was told. . . . The decision was the school was to be continued, if the supplicant could get scholars enough to supply her with food, which was almost doubtful" (101).

Such evasion demonstrates more than an experimentation with rhetorical strategies; it clarifies more than Stewart's persistent discomfort with the projection of herself as the historical subject of her own discourse. Stewart appropriates sentimentalized fictional conventions in telling a segment of her life to circumvent the portrait of a life of which she is no longer fully proud. During the early years of her career, Stewart used a variety of expository and narrative forms but rejected the autobiography as a viable mode for the expression of her convictions and the experiences that forged them. Conversely, in her maturity, she published an autobiographical revision of her earlier works, apparently convinced that a narrative reconstruction of the events of her life during her twelve-year hiatus from the literary world was precisely the form her ideas should take. In that interim, however, Stewart's situation drastically worsened. Despite the meaningful work she performed in schools and among freedpeople during Reconstruction, Stewart implies in her autobiographical narrative that poverty and politics tarnished her persona and eroded her value system from one that privileged Afrocentrism and Christianity to one that deserted African Americans in the name of Christianity. For the *Meditations* reveals that, even though she was an African American in race-conflicted Baltimore, the elder Stewart worshipped primarily among white Episcopalians. In contrast, her lectures in Boston had ardently espoused her commitment to African American education and self-determination. Presenting the early jeremiads alongside the postbellum sketch, the *Meditations* elucidates Stewart's dilemma: she could abandon her religious sect, or she could continue to support and provide education for her people. Steadfast and faithful to her religious sect, Stewart replies, "Well, before I will give up my religious sentiments for dollars and cents I will beg my bread from door to door" (101).

Forced to choose between changing her religious creed, on the one hand, and transforming her activist message about the importance of education for racial uplift, on the other, Stewart chooses the latter option when she casts her lot with those class-conscious blacks and whites who want "to have nothing to do with the colored school." As Richardson notes, "Her allegiance to the Episcopal church . . . removed her from the funding subsidies for her classes which might have been available through other denominations" (131 n. 28). This crucial choice is only somewhat justified by a supporting document that alludes to Stewart's dilemma. The letter from the Reverend Henry Bailey commends her refusal to forsake her faith, although he served on the committee that discharged Stewart from her teaching duties, effectively expunging her income. His understatement that "many persons like myself preferred to pay for their children's instruction, and thus have them taught by Mrs. Stewart" (96) does not adequately resolve the issue of her apparently perfidious choice. Perhaps the digressive, circuitous design of "Sufferings During the War" derives precisely from Stewart's own lack of resolution—or nagging doubt—about the lamentable dilemma none should have faced in a free nation that was in the process of renewing its commitment to liberty and justice.

Stewart's intricate digressions and disruptions work to explain her relationship with the Reverend Dr. C. H. Hall. Her statements that she placed herself "under his parochial care" (103) and sought his assistance with the establishment of a local parish (105–6) enable her to separate an account of her appeals for spiritual direction from her disclosure that Hall "was in sympathy with the South" (103). In fact, she contextualizes this revelation so as to cast Hall in the best possible light, by juxtaposing him against two (other?) white men who were ill-regarded by the black community: "The minister of Trinity Church, Rev. Dr. Syle, was so much in sympathy with the South that an objection was raised by some of my Episcopalian friends. . . . The colored people were not altogether pleased with. . . . Rev. Dr. Payne . . . and although Dr. Hall was in sympathy with the South, *he was considered the best man of the three;* in sympathy with the South because he had resided there; it was thought natural that he should be" (103, italics added). Stewart furtively rationalizes Hall's allegiance to the South, shrouding it in passive constructions. Apparently, she felt obligated to include in her narrative an expression of gratitude and devotion to the minister who quite possibly saved her life (and more than once), whatever his racial identity.[5] In contrast with the impervious tone of her 1835 writings, in which she rhetorically disparages her "unworthiness," her 1879 revision exposes the author's genuine sense of unfitness. The latter text indicates her profound ideological and psychological suffering and narrative dis-ease that render Stewart's *Meditations* profoundly effaced.

Stewart's writings participate in the nineteenth-century black women's literary tradition in which African American women wrote the stories of their lives while existing under ideological, emotional, financial, and social duress. In her early writings, Maria Stewart's deployment of the jeremiad requires—or *permits*—her to avoid references to her life, allusions that she apparently considers both private and superfluous. But Stewart transforms the jeremiad not only with her blackness but also with her womanness. Her own mentor, David Walker, had participated in the Africanization of the American Puritan jeremiad with his 1829 *Appeal to the Coloured Citizens of the World*, wherein he embellished the prophetic and passionate form with an incisive analysis of the impact of race upon the destruction of the world, which the genre typically predicts. Under Stewart's steady hand, the revision of the jeremiad includes the introduction of the critique of both racism and *sexism*. Her jeremiads contemplate and excoriate differently in comparison with more traditional jeremiads written by American men of both African and European heritage because she meditates more on individual destinies, especially of her family and close friends, than on depersonalized institutions. And while Walker's *Appeal* considers the fate of African manhood throughout the world, Stewart's concerns are more confined, more "domestic," and chiefly involve Africans in the diaspora. She chooses to focus upon the New World "home" and the African American home under the care of republican "daughters of Africa." Still, both Walker's *Appeal* and Stewart's own writings can be properly called jeremiads. Although in her later writing, her dis-ease with autobiography manifests itself in sentimentality, anxiety, and circumvention, as an "I-witness" of her time, Maria Stewart is able to call the spiritually and politically recalcitrant to conversion and transcendence through the example of her own life story.

TWO

Sin-Sick Souls:
Jarena Lee and Zilpha Elaw

Possessing no political rights or broadly sanctioned social status, black women—slave and free—usually petitioned religious morality to justify their rights as mothers and to solicit public sympathy for their plight. Going public, however, demanded a vehicle. Some . . . used the written word as the means to transform their private and personal struggles into public testimony; their writing violated gender conventions as well as crossed social boundaries between white and black, free and slave, public and private.

CLAUDIA TATE, *Domestic Allegories of Political Desire*

African American literature is intrinsically a revisionary literature. Because of the social and rhetorical construction of racial identity and the difference it posits between African Americans and others and the racism it has wrought, African Americans generally do not—*cannot*—write in English without transforming existing genres or developing new ones. One of the earliest works of African American literature, the *Narrative of the Uncommon Sufferings and Surprizing Deliverance of Briton Hammon* (1760), arguably the first slave narrative, transforms the genre of autobiography by deploying conventions used in many of its subgenres and other related prose forms, such as the picaresque novel, the Puritan relation, and the Indian captivity narrative. Although the authorship of Briton Hammon's *Narrative* remains unconfirmed and controversy as to whether it was dictated or self-authored continues to this day, its form nonetheless authenticates the racial identity of the storyteller, for hybridity and a racialized consciousness are distinctive characteristics of virtually every text by Hammon's literary descendants.

In my discussion of the writings of Maria Stewart, I highlighted the multiplicity of generic forms she integrates in her writings, which appeared in the century following Hammon's narrative. Stewart's 1835 *Productions* contains jeremiads and meditations in the tradition of the Old Testament prophets and poets, and her 1879 *Meditations* adds to those forms elements of (auto)biography and sentimental fiction. Two of Stewart's contemporaries, Jarena Lee and Zilpha Elaw, African American itinerant ministers living and preaching in the antebellum northeastern United States, revise the traditional early American spiritual autobiography. Lee, born in Cape May, New Jersey, in February 1783, is believed to be the second African American woman to preach the Gospel. (The first known black woman preacher, an evangelist known simply as Elizabeth, is discussed in chapter 4.) Zilpha Elaw was born seven years later, near Philadelphia. Although Elaw would spend most of her ministerial life in New England and Lee lived her adult life in Philadelphia, traveling mostly in the mid-Atlantic states, the two women's paths did cross, and Elaw's autobiography reports that they once shared the same pulpit. Like Maria Stewart, their spiritual autobiographies appropriate essential conventions to construct texts that are, like the classic jeremiad, sentimental. Whereas the impassioned rhetoric used in the jeremiad is engaged by the writer to effect far-reaching societal and spiritual reforms, the sentimental pedagogy used by the traditional spiritual autobiographer depicts her radical conversion from a sin-sick soul using a heart-wrenching representation of her transition from sin to sorrow and salvation.

The spiritual autobiographies of Jarena Lee and Zilpha Elaw express what contemporary theorist M. Shawn Copeland calls a *theology of suffering.* Copeland defines this particular theology as one that "remembers and retells the lives and sufferings of those who 'came through' and those who have 'gone to the glory land'" (123). Both Lee's and Elaw's autobiographies reconstruct not only their own physical suffering, but the sufferings of others, including their relatives and friends. Moreover, each uses the image of her own body to develop an *incarnational* theology, that is, to inscribe her certitude that "the Word was made flesh." However, the body they depict is frequently dis-eased and in pain. Throughout their texts, they connect physical well-being with spiritual health. In addition, both graphically portray the death of at least one unsaved sinner. This particular theology functions to denounce religious skeptics and to hearten Christian readers confronting death.

In the *Religious Experience and Journal of Mrs. Jarena Lee* (1849) and the *Memoirs of the Life, Religious Experience, Ministerial Travels and Labours of Mrs. Zilpha Elaw* (1846) the respective authors compound the rhetoric of

Christian Protestantism with three major sentimental tropes: chattel slavery, the figure of the sick (black) woman's body, and the dying or dead sinner. Each of these tropes is also adumbrated in the writings of Maria Stewart, as I discuss in chapter 1. For example, in the *Meditations* Stewart represents death as the natural conclusion to her prophesy: once her forecasts have come to pass or once her society ameliorates itself to avoid the devastation and destruction that she has foretold, then the jeremiah is free to die: she writes, "[C]ould I but see young men and maidens turning their feet from impious ways, rather choosing to suffer affliction with the people of God than to enjoy the pleasures of sin for a season . . . then could I say, now, Lord, let thine unworthy handmaiden depart in peace, for I have seen the desire of mine eyes, and am satisfied" (10). Stewart also appeals to the sense of tragedy her readers share with her in reconstructing the deaths of her mother, father, mentor, and husband. In arousing readers' sympathy for her losses, Stewart performs the sentimental work of teaching readers to value and to act on their (capacity for) deep feeling. Lee and Elaw also describe the deaths of close family members, but because their spiritual autobiographies are more conventional than Stewart's sacred writings, they go beyond teaching readers to grieve for others. Both Lee and Elaw theologically illustrate the plight of the unsaved: each author didactically reconstructs the pitiable death scene. More moving is their reconstruction of the death of someone who has long known salvation; this figure's admirable, even beautiful preparedness for death inspires readers to long for precisely this kind of sanctified death. In their appropriation of sentimentalism and of other literary conventions, Lee and Elaw make the spiritual autobiography a form amenable to the reconstruction of African American women's particular experiences, both sacred and secular.

"The Lord Touched My Tongue"

In many ways, Lee and Elaw revised the traditional spiritual autobiography. Specifically, they transformed the genre into one that enabled them to identify the peculiar experiences of African American holy women. By combining a secularized protest against injustice with the sacred issues of their evangelicalism and the travel details of their respective itinerant ministries, Lee's and Elaw's spiritual narratives are hybrid texts in the tradition of Briton Hammon's *Narrative*.

In *The Puritan Conversion Narrative*, Patricia Caldwell identifies the traits of early spiritual autobiography. Specifically, she describes the formal seventeenth-century conversion "relation" as "a testimony of personal religious experience" that detailed the saved person's progress "from ignorance and self-deception," through an "excruciating vacillation" between despair and redemption, to hope and faith (1–2). According to Caldwell, the "skeletal structure" of one conversion narrative "looks indistinguishable from that of any other conversion story"; each bears "the expectable sequence of sin, preparation, and assurance" (2). Plainly, the autobiographies by Lee and Elaw descend from conventional seventeenth-century Puritan conversion narratives. The black women's narratives argue that they are indisputably fearless, frank women of God. They also go beyond that to establish the authors' right to preach, in spite of their being female, and to proclaim their work—that is, the autobiography and the itinerant ministry that generated it—to be sanctioned by God.

In their attention to race, gender, and nation, Lee's and Elaw's respective narratives depart from traditional early American spiritual autobiographies. Reflecting the Puritan resistance to individuality, each narrator resists distinguishing themselves from other members of the religious community, the African American community, and the women's community to which she belongs, to assert instead a collective identity. Moreover, unlike Maria Stewart, who in her later life succumbed to religious factionalism and found herself embroiled in postbellum denominational disputes, both Lee and Elaw revere interdenominationalism. Lee's *Religious Experience and Journal* especially rejoices in the integration of sects and races. Perhaps the best illustration of her commitment to a multiethnic religious community is her report of her experiences with Native American Christians in late March 1828, at Fort George, New York, which teems with excitement. Prior to this visit, she also recalls, she "spoke . . . to a quiet congregation, and the Lord was with us, though composed of all denominations" (50). Whereas Stewart's jeremiads of the 1830s rhetorically establish a great gulf between the prophet and her audiences, in the same decade Lee offers the Gospel to every group that will embrace her. The role of jeremiah necessitates Stewart's estrangement from other people; conversely, Lee's and Elaw's narratives reveal their respective sense of collective identity. Both Lee and Elaw record religious experiences of other people of color, and, as African American spiritual autobiographers, both conscientiously assume responsibility for verifying for white readers the validity and necessity of discussing spiritual matters with regard to all people. This, too, contributes to their inclusive theology.

Lee's regard for multidenominationalism is further illustrated by the narrator's account of her search for a church home. Between 1804 and 1811, she attended Presbyterian, Roman Catholic, "the English Church," and Methodist services before attending a worship service led by Reverend Richard Allen of the "African Episcopal Methodists" and determining immediately "that this is the people to which my heart unites" (5). Although she remained steadfastly committed to this denomination, despite the opposition of its leadership to the idea of women interpreting Scripture, Lee celebrated multiethnic and inter-faith Christian worship. Alternatively, Elaw developed a more expansive idea of congregation, and eventually left the AME Church, resisting their custom of non-affiliation with other denominations. As she joyfully describes one camp meeting, "There many thousands assemble in the open air, and beneath the overspreading bowers, to own and worship our common Lord" (64). In her ec-static spread of the Gospel, Elaw manages to convert a Jew to Christianity: "One of the seals of my ministry [in South Shields, England], was a descen-dant of Abraham, according to the flesh—a Jew outwardly, who, believing in the Lord with the heart unto righteousness, became a Jew inwardly also" (155). Thus, the Jewish convert, at first associated with Christ only by race, becomes Christ-like spiritually upon conversion to Christianity. Elaw's jubilation at this triumph of Christianity sings on the page even as it invokes a racial essential-ism based on phenotype that she elsewhere denounces.

To refute anticipated attacks on their work, Lee and Elaw, like Stewart be-fore them, turn to scholarly and scriptural sources to validate their mission. For example, despite her own advancement of traditional gender roles, manifested in exhortations to African American mothers to "bring up our children in in-dustry" (50), Lee compares preaching women, herself included, to "Esther the Queen, who fasted and prayed, and commanded the men of Jerusalem and the women of Zion to pray" (44). Stewart also cited the exemplum of Esther when she asked in her narrative, "Did not queen Esther save the lives of the Jews?" (75). For her part, Elaw compares herself without hesitation to numerous signi-ficant figures of the Bible, Old and New Testament, including Phoebe. When Phoebe visited Rome from Cenchreae, Corinth's seaport to the east, Paul asked the readers of his epistle to take care of her because, as a footnote in *The New Oxford Annotated Bible* states, "ancient inns and hotels were often infested with prostitutes and bandits" and therefore it was safer for her to stay with Christian hosts (NT 227). He writes, "I commend unto you Phebe our sister, which is a servant of the church which is at Cenchrea. That ye receive her in the Lord, as becometh saints, and that ye assist her in whatsoever business she hath need of you: for she hath been a succourer of many, and of myself also" (King James Bible, Romans 16:1–2). John Updike has recently reminded us that the New Revised Standard Version of the Bible translates Paul as referring to Phoebe as a deacon, "applying to her the Greek word, *diakonos,* that he applies to himself and Timothy" (95). Elaw, Lee, and Stewart very purposefully allude to Paul in their works because of his conflicting attitudes toward women (both that women should not speak or preach publicly and that women contributed significantly to the early Christian Church) that emerge in his epistles. One of their goals is to justify their life's work to their religious adversaries even as they condemn the opposition against them as unholy. In countering these nay-sayers, Lee and Elaw both inscribe a theology of inclusiveness, insisting that all persons are welcome in God's family. Lee's Scriptural epigraph advances this overt instruction: "And it shall come to pass . . . that I will pour out my Spirit upon all flesh; and your sons, and your *daughters* shall prophecy" (3). Ironically, poignantly, the verse is taken from Paul's letter to Joel.

The publishing history of Lee's 1849 autobiography summarily illustrates the kind of sexism both Lee and Elaw faced. The *Religious Experience and Journal of Mrs. Jarena Lee* is a revised edition of Lee's 1836 narrative, which she published against the express objection of church leaders. Despite her initial fear that "to sell them appears too much like merchandize" (77), Lee felt blessed by God when she earned more than $60 in the first four months of selling her tracts on the road as an itinerant minister. In Cincinnati in the spring of 1839, Lee noted in her journal, "My pamphlets went off as by a wind, the Elder recommending them very highly, and also encouraged me to have the 2d edition printed, which I had done—there being one thousand more for sale, in which I was successful" (85).[1] However, during the following year, "the General Conference [of the AME Church] passed a resolution which declared that 'no travelling preacher is permitted to write or publish any book or pamphlet without the approbation of the annual conference to which he belongs or a committee chosen by them'" (Walker 25). That same patriarchal body voted against licensing women to preach in 1844, 1848, and 1852 (Walker 25–26).When black Methodist preachers convened in 1890, after decades of refusing to license women preachers, the men asked, "Is woman inferior to man?" The chairman of the Washington Annual Conference that year pronounced the conclusion that had been evident for generations: "Sad as it may be, woman is as inferior to man as man is to God" (qtd. in Collier-Thomas xiii–xiv). Given the anti-feminism of the 1840 Conference, it is not surprising that when Lee sought permission to publish an enlarged edition of her autobiographical tract a few years later, the AME Book Concern refused her.[2] Nor is it surprising that Lee defied its ruling. Although Elaw's book apparently did not undergo similar scrutiny and rejection, she did publish her autobiography in Great Britain rather than in the United States. She had left the AME Church of her youth long before she left for England, preferring interdenominationalism rather than remaining in any particular sect. However, Elaw would certainly have known the Book Concern's stand against women preachers and against the publication of their spiritual narratives; a dispute with them about her text would probably have been impossible for her to avoid.

In their autobiographies, Lee and Elaw name names: they make sure to identify their detractors as well as their supporters. They criticize many whose opposition to female ministry stems from patriarchal codes of female conduct for interfering with their ministry. In her 1849 autobiographical revision Lee describes the endorsement of her ministry by respected leaders—especially by men like Reverend Richard Allen, founder of the AME Church, and Lewis Tappan, a New York abolitionist who promoted quality education for blacks. Lee documents her efforts and her triumphs. Initially, even Allen opposed Lee's preaching, permitting her only to exhort sinners to conversion. After she demonstrated her ability, however, by speaking extemporaneously and taking over for an uninspired minister, Allen publicly acknowledges and honors her calling, thereby rendering Lee the first female minister of that faith. Allen's recognition of Lee as divinely inspired hardly ends the antagonism toward her work, however. As she traveled, Lee was often attacked as indecent and unnatural. She notes that one of her first congregations, ironically located at a place called Newhope, was composed of "some very ill-behaved persons, who talked roughly, and said among other things, 'I was not a woman, but a man dressed in female clothes'" (23). Like Lee, Elaw was also "greatly encouraged" by male clergy members to proceed in her ministry when she first began to act on the impulse to preach. But immediately thereafter, she recounts, jealousy and gossip arose among the other congregants, much to her sorrow (83).

Lee met opposition to her work from both blacks and whites, since her congregations were as likely to be composed of both races as to be comprised of various denominations. Though hurt by the defamation, she declares, "[T]he Lord supported the 'woman preacher' and my soul was cheered" (33). Indeed, the narrative carefully accounts for the fate of most persons who criticized women's preaching. According to her testimony, almost no one who condemns her ministry escapes the hand of God. At one point Lee does not even wait to see how God will punish her opponent; instead, she *prays for* his demise. Her antagonist owns the building that houses a new church in Lancaster, Pennsylvania. When the worshippers cannot pay their rent, he takes their keys away. Lee writes, "I felt a great zeal for the cause of God to soften the man's heart, or kill him out of the way; one had better die than many." She continues dispassionately, saying, "Brother Israel Williams, a few days [later], called to converse with him on the subject, and he gave him the key; he was then on his deathbed, and died in a short time afterwards, and we must leave him in the hands of God, for he can open and no man can shut" (41). Apparently, Lee intends the final clause to absolve her of any personal culpability for the man's death. But the incident is undoubtedly reconstructed to signify to readers not only the power of God but also the power of God's chosen. Her assertion that "we must leave him in the hands of God" is particularly ironic, of course, in that her initial prayer betrays her impatience with passivity; only after she has actively solicited "the hand of God" does she sit with her own hands quiet.

For the most part, Lee merely praises God's vengeance rather than importunes him for it. Her opponents, usually men, simply reverse their opinions after hearing her preach. She has absolute faith that God will not tolerate those who oppress her, particularly when the oppressors are themselves ministers. For example, the narrator describes an African American minister who "could not reconcile his mind to a woman preacher—he could not unite in fellowship with me even to shaking hands as christians ought" (24). However, after being persuaded by others to attend a service where she says, "We had a wonderful display of the spirit of God among us," the elder invited her to preach in his church. Lee writes, "He had said he did not believe that ever a soul was converted under the preaching of a woman—but while I was laboring in his place, conviction seized a woman, who fell to the floor crying for mercy." The paragraph-long account concludes with the narrator glorifying God, but the last sentence reveals her personal pleasure in this triumphant moment: "I never felt a doubt . . . of my acceptance with God, but rested my soul on his every promise. The elder shook hands, and we parted" (24). So the vignette serves both to praise God for taking care of her *and* to warn those readers who are still skeptical of God's protection over her. Other passages further illustrate Lee's paradoxical piety. Her reportorial tone sometimes becomes embittered and uncensored, indicating the depth of her security in her sanctification. Empowered by the conviction of her intimacy with God, the narrator boldly exposes her detractors to illustrate God's wrath and his glory.

Lee is less ambiguous in her rhetorical treatment of the Reverend James Ward, who, she writes, "was so prejudiced he would not let me in his pulpit to speak" (44). When a group of women "tried to open the way[,] the men of color, with no spirit of christianity, remained idle in the enterprize" (44). The women triumphed over the men, and Lee "spoke with the ability God gave [her]" to a large congregation of diverse races and religious affiliations (44). Moreover, she was so impressive that, Ward's initial discouragement notwithstanding, she was granted a donation by Ward's community, whom she "left in friendship" (44). Lee concludes the lengthy paragraph with a single statement describing Ward's plight: "It is to be lamented, that James Ward, colored, with his over-ruling prejudice, which he manifested by saying no woman should stand in his pulpit, and with all the advantages of a liberal education, was in a few weeks after I left there, turned out of the Church" (44). Although she asserts the shame of Ward's dismissal, nothing in her tone or diction suggests that she heavily grieves his going. The very structure of her passive sentence—periodic or irmus, with each phrase or clause identifying one more contemptible element of Ward's behavior—undercuts the sense of remorse the opening clause declares. Lee's final "sentence" regarding Ward expresses more scorn than sympathy.

Yet, on the whole, Lee's *Religious Experience and Journal* is straightforward and unswerving. Elaw's *Memoirs* is no less so. Neither author flinches from giving a full account of the persecution against her, which she implies is tantamount to persecution against God and to an important opportunity for the glory of God to be revealed through both His protection of her and her endurance of the abuse. While the traditional spiritual autobiography divulges an author's conversion experience in close detail, Elaw confines the reconstruction of her own conversion to a scant two pages (pages 66–67, as it is reprinted in *Sisters of the Spirit*). Like Lee, Elaw devotes the bulk of her text to exposing the wrongness of xenophobia, especially as it occurs in the form of racism and prejudice against foreigners. (Addressed to British Christians by an American, the *Memoirs* also explores the theme of patriotism.) And like Lee, she documents numerous conflicts she had with other ministers and with other women who were opposed to the idea of women preaching and harassed her personally for her evangelism. For example, Elaw writes, "When it was first announced that a female would preach in that chapel [at Albany, New York], a gentleman in the vicinity had a strong desire to come and hear me, and proposed to his lady to accompany him; but she objected, that it was unbecoming in a woman to preach; and also, that God never commissioned women to preach" (131). The two do attend the service, however, and the demure woman's "former sentiments became completely reverted" (131–32). Reconstructing this episode enables Elaw to acknowledge her awareness of the objections to her ministry that were predicated on the charge that it violated both the divine order and the social code for proper womanly behavior. She also uses this incident to instruct those readers with lingering doubts. Speaking of the same woman, she writes, "when she got home, she read of Christ sending the women to inform the disciples and Peter, that he was risen from the dead; she then reprobated the folly of her former objections; for said she, I now perceive the first preachers of the resurrection were women" (132). Thus Elaw adroitly narrates her story, protests the patriarchal subjugation of women (especially by women), inscribes an inclusive Christian theology, and praises God's glory.

Ironically, Elaw's own husband proved to be one of her chief detractors. In an extended passage near the beginning of her autobiography, Elaw sanctions the patriarchal reading of Genesis as calling for the domination of women by men. It seems surprising that an independent woman would believe, much less assert, such male-centered ideas as, "formed as she is by nature for subordination, [woman] becomes the endowment and is subject to the authority of her husband" and "that woman is dependant on and subject to man, is the dictate of nature" (61). However, these pronouncements appear in a lengthy paragraph in which she reflects on her marriage to her infidel husband. While she knew that he was not saved before their marriage, she naïvely hoped to convert him. As she miserably confesses, "I am aware that when once the carnal courtship is commenced, the ensnared Christian fondly imagines that he shall soon be able to persuade his unregenerate companion to think as he does, and also to love and serve God with him. . . . I am sorry to say, I know something of this by experience" (62). Throughout their marriage of twelve years, Joseph Elaw not only never converted, but continually attempted to obstruct the ministry of his wife that he found so offensive. Yet despite the fact that he "was extremely hostile to religion, and had an extravagant prejudice against camp-meetings" of the sort his wife led (79), Zilpha persevered in her evangelism. Her autobiographical accounts of his impediments clearly function to cast her story as the more laudable, her God the more impressive.

Elaw's adversaries occasionally came near to threatening her with physical violence, so vehement was their opposition to her ministry. The *Memoirs* uses many sentimental conventions to reconstruct these incidents. In one powerful instance, Elaw demonstrates how multiple systems of oppression combined to frighten her and to threaten her ministry. In Utica, New York, she had recently been reunited with one of her surviving blood brothers after about twenty-five years apart when "a number of young men" attending a crowded worship service at a large chapel where she was to preach conspired to pelt her with stones. Although the situation is fundamentally pathetic, particularly with its echoes of Jesus' decree about casting stones, Elaw undercuts some of its pathos with sarcasm and irony. For example, she refers to the men alternately as "gentlemen" and "tyros" and dismisses their judgment of her as "petty opinions" (133).

In the end, however, Christianity reigns, for Elaw implies that God devised a miracle through her to save her: "The presence of the Lord overshadowed the assembly." Her brother later overhears the miscreants "confess that they knew not what ailed them when they entered the chapel; but their arms seemed bound and held down, and were so paralized [sic] that they dropped the stones upon the floor, and that their emotions were such during the service as they had never felt before" (133). Because she does not specify the men's racial identity, it is unclear whether the men were white; what is clear is that their resistance to her was both sexist and irreverent. In another incident, Elaw reports that she left her brother shortly after the incident with the "tyros," hoping to travel by steamer. But the captain of the boat denied her passage, and she observed that her "complexion appeared to be the chief reason for his refusal" (133). Thus, though she celebrates the fact that "the number of white brethren and sisters who flocked to my ministry increased daily" (83), Elaw also uses her spiritual autobiography to condemn the multiple forms of abuse she suffered and survived and to demonstrate the impossibility of true piety in the xenophobic.

While the *Religious Experience and Journal* records Jarena Lee's deep disappointment in black preachers who persecuted her, the most grievous and threatening opposition to her ministry originates with whites. At Sinapuxom, Maryland (i.e., slave territory), in the summer of 1824, she is hunted and harassed by "10 or 11 white men." She becomes significantly "sick" before the men search the home of "Mr. J. B.," the elder with whom Lee is lodging, knowing "it was me they were after" (36). The men challenge the legality of both J. B.'s and Lee's authority and insist on a judiciary hearing. One court official in particular was, Lee writes, "anxious to get hold of my papers, very much opposed to our being in the state, [and] tried hard to frighten us out of it" (36–37). Though the magistrate upholds the validity of her credentials, Lee prophecies to friends "that God would make an example of [the men] before one year" (37). Dozens of miles and sermons later, Lee reports: "I was informed that the constable who was so enraged against me before then was dying; the other white man who came and set [sic] at the end of the table twice while I was laboring, thinking I would say something to implicate myself and wanted me arrested so bad, had been sold and his family broke up; it is thus the Lord fights for Israel" (37).[3] The paragraph concludes with a succinct statement of God's steadfast love for those women he has chosen for the ministry, who are metonymously represented in this instance as "Israel." Clearly, her confidence in divine intolerance of the persecution of women apostles strengthens Lee's sense of self-righteousness and of justice. Moreover, like Maria Stewart, who often declares herself "enlisted in holy warfare" (*Productions* 59), Lee uses a military trope to indicate the divine support for her mission. Interestingly, she uses this imagery even to praise God's use of her as His instrument. For example, it appears in her reconstruction of the conversion of the "white gentleman . . . [who] had become almost glutted with the cares of this world" (92). Lee extols the effect of God's "awakening power" as she describes with quiet amusement the man rejoicing "louder than others, telling me he was glad the Lord had sent me . . . and all of this while Irael [*sic*] shouted for the battle" (93). So while many of the whites she and Elaw encounter believe themselves superior to the black women ministers, Lee continually documents God's revelations that He knows differently.

Undoubtedly, Lee's and Elaw's most sobering interactions with European Americans revolve around chattel slavery. The figure of the slave is a fundamental device used by sentimental writers, and Lee and Elaw portray it and draw upon it with skill and authority. Robbed of possession of herself and often ripped from her family, the slave figures as an orphan, another key sentimental trope; because of the orphan's presumed lack of cultural—and thus, political— guidance, she is unable to function as a member of the state. (Harriet Wilson's eponymous Frado, the *de facto* slave heroine of *Our Nig,* is one embodiment of this trope.) Moreover, since the question of whether slaves should be exposed to Christianity—indeed, the debate as to whether Africans possessed souls at all—raged on so in early nineteenth-century America that the figure of the slave was also sentimentally constructed as one lacking spiritual guidance, one in need of God and salvation. In portraying their confrontations with slavery, Lee and Elaw focus more on slaves themselves than on the slaveholders. In particular, Lee illustrates her commitment to improving slaves' welfare by reconstructing several poignant instances in which she preached to them. For her, slavery is "that wretched system that em[a]nated from the bottomless pit [and] is one of the greatest curses to any Nation" (63). At one point, too, she proudly helps hide a runaway slave girl. But Lee's devotion to helping slaves is most conclusively illustrated by her powerful reconstruction of an occurrence at Milford, Maryland. She "was sent for by a slave-holder to come to his house to preach" a funeral service for three slaves, "two grown persons and one child," all of whom "had been dead about a year" (39). Her syntax and tone substantiate her pithy report that "it was a solemn time." Vividly, she recalls being affected by the implacable grief of two young girls whose mother was among the deceased. Her own palpable anguish, like that she observes in the slave girls, evidently results from the slaves' bondage, from the girls' loss, and from her abhorrence of an institution that permits newly deceased blacks to remain improperly buried for months without permitting their families to bury them decently. Lee's decisions to preach the sermons and subsequently to publish her account of the incident show her sense of duty to her people, particularly since she could expect many whites to read her narrative. By invoking such sentimentalized figures of oppression to represent her personal observations of the dehumanizing effects of slavery (especially on white slaveholders), she hopes to arouse northerners' abolitionist efforts.

In the same paragraph, Lee notes that slaves "walked from 20 to 30, and from that to seventy miles, to worship God" at camp meetings where many were converted to Christ. She takes no credit for the success of meetings at which she preached, but gives "all glory to God, for the good done at Camp meetings" (39); such meetings were often the slaves' only source of religious instruction and experience. Throughout her Maryland remembrances, Lee implicitly condemns not only the institution of slavery but also any society that inhibits or otherwise fails in the spiritual development of its members. For the narrator reports that prior to the slave funerals, she visited the Georgetown jail, where she witnessed two black men and two white ones sentenced to be hanged. She cites a hymn to signify her sympathy for them: "But O, their end, / Their dreadful end!" (38). Though concise, the reconstruction of the incident especially serves whites. She relates the peril of white spiritual negligence by remembering that "one of the white men, by the name of Sharp had killed all his family, except his oldest daughter; she was the most hardened wretch I ever saw."[4] When Lee reads a chapter from the Bible with the prisoners before the three are hanged, "Sharp treated it with contempt, but the other [sic] answered with a degree of humility" (38). So the details about Sharp, the only impenitent prisoner, serve to warn Lee's white readers of the harm the deprivation of spiritual instruction can have on whites. Furthermore, the vignette performs the sentimental work of collapsing the emotional and material gulf that readers might presume lies between themselves and literature. As Elizabeth Barnes asserts, "Rather than teaching readers to appreciate differences, sentimental lessons reinforce for readers the idea that recognition relies on likeness—that one is bound to love whatever or whomever appears most like one's own" (*States* 97). By pointing to the example of Sharp, Lee does not suggest that her white readers *necessarily* share his impenitence; that is, she does not essentialize whiteness as inherently impious. Instead, she insinuates the racial divide separating the black prisoners from the white and the black prisoners from her white readers and implies that white readers have likely been socialized to respond to African Americans—the other prisoners and Lee herself—as Sharp does. It is the cultural proclivity of her white readers for sharing Sharp's wickedness and the possibility that they *do* share his impenitence that Lee tacitly underscores to inspire not their love for "whomever appears most like one's own" but their fear that Sharp's inhumanity may be manifested in their own hearts.

Neither Lee's reconstruction of the slave funerals nor her account of the events she witnessed at the Georgetown jail in the mid-1820s ends sorrowfully, as a reader accustomed to sentimental literature might expect; rather, the accounts end in jubilation. In one sentence she mourns slaveholders' penurious hindrance of slaves' Christian worship; in the next, she asserts, "My heart glows with joy while I write; truly God is inscrutable" (39). Lee's jubilation derives from the conversion of the sinners. By sentimentally reconstructing her experiences in Maryland, Lee adds to a primary goal (specifically, the promulgation of the author's own conversion experience) of the traditional American spiritual narrative a significantly recurring sign of African American spiritual autobiography (namely, the collective identity emergent in the testifying to others' conversions). Evidently, Lee intends her autobiography to inspire in all of her readers empathy and emulation, respect for the saved, and respect for the Christian God who saved them.

Like Lee, Elaw often went into the United States slave territory to preach; she also uses her autobiography to present key incidents from an abolitionist perspective in order to condemn slavery for its violation of Christian principles.[5] Elaw traveled around Maryland four years after Lee's earlier itinerancy there. One of the most compelling accounts in her autobiography shows how multiple systems of oppression undermine evangelism among slaves. Specifically, the *Memoirs* describes her ministerial experiences at Baltimore and at Annapolis in the winter of 1828. One particularly funereal sermon she preached on mortality was followed by the exhortations of "a local preacher, a coloured brother and a slave," who was beloved among the enslaved population (98). Elaw grieves for the man's desperation for freedom and at the same time denounces slavery: "This poor brother in bonds . . . was very impatient of slavery, and anxiously sighed for liberty. Alas! His life and spirit, his body, his bones, and his blood, as respects this life, were legally the property of, and at the disposal of his fellow man." By highlighting the bondsman's corporeality, Elaw reinforces his spirituality: though the legal property of "his fellow man," he is eminently a man of God. Either Elaw's sermon on death that Sabbath proved auspicious or the slave preacher was finally vanquished by his acute desire for release, for

within one week of their sharing the pulpit, he sickened and died. To accentuate the depth of the tragedy, Elaw turns momentarily to the lamentations in Job
3.17–19, which state in part that in the afterlife, "the servant is free from his
master" (qtd. in Elaw 98). She then describes the funeral service, with a crowd
so grievous, the congregation's "wailings . . . so intense," that the officiating
minister cannot complete it. To suggest the otherworldliness of the scene she
sentimentally invokes unreal dreamscape: "The suddenness of the [deceased
man's] stroke was surprising; and the loss of their beloved minister appeared
to his sorrowful flock more like a dream than a fact." Her allusions to transcendent states of being—the fatal stroke, then death itself followed by "intense" lamentations for an overwhelming and unfathomable loss—inspire
Elaw's corollary rhetorical transcendence: she slips out of the past indicative to
the present subjunctive tense when she meditates on "the abominations of slavery!" Concluding that "in every case" slavery "involves a wrong, the deepest in
wickedness," Elaw closes her reconstruction of the episode with the remon-
strance that slavery is unchristian (98). She deftly deploys sentimentalism to
elicit the reader's meditation on the deleterious and tragic consequences of
chattel slavery like the one that the remembrance has occasioned in her. The
"immediacy" of her own reflection calls for a similar spontaneity in readers,
playing upon our common senses of pathos and grief in the face not only of
great loss, but also of great depravity. When Elaw writes that the dead man's
interment was "a remarkably afflictive occasion," she cues us that only the
heartless—unlike us—would fail to mourn his loss. Moreover, the rhetorical
power of her reconstruction of this man's death foreshadows the kind of sentimental power that penning the death of Uncle Tom would provide Harriet
Beecher Stowe four short years later. Both Elaw's unnamed slave preacher and
Stowe's Uncle Tom are Christian martyrs, triply pathetic and sentimental for
their slave status, their splendid piety, and their stunning deaths. Providing
Stowe an even stronger model, Elaw gains additional momentum for her linking of sacred and secular ideals in this passage: the Christian love of "right" feeling is fortified in her account by the abolitionist stance against iniquity with
which she couples it. In a bizarre way, Elaw anticipates Stowe further still in her
affectation of immediacy, for her discourse suggests that Elaw did not personally attend the "afflictive occasion" of the funeral any more than Stowe was
an eyewitness to the deaths of "Uncle Tom" or other slaves she narrates in *Uncle
Tom's Cabin*. Yet everything about Elaw's vignette underscores the irrelevance
of her own—or her readers'—firsthand witnessing of such grave scenes. The
vignettes' affective power presumably transcends the need for eyewitnessing

and moves us into the realm of faith—from affect into effect and on to social change for the sake of the living.

"A Sickness Unto Death"

The exemplary lives commemorated in early American spiritual autobiographies are characterized as much by uncommon physical endurance as by rare piety. Both Lee and Elaw demonstrate extraordinary stamina as itinerant ministers, and both chronicle numerous bouts of illness. Concerning Lee's physical fortitude, Frances Smith Foster has remarked that Lee "has more in common with the characterizations of women in seventeenth- and eighteenth-century literature as 'forthright, earthy and capable,' than the frail, dependent, emotional nineteenth-century creatures who must be protected by men from the rigors of the outside world" ("Neither" 145). In fact, Lee and Elaw exploit both stereotypes of women. Dueling self-images are at work in their spiritual narratives, whose theological imports are paradoxical. While the two autobiographers paradoxically claim that their travels were directed by God and thus made in submission to Him, the opposition to their ministry was formulated repeatedly on the grounds that Lee and Elaw were not submissive enough in accordance with the cult of true womanhood. In other words, each autobiographer asserts that when she was most vehemently admonished by society for insubordination, she was actually acting most submissively, for she fulfilled the patriarchal mandate that women submit to male authority, God's authority being the highest. Similarly, both Lee and Elaw posit that only by exposing themselves to unsympathetic elements—from inclement weather to the "chill" of adversarial attitudes—could they counter the incriminating charges against them of blasphemy, impudence, and unwomanliness, and only by narratively exposing their readers to the illnesses they suffered from such antagonism could they justify their evangelism and gain other Christians' sympathy.

In her introduction to a twentieth-century publication of Lee's *Religious Experience and Journal,* Sue Houchins states, "Images of the body abound and, indeed, are appropriate in texts [like Lee's] dealing with incarnational theology, which asserts that 'the Word was made flesh'" (xxvii). The body depicted by Lee and Elaw, however, is frequently dis-eased: a (black) woman's sick body becomes as significant in their narratives as the Incarnation itself. Throughout their texts, they intertwine physical well-being with spiritual health; an unwell body almost invariably signals a dis-eased spiritual condition.

Lee seems purposefully to draw on nineteenth-century notions of woman-hood as a social and biological construction in order to garner sympathy from those who might otherwise have disdained her as unfeminine and thus unnat-ural. In the 1840s, the black woman was generally believed to be biologically different from her white counterpart, especially in the southern United States, where, as a slave, black women "plowed, planted, and hoed, did as much work as a man, endured the brutal punishment meted out by slaveholders and their overseers, and also fulfilled her ordained role of motherhood" (White 14). Lee's careful self-designation as a "coloured lady" in her subtitle momentarily sup-plants the image of the black woman as field hand with the image of her as the "angel in the household." Thus, Lee is able to include herself in the societal conception of women as frail, sickly creatures. As Sandra Gilbert and Susan Gubar argue in *The Madwoman in the Attic,* "nineteenth century culture seems to have actually admonished women to *be* ill"; so-called "female diseases" formed the *consummation* of Victorian women's training in femininity as much as its cause (54). In other words, Lee transforms her genuinely suffering self into the trope of the sick woman and exploits this trope in the representation of herself as an exemplary Christian. The convergence of infirmity, femaleness, and self-effacement in Lee's autobiography yields one of her most powerful rhetorical tools, the sentimental trope of the sick black woman's body. By doc-umenting her illnesses, Lee obliquely describes occasions on which she nearly succumbed to clerical antifeminism, thus illustrating the pernicious power of faithlessness, on the one hand, and the magnificent power of God, on the other.

Lee describes her physical suffering from the beginning of her text. On the second page, she records her desperation as a child of nine who is burdened by "the weight of [her] sins, and sinful nature." She notes that "so great was the la-bor of my spirit and the fearful oppressions of a judgment to come, that I was reduced as one extremely ill, on which account a physician was called to attend me, from which illness I recovered in about three months" (4). This report of her protracted bout of illness highlights the overlay of physical debility and emotional and spiritual decay present in her text. Twenty years later, having married Joseph Lee, a minister, and relocated with him to Snow Hill, Pennsyl-vania, Jarena's mental health collapses again, this time under the weight of her repressed desire to preach. Marrying a minister, she discovers, is *not* as satisfy-ing as becoming one. She writes, "From this sickness I did not expect to re-cover" (14). Provocatively, Lee devotes most of the chapter entitled "My Mar-riage" to her recollections of the "great trial" and physical affliction that the nuptial move to Snow Hill induced in her. Despite her aversion to moving and her fears of death, however, Lee survives her breakdown in Snow Hill, Joseph's death, *and* the deaths of four other loved ones in her six years there.

Just as Lee's sufferings reportedly increase as she ages, the discourse she uses to narrate her maladies intensifies as well. This is especially apparent in a series of descriptions of dis-eases she experiences that are caused by spiritual unrest. After she has been preaching for several years, for example, on one Sabbath she experiences a profound physical reaction to speaking from Matthew 26:26–27, which proclaims the transubstantiation of the Christ ("Now as they were eating, Jesus took bread, and blessed, and broke it, and gave it to the disciples and said, 'Take, eat; this is my body'"). This text momentarily affects Lee in body and spirit, she says. In fact, her corporeal reaction illuminates her association of a failing faith with a deteriorating body: "My faith it seemed almost failed me, for when I got in the stand, so hard was the task that I trembled, and my heart beat heavy, but in giving out the hymn I felt strength of mind, and before I got through, I felt so much of life and liberty in the word, I could but wonder" (41). Whereas this brief physical dysfunction results from her spiritual passion and her feelings of ineptitude, Lee more often and more severely suffers physically in response to opposition to her vocation. For instance, she notes, "I was taken sick for a few days" after having "to withstand a beast in Princeton" in the mid-1820s (46). Specifically, Reverend Thomas Voris preached a Sabbath sermon with her, then invited her to hold prayer meetings at his home throughout the subsequent week. That week Lee lay ill, however, while Voris consorted with other pastors, apparently in an effort to prohibit her from preaching in Princeton altogether.

By 1829, Lee's "health was much destroyed by speaking so often and laboring so very hard, having a heavy fever preying upon [her] system" (58). Because she continued to travel, to preach, and, ironically, to visit the sick, she developed bilious fever and delirium. This demanded a cessation in her work and constant medical attention; however, she returned to the ministerial circuit after a brief month's retirement. In words that suggest her exasperation at the severity of her illness, she writes, "After a lapse of four weeks I was able to get out of that house, but very weak" (58). During the winter of 1833, Lee fell ill again while traveling through northern New York in inclement weather. The narrative registers a repeated impatience with this particular malady; for example, she says, "The road was so rough that it caused me to be quite sick. I could not stand to ride 200 miles [in] that cold weather, and I continued to preach in and out of town to different denominations through frost and snow" (68). Later, the narrative provides no specific details about what may well have been the worst of her illnesses. Cryptically, Lee writes: "I returned to Philadelphia in December [1836]. After I arrived my health was much impaired, and I had a severe spell of sickness. So ended 1836. I commenced travelling March 11th, 1837" (79). In other words, Lee's narrative both meticulously details her activities for weeks at a time of her life as a minister and at the same time enigmatically leaves months of her life unexplained.

Yet, despite imaging herself as a sufferer of frequent illnesses, or perhaps through her depiction of her endurance of them, Lee emerges as a woman of exceptional moral and spiritual strength in her narrative. Her use of the trope of the physically frail woman paradoxically repudiates the stereotype of the nineteenth-century weak woman by demonstrating Lee's capacity for wellness and endurance. Juxtaposed against one fictional white religious heroine of the era, for instance, Lee survives, whereas Eva St. Clare in Stowe's *Uncle Tom's Cabin* does not. Jane Tompkins has cogently argued that "Little Eva's death enacts . . . the idea, central to Christian soteriology, that the highest human calling is to give one's life for another" (86). Lee's life and her autobiography, in contrast, dramatize the Christian ideal of apostolic self-preservation to perform God's bidding. Her endurance is portrayed in terms that depreciate individual value and suggest that personal strength is a metaphor for collective Christian triumph over sin and flesh. Paradoxically, her endurance is also demonstrated by the repetition of the pronoun "I," the sign that Lee has taken pen in hand to assert her story. Lee's account of the restoration of her health provides her with an opportunity to honor God.

Like Lee, Zilpha Elaw experienced many critical illnesses that, diagnosed as fatal, she expected would end her life. In recounting her first near-fatal illness, she reflects on the ways that illness signifies the mystical. For although she asserts that her internal injuries resulted from an accidental "severe fall," she also implies that divine intervention, not coincidence, caused her literal "fall" in order to reveal her duty to preach and to punish her for her fall from grace. In the week prior to this "fall," she had informed her spiritual leader that she felt destined to desert the "family or household ministry" she had been conducting for five years in Burlington, New Jersey (71). In spite of her physician's pronouncement that as a result of her injuries from the fall it was "impossible that [she] could live . . . God ordered it otherwise to every expectation" (70). Thus, Elaw considers herself divinely protected not only in this instance of illness, but also blessed in her "presentiment" that she should travel in His name. Elaw further reports that during this illness "a preaching Quakeress" (70) came to pray for her. This figure recurs in her subsequent reconstructions of her near-fatal illnesses or injuries. For example, after the death of her sister Hannah in 1816, for *fifteen months* Elaw again "lay upon a bed of affliction, with a sickness, which, to all appearance, was unto death . . . and I grew worse and worse" (76). This time, the narrator has no doubt but that God has made her sick to signify His displeasure and "to bring [her] into subjection to our Master's will." Again, "a kind Quaker lady" figures in her recovery, visiting her often (77). Perhaps this repeated image serves to emanate Christian virtue and benevolence, the "inner light" so intimately associated with early Quakers. Moreover, for both Elaw and Lee, in whose autobiography the same trope also appears, the white Quaker woman preacher offers a juxtaposition: even though—or because—she is doctrinally marginalized from the dominant culture because of her beliefs, the woman's whiteness and the tranquility and quiet associated with her sect run counter to the African American ministers' blackness and the mythic audacity and recalcitrance associated with their race. Elaw also writes that while living among Quakers in antebellum Virginia years later, she contracted "a very severe attack of the fever" that is endemic in that climate and was then pervasive in northern Virginia; she is expertly nursed back to health "by a physician of first rate eminence, and by several kind and most anxious nurses." She significantly concludes the account by stating, "and the Lord was pleased speedily to raise me up again" (93). Clearly, though nondenominational herself, Elaw exalts Quaker dogma as exemplary for her readers. In every instance of personal ill health, she reads sacred implications in the debilitated state of her body.

Reconstructing the fifteen-month illness that she suffered after her sister's death, Elaw suggests that though she was not a Quaker her poor health sometimes provided her with a sort of "inner light"; although she was physically diseased, she often developed extraordinary insight. From an early age, she experienced visions of God, Jesus, and angelic presences. Whenever she becomes weakened by sickness, she gains a paradoxically vigorous sense of her own sacred power: "my debility was long protracted; but at times the presence of the Holy Spirit was so powerful within me, that I seemed quite invigorated and strong; and in this illness, I received another striking communication in reference to my future employment in the ministry" (77). In the paragraph in which she analyzes this clairvoyance, Elaw disrupts her linear chronology to condemn religious skeptics who are incredulous of the reality—to say nothing of the verity—of visions. For herself, however, she is confident of the clarity of her insight. She writes, "From that moment I was assured of my ultimate recovery" (78), obviously intending "recovery" to signify both her physical restoration and her spiritual salvation. One recovery finds her "holding sweet converse with my God, as a man converses with his friend" (71). Thus, illness paradoxically proves empowering to her, and, in addition, signifies her personal friendship with the divine.

Another episode concerning illness offers a masterful illustration of Elaw's narrative skill as a subtle, effective sentimentalist. In this account, she receives an important sign, manifested also as a sacred vision, of God's will for her life and His divine protection over her. This time, however, the setting is not a sick bed but a predominantly Presbyterian chapel in Connecticut whose opposing denominational factions are at war over the costs of maintaining the "union chapel" building (108). At the time, Elaw was still a Methodist; thus, part of the jealousy and marginalization that she suffers results from interfaith competition. Here, too, she inscribes a compelling paradox: ultimately, she interprets her lengthy illness as a sign of God's satisfaction with her own actions and His displeasure with those of her sexist antagonists. Elaw skillfully constructs the episode around the notion of silence, thereby emphasizing the patriarchal subjugation of women accomplished in part through the suppression of women's voices. Specifically, in an effort to curtail church expenses, some ministers at the chapel were relieved of their clerical duties. Needless to say, as the only woman preacher and the object of "a great jealousy [that] was excited, fostered, and hatched under the influence of the rulers" (108), on Sunday Elaw is dismissed — not explicitly, but stealthily. Several of the ministers advise her "not to enter the pulpit" as arranged, while others, their adversaries and "our friends," desire her "to ascend the pulpit according to the recent arrangements." Their misuses of her in their tug-o'-war, particularly given that she is the only woman among them, renders her speechless with emotion. However, the faithful congregation insists on her continued participation, about which Elaw writes, "And when I appeared in the pulpit I was obliged to vent my feelings in a shower of tears, *before I could utter a word;* and my dear flock were very much affected at the sight" (108, italics added). At this point in her recapitulation of the event, then, Elaw clarifies the difference between being silenced and being inexpressive: she effectively communicates her frustration and sadness to her "flock," in spite of the leaders' efforts to dismantle her ministry. In addition, in this context her emotional "venting" implies that inner turmoil is a form of illness. Thus, through the sentimental invocation of holiness shunned and the figure of the sick (holy) woman, Elaw argues against clerical chauvinism, patriarchal subjugation of women, and hegemonic rule over the disenfranchised. Her true confession of her own "weakness," suggested by what some no doubt disparaged as "dumb tears," argues for the obliteration of these evil forces from a holy and just world.

Recovering her voice in the chapel, Elaw eventually asserts herself into the service by breaking the congregation's "profound silence" to call forward those "who feel anxious for their souls." But again, though "a great number then came forward," the male ministers obstruct her access to the congregation and close the meeting, in Elaw's decisive phrasing, "without giving [her] an opportunity of saying a word" (109). Moving in and out of chronicle and analysis, narrative and inference, Elaw grieves the display of "gospel rivalship," and quotes Phillipians 1:16 to liken her "affliction" to Christ's, noting that before her invitation, the other ministers had "all sat waiting in mute silence." In Elaw's interpretation, such an act against God calls for His retribution, for at mid-week He visits her with a promise she cites using Ezekiel 3:25–27, including, "I will make thy tongue cleave to the roof of thy mouth, that thou shalt be dumb." In the same triumphant spirit as Jarena Lee's remembrance of the fate of men like Thomas Voris and James Ward, Elaw celebrates God's victory over the failure of that "rebellious house"—even though His conquest necessitates her muteness. She notes that she becomes sick as well: "I was suddenly attacked with a very severe fit of illness, and confined by it for five weeks, so that I became dumb to them indeed" (109). What is astonishing in Elaw's reconstruction of this incident featuring the sick (black) woman's body is its reversal of mystical signs. In other instances she interprets her weakened physical state as punishment for a particular sin she has committed, such as when she later recalls, "as I began to get myself ready . . . I was seized with a fearful tremour and loss of strength. I sunk down upon a chair, and pondered within myself the reason for this visitation, and it occurred to me, that my design of going . . . was taken without the permission of God being first obtained" (154). Sickness for her heretofore always signified God's disapprobation with her. In this case, however, it serves paradoxically as a sign of His love for her and His dissatisfaction with others. The depth of His love, Elaw implies, is apparent in that through her He fulfills the Scriptures. Moreover, the other ministers disrespect her in a distinctly gendered way: by effectively silencing her. As Elaw interprets her illness, when God Himself renders her mute, in fulfillment of the pledge in Ezekiel, He demonstrates for her the difference between mortal (and petty) silencing, which hurts her physically and psychically, and sacred silencing, which exalts her and her ministry specifically by elevating the sick holy woman over the men who so incisively derided her.

The magnitude of the trope of the sick woman is unmistakable in Elaw's account of the death of her sister Hannah in Philadelphia, for it simultaneously describes how she came to act on her call to preach. In a lengthy paragraph Elaw deploys classic conventions of sentimentalism to describe the death of her last surviving sister; apparently, the only remaining sibling of their mother's twenty-three children she had at the time was the brother with whom she is reunited at Utica. The trope of death, especially a woman's or an infant's death, as I have suggested, is integral, even endemic to American sentimental litera-ture. Early sentimental literature specifically argued that no death is without eschatological significance for the living; in other words, no one simply *dies* and that is the end. In her case, her sister's death becomes the impetus that propels Elaw into the ministry. Moreover, her extended reconstruction of Hannah's death—running four pages in Andrews' edition of the *Memoirs* (published in *Sisters of the Spirit)*—provides an important forum near the beginning of the autobiography for Elaw to develop a theology that is inclusive and revisionary, thus subverting both orthodox theology and the traditional spiritual autobiog-raphy. By using her depiction of Hannah's death as the basis of her theological argument, Elaw brilliantly performs the primary responsibility of theologians who are privileged by their education and masculinity in a way she is not: spe-cifically, the development of a treatise that is both philosophy and praxis. Through her calculated rhetorical strategy for this theology, she sentimental-izes the sacred and establishes her ecclesiastical authority.

Hannah's death is replete with the trappings of traditional sentimentalism. At the outset, Elaw employs two female figures: that of the "very pious" dying woman and of her grief-stricken sister. The two figures hold our attention as the narrative shifts focus from one to the other. Other women—nursing "sisters" and an ethereal "Quakeress"—as well as the soon-to-be widower are present as minor characters. From the first it is clear that Hannah looks like the oxy-moronic picture of the "beautiful dead": Elaw marvels that she appeared "so emaciated and altered in appearance, that I scarcely knew her; but in so happy a frame of mind, that the body seemed almost unable to detain so heavenly a spirit" (71). This is true at least for a while: then Hannah experiences a classic "dark night of the soul"—except that "this horrible state" lasts a full week. Hav-ing narrated her sister's illness and served as mediator for her discourse, Elaw suddenly provides the dying woman's words directly for dramatic effect: Han-nah says to her, "My dear sister, I am going to hell" (72). Elaw reports that she "had not either spoken or sat down in the house; but upon hearing this, I kneeled down and tried to pray; but she [Hannah] instantly exclaimed, 'Oh, do not pray, for you will only send me the sooner to judgment!'" (72). While Hannah retreats from the sounds of prayer, her disconsolate sister and the circle of weeping "sisters" enact sentimentalism's supporting cast of mourners; their physical presences in the sick room stress the confinement of the domestic scene. When their prayers prove effective, Elaw rejoices that God "was pleased to burst through the gloom, and set the captive free" (72). Hannah, released from the specter of death, revives her piety and not only speaks, but *sings* in tongues: Elaw marvels that "the language in which she sung was too wonderful for me . . . her voice was as clear, musical, and strong, as if nothing had ailed her; . . . it was indeed a song of praise, and the place was full of glory" (73). The narrator writes that Hannah reports that this achievement of the Spirit brings her visions of Jesus and the angels. In one angelic visitation Hannah is told of "a lady named Fisher, a Quakeress," whom Zilpha should seek for guidance about the ministry Zilpha should pursue. (The name Fisher refers, perhaps, to the Apostles, those "fishers of men.") Elaw confesses that she retreated at this commission, mute with amazement. But upon Zilpha's return the next day, Hannah persists, even to an anguished and piercing confrontation when the sisters are next alone: Hannah tells her, "[A]nd oh! how you hurt me last night by not going where I told you" (74). Elaw further writes, "After my sister had lain in a swoon for some time, she revived, and said . . . 'I have overcome the world by the kingdom of heaven'" (73). Oblivious to her sister's faithlessness, Hannah "continued in this happy frame of mind until her soul fell asleep in Jesus." Of course, that we are holding the spiritual autobiography of the reverend Zilpha Elaw indicates that Hannah's sacred vision was both authentic and realized.

This episode in Elaw's *Memoirs* asserts a definite theological perspective: what distinguishes the event for Elaw is not that her sister was about to die (and death is an act that she presumably would have considered private anyway). To be sure, we are not told about the deaths of anyone simply because she or he is dying; Elaw is not that morbid. Rather, she recounts Hannah's death using the Christian concepts of conversion, salvation, deliverance, exultation, and so on because the incident can teach readers about God and about the distinctive kind of relationship they should cultivate with God. Furthermore, this particular passage demonstrates the propriety and naturalness of a certain amount of fear of God. The narrator is confused, distraught, abashed, and humbled when her sister reports that angels have instructed her to tell Elaw to preach. The sister is, paradoxically, both "hurt" and "happy" because, the narrator implies, she is joyful that God has chosen her to inform Elaw of her calling, but then she is anguished that Elaw rejects God's choice of her to spread the Gospel to others.

Besides chronicling the events in the last weeks of her sister's life, in this portion of the *Memoirs* Elaw explores some of her most important theological tenets. Twice in the course of the recapitulation of Hannah's death, Elaw disrupts her narrative to assert and analyze the implications of her own text. These disruptions assert her theology. And the particular theology serves a dual purpose: both to condemn skeptics and detractors and to inspire faithful Christians facing either their own deaths or the death of a beloved. In the first of these shifts, which are positioned after Hannah swoons away following her descent into fear of death and retribution, from past recollection to her present contemplations, Elaw abruptly ponders, "What will infidelity say to this?" (72). She continues by condemning those who would charge her or her sister with "hypocrisy" or "fanaticism," and discourses on "the natural cause and effect of exercise of Christian faith, in collision with forces asserted by the gospel to be engaged in hostile action to it" (73). Arguing that Christianity's denominations are "too uniform" in their tenets to be dismissed as "the wild and fluctuating uncertainties of fanaticism," she ultimately denounces religious doubt as the "luxuriant, bewitching, and arrogant" stuff of "The Age of Reason," which she scoffs as altogether unreasonable (73). The second digression follows a marvelous description of glossolalia, the tongue(s) in which Hannah sang before her death, which Zilpha describes as "a pure language, unalloyed by the fulsome compliment, the hyperbole, the tautology and circumlocution, the insinuation, double meaning and vagueness, with which all human languages are clogged" (74). Having characterized this heavenly tongue as the sign of the fulfillment of Jehovah's covenant, Elaw explains why she has attended to Hannah's death in such detail; thus, she clarifies the practical purposes to which good theology ought be put: "It may possibly meet the cases of others tempted in a similar manner [as Hannah's initial fear and rejection of prayer]; that they may take encouragement from her happy and triumphant end." In the end, Elaw argues for the verity of her account by speculating about the suspicions readers might develop. In positing the rejection of Hannah's vision and deathbed prophecy, she confirms the authenticity of those experiences. And, indeed, the whole narrative, most of which follows this early reconstruction, disproves and invalidates religious skepticism. Elaw thus performs the work of traditional theologians: she constructs an argument in defense of Christianity rooted in personal witnessing, doctrinal concepts, and the glory of the divine.

Like Elaw's *Memoirs*, the *Religious Experience and Journal of Mrs. Jarena Lee* asserts an inclusive theology, often by a similar manipulation of the reconstruction of the author's intimate relationships, especially with her immediate family and especially in the face of death. The details Lee confides about her ties to her son James—for example, her joy when he "embraces religion," their shared grief at the death of his son and later his daughter, her anxiety about illnesses he suffers, and so on—demonstrate not only her mother-love for him, but challenge the charges against her of unsexing herself by performing in the pulpit. Moreover, Lee and Elaw, like Maria Stewart, the black holy woman whose spiritual writings predated theirs by a single decade, show themselves literally willing to die in the fulfillment of God's holy command. Opponents momentarily incapacitate them, but ultimately they cannot vanquish the Spirit that empowers and sustains them. Lee's *Religious Experience and Journal* concludes with Lee still very active at age sixty-six, continuing her recurring pattern of infirmity, healing, and evangelism. Blending the discourse of Christian witness with folk wisdom, she testifies on the penultimate page of her text: "My health being very much impaired, I knew not but that I should be the next one called away, but the Lord spared me for some other purpose, and upon my recovery I commenced travelling again, feeling it better to wear out than to rust out—and so expect to do until death" (96–97). Elaw's end, however, remains unknown; thus, the *Memoirs* she generously and lovingly inscribed for London's "Saints and Faithful Brethren in Christ" (51) literally became her last public utterances.

THREE

Rejecting Sentimentalism: Nancy Prince

As with all counterdiscourses, the assumption that there exists one
essential victim suppresses internal power divisions. To [Richard]
Terdiman's "no discourse is ever a monologue," we should add, the
site of counterdiscourse is itself a contested terrain.

E. FRANCES WHITE, "Africa on My Mind"

Central to the theology of Nancy Prince is the practice of self-respect and the
censure of unrighteousness: performances that cannot be severed one from another. For Prince, to honor God is to honor His creatures. The conclusion to
her largely secular *Narrative* overtly glorifies the goodness of God. Implicitly,
each sentence of the *Narrative* affirms her own goodness. In this way, it overtly
opposes the multiplicity of negative stereotypes and myths circulating about
African American women, particularly the freeborn. Traveling not only provided Prince with stories that she could literally and figuratively transform into
an "account" of a life of independence if also of poverty; it also fulfilled the
republican missionary's cultivated sense of religious, civic, nationalistic, and
maternal duty toward others. This sense of duty is the primary precept of her
theology.

In 1850, an African American Bostonian published the first of three editions
of *A Narrative of the Life and Travels of Mrs. Nancy Prince*. Two decades before,
in 1831, *The History of Mary Prince, A West Indian Slave, Related by Herself* had
been published simultaneously in London and Edinburgh; it remains "the only
known English-language testimony by a West Indian slave woman" (Sharpe 31).
These two black women's autobiographies share a number of common characteristics with each other, and together they differ dramatically from the narratives by Maria Stewart, Jarena Lee, and Zilpha Elaw. Strictly speaking, the

autobiographies by the two Princes are neither jeremiads nor spiritual auto-biographies; they do not prophesy national devastation nor do they implore readers' religious conversion. Furthermore, they generally lack the deployment of sentimentalism that characterizes the autobiographies by Stewart, Lee, and Elaw. However, the narrative of each Prince offers specific types of sentimen-talized womanhood. *The History of Mary Prince* not only features the senti-mentalized trope of the slavewoman victimized by physical and psycho-sexual dominance, but it also offers a vivid portrait of the monstrous slave mistress who would become a stock figure in abolitionist literature of the antebellum era. In *A Narrative of the Life and Travels,* Nancy Prince depicts her fallen sis-ter and her disconsolate mother, both standardized to correspond to sentimen-tal literary types. These images aside, though, each Prince seems impatient with sentimentalism's pathos, and each rejects self-portraiture rooted in senti-mentalized victimization and Christian lamentation. While both women pro-fess Christianity and appropriate the Protestant evangelical discourse that per-meated western *belles-lettres* of their day, each is also incisively critical of the moral shortcomings of white Christians. In addition, each uses her autobiog-raphy to condemn slavery, to urge abolition, to expose the multiple fallacies that inhere in the ideology of true womanhood, and, most audaciously, to speak for slaves to a slaveholding society.

Because of the characteristics the women share in common, readers have routinely confused the identities of Mary Prince and Nancy Prince. This is partly a result of the fact that their works were published closely together, but of course the confusion stems more so from their common surname. This name was prevalent among eighteenth-century New England blacks: Nancy Gardner took the surname of her husband, Nero Prince, who, before becom-ing an escort in the Russian courts, succeeded the revolutionary Prince Hall as Grand Master of Boston's African Lodge of Freemasons. For her part, as Moira Ferguson notes, "Mary Prince's surname [was] taken self-consciously from her own father's Christian name": this "Prince" "was jointly owned by Frances and David Trimingham" (4).[1] Moreover, both narrators were associated with slavery—Mary because of her own bondage and Nancy due to her abolition-ism. Finally, the Princes have often been unwittingly misidentified since 1988 because their autobiographies were concurrently reissued as volumes in Oxford University Press's Schomburg Library of Nineteenth-Century Black Women Writers series.

But these are superficial similarities seen from a late twentieth-century per-spective that dehistoricizes the two texts; their differences are far more profound and more apparent when the texts are examined in an historical context. The most critical difference between the two is that Nancy Gardner (Prince) was born free in the United States in 1799 roughly eleven years before Mary Prince was born into slavery in Brackish Pond, Devonshire Parish, Bermuda. Obviously, the women were not blood-kin, and although each spent several years in the West Indies, they probably never met. Moreover, though she was well-read, Nancy Prince quite likely never read Mary Prince's *History*. Their respective life narratives offer sharp insights into the class, caste, religious, and national differences between black women in different parts of the African diaspora. On the one hand, *The History of Mary Prince* reports the experiences of a woman enslaved in the West Indies; in fact, it appears to be the first female slave autobiography written in English. Mary Prince narrated her story to white abolitionists, who insisted on highlighting her Christian chastity in order to promulgate her plea for emancipation. On the other hand, the *Life and Travels of Mrs. Nancy Prince* narrativizes its subject's life and travels as an American Baptist missionary to convert and to "christianize and civilize" in accordance with the missionary's motto precisely the kind of slave(woman) that Mary Prince represented.[2] Contrasting their autobiographies, therefore, enables us to examine the life conditions of antebellum black women who lived outside Africa. Perhaps even more important, analyzing the two texts together allows us to observe the differences that literacy made for nineteenth-century black women. Specifically, while Mary Prince was forced to rely on those rhetorical strategies her amanuenses deemed most appropriate for the reconstruction of her life, Nancy Prince formulated her own means of self-assertion. Rather than deploy the sentimentalism so readily adapted by well-intentioned white writers of early "black" narratives, Nancy Prince resisted literary modes that pathologized black people as victims. Her narrative endorses self-reliance and depicts African Americans as figures of agency and accomplishment.

A Narrative of the Life and Travels of Mrs. Nancy Prince was first published in 1850. Its narrator describes herself as brave and independent. Other antebellum African American women writers, such as Jarena Lee and Zilpha Elaw, used sentimentalism to revolutionize white-authored stereotypes of African American women as soulless and insentient, in part by depicting their autobiographical narrators as alternately divinely defended and mortally oppressed. Adapting the archetypal sentimental plot of a story of a (white) woman's beset chastity, these black holy women writers portrayed themselves as not only possessing such Christian virtues as charity and purity, but also as protective of their virtue(s) when they were under attack by whites and by black men. As

I argued earlier, the spiritual autobiographies of Lee and Elaw both embrace and eschew the image of the true woman as fragile and delicate. They write themselves as being ill as often as being well, proclaiming a physical and metaphysical tenderness that nearly buckles under the weight of patriarchal abuses, especially clerical chauvinism. As itinerant ministers equally subject to the severities of nature and the brutalities of sexism, they were as likely to suffer from an opponent's beastly conduct as from bilious fever. By appropriating sentimentality, Lee and Elaw posit the capacity for transcendence and for nobility as always already present in African identity. The physical responses inspired by their sentimentalized narratives could perhaps "move" even the most intractably negrophobic of readers to regard African Americans as deserving of pity and support.

Conversely, Nancy Prince avoids sentimental strategies when writing of herself at home and abroad, expressly because she wishes to avert the archetypal requirement of sentimental literature that the heroine's virtue be *besieged*. For Prince absolutely no aspect of her autobiography should imply that she was anything less than steadfastly self-reliant. Instead, her *Narrative* suggests that, blessed by the Holy Spirit, she prevails over worldly worries. Prince rejects sentimentalism because she assesses the political price of the rhetorical strategy as too great: she implies that sentimentalism costs black people, especially black women, nothing less than their dignity and their rights. Because sentimental literature profusely solicits readers' pity, then proclaims the bodily signs of that pity—a lump in the throat, tears, sighs, swoons—to be definitive evidence of readers' moral virtue (Barrett 424),[3] Prince's resistance to sentimentalism denies readers' facile, gratuitous catharsis. Although she briefly and effectively appropriates a sentimentalist poetics at the beginning of her autobiography (when reconstructing the social failures of her mother and sister), Nancy Prince develops her *Narrative* using a strategy that resists the sentimentalization of the black woman.

One of the most arresting features of the *Life and Travels of Mrs. Nancy Prince* is its construction of the narrator's problematic internal class hierarchies: the world-traveler narrator intimates an ambivalence toward other persons of African descent, especially those "folk" whom she encounters in her two religious missions into the West Indies.[4] As an American, though one born only "nominally free," Nancy Prince seems to have regarded herself as superior to black persons born outside of the United States. In spite of her own lowly status as a poor black woman, Nancy Prince was influenced by American Protestantism, which, as Mary De Jong asserts, had by "the late eighteenth century entered an aggressively evangelical phase, [such that] it became a Christian imperative to include, not exclude, 'heathen'" (259). Prince's *Narrative* is marked by a classist pride and colonialist arrogance comparable to that of her European American cohorts in the nascent Christian mission movement. It is this elitism masking as benevolence that Mary Prince repeatedly confronts among the whites with whom she interacts in Antigua and England and that she exploits and subverts in the narration of her story. In this chapter, I address first Mary Prince's dictated autobiography and analyze its use of double-speak to distinguish the narrator's voice from her amanuensis's and to study their disparate deployment of Christian rhetoric. Then I will turn to Nancy Prince's self-authored autobiography, analyzing it also for its ambiguity, double-speak, and ambivalent deployment of the trope of Christianity.

Rejecting Christianity

If Nancy Prince's religious and imperialist training taught her to condescend to "heathens," even those "pre-Christians" who either looked like herself or who, by fictions of law and custom, were similarly declared "black," then Mary Prince had also learned a thing or two about "good Christians" by the time she authorized her *History*. While each of her "owners" professed Christianity, Mary had learned some of these lessons quite literally in the school of hard knocks. For the most remarkable aspect of *The History of Mary Prince* is the extreme violence and psychosexual sadism to which its narrator was interminably subjected. In a typical report of what she suffered, the narrator asserts, "[My mistress, Mrs. I———,] caused me to know the exact difference between the smart of the rope, the cart-whip, and the cow-skin, when applied to my naked body by her own cruel hand. And there was scarcely any punishment more dreadful than the blows I received on my face and head from her hard heavy fist. She was a fearful woman, and a savage mistress to her slaves" (66). Thus, Henry Louis Gates Jr. concludes, "Prince's account makes her readers acutely aware that the sexual brutalization of the black woman slave—along with the enforced severance of a mother's natural relation to her children and lover of her choice—defined more than any other aspect of slavery the price of her bondage" (xv). Two sentimental figures emerge in Prince's memoir: the victimized slavewoman and the monstrous white woman who dominates her. The latter figure specifically served to caution white women readers, like "the women that are at ease . . . the women of the North," to whom Harriet A. Jacobs appeals in her 1861 fugitive slave narrative. The jealous and malevolent mistress of

Prince's and Jacobs's autobiographies would become standard in such novels of the 1850s as Harriet E. Wilson's *Our Nig* and Harriet Beecher Stowe's *Uncle Tom's Cabin*. Moreover, that corporal, psychosexual, and homoerotic violence formed the most dominant traits of slavewomen's bondage has been established by other enslaved women's accounts of their lives. From Jacobs's two hundred-page *Incidents in the Life of a Slave Girl* through stories of bound life slaves related to interlocutors of all sorts, *thousands* of black women have left an enduring discursive legacy of the multiple ways they were deprived and debased as chattel slaves.[5]

The representation of violence is a staple of sentimental literature, particularly in slave testimonials dictated to white transcribers of black narratives in the abolitionist movement. As I have already stated, sentimental literature evolved alongside the seduction novel, a subgenre based on the concept of chastity under *siege*, of moral virtue under *attack*. Whereas Susanna Rowson demurely protects her readers by staging Charlotte Temple's ruin off-page (in the bowels of a vessel on the Atlantic Ocean, away from readers' direct gaze), abolitionist authors customarily showcase the corporal violence experienced by slaves to arouse the readers' moral indignation and to provoke them to expressions of sympathy and abolitionist efforts. Frederick Douglass's reconstruction of the beating of his Aunt Hester in his narrative of 1845 and Stowe's narration of the death of Uncle Tom famously illustrate this convention; the kinship implied by the use of the terms "Aunt" and "Uncle" before the characters' names insinuates a familial bond that sentimentalism prompts readers to honor and protect. Abolitionists apparently reasoned that including slaves' eyewitness accounts blazoning the barbarity of slavery would prove effective in ending the peculiar institution—and the more sentimentalized those accounts were, the greater aid they would be to the abolitionist cause. The transcriber of *The History of Mary Prince* clearly thought so.

That many testimonials of slave atrocities reconstructed white savagery in terms of black lack is both unsurprising and paradoxical. For they accounted not only for the ways of wicked white folks but also for the capacity of the enslaved African (convert) to be saved from sin. Intolerant of deeds that defied the Protestant ethics of both work and comportment, white Christian abolitionists, as Sharpe asserts, "located the moral deficiency of black slaves in both the negative influence of slavery and their 'Africanness'" (33). It would seem that white violence, perversely, redeemed black recalcitrance. Nancy Bentley has suggested that "for women's bodies and black bodies the infliction of violence or abuse can be a means by which the individual achieves a transcendent grace or enriched dignity" (503). Put another way, reading the incontrovertible violence inflicted upon figures like Uncle Tom and Aunt Hester enabled some antebellum readers to endow such figures with transcendence and dignity. That is, for these readers, their own emotional response to the rhetorical (re)construction of legal corporal violence, manifested in the familiar physical signs/sighs of sympathy, authenticated the possibility of slave sentience and humanity. Such a conclusion lay predicated on an initial belief in black baseness. Writers of slave narratives thus sentimentalized the slave body, as it were, for political ends. However, as Lindon Barrett cogently cautions, "it is paramount to recognize that the body in question in the sentimental literary transaction *never* enters the transaction on its own terms [but] foremost and always, as a measure of a prioritized, immaterial sensibility or character, as an emblem of a state of mind and consciousness" (424). Undoubtedly, slaves like Mary Prince who were forced to rely on white Christian amanuenses for the promulgation of their stories knew that they not only risked a truncation of the full complexity of their experiences, but that they actually required a discursive exploitation— or obliteration—of their "bodies" as well. When Methodist poet Susanna Strickland penned Prince's body in pain in Prince's *History*, she transcribed the slavewoman's subtle paradox and argued at once for the actual corporeality of the black body *and* for the utter disembodiedness of blackness. Following Prince's locutionary lead, Strickland could argue for the release of Prince's black body from bondage only by challenging the materiality of the blackness of Prince's body.[6]

Prince, in many ways a representative slavewoman, was clearly cognizant— and contemptuous—of the equation of blackness with depravity and deficiency when she dictated her story to Strickland around 1830. Such an equation seems as prevalent among abolitionists at the time as among slaveholders. Prince worked with Strickland while the latter was a guest in the home of Thomas Pringle.[7] Secretary of the Anti-Slavery Society in Aldermanbury, London, Pringle had hired Prince into domestic service in December 1829, a year after she first appealed to the society upon leaving the Woods family, tyrannical slaveholders who had brought her from Bermuda. *The History of Mary Prince* indirectly denounces those who mistake the preliterate for the imbecilic; the narrator exclaims, "Oh the Buckra people who keep slaves think that black people are like cattle" (71). Furthermore, the narrator implies that slaveholders will ultimately suffer for those sins they compel their slaves to commit. At one point, enumerating the cruelties of slavery in Antigua, she tells her evangelical amanuensis, "It is very wrong, I know, to work on Sunday or to go to market;

but will not God call the Buckra men to answer for this on the day of judgment—since they will give the slaves no other day?" (82). Prince's reproach of
Christian hegemony undercuts the *History*'s chronicle of her religious conversion, an experience that simultaneously teaches orthodox religious doctrine and
exposes white Christian hypocrisy. The narrator reports:

> After a while I was admitted a candidate for the holy Communion.—I
> had been baptized long before this, in August 1817, by the Rev. Mr. Curtin,
> of the English Church, after I had been taught to repeat the Creed and the
> Lord's Prayer. I wished at that time to attend a Sunday School taught by
> Mr. Curtin, but he would not receive me without a written note from my
> master, granting his permission. I did not ask my owner's permission,
> from the belief that it would be refused; so I got no farther instruction at
> that time from the English Church. (83–84)

Thus, Prince, ironically, demonstrates through Strickland that Christianity
buttressed slavery in two significant ways: through a coalition between ministers and slaveholders and through active deterrent of the pursuit of salvation
among slave converts.

The narrator further reports that her conversion to Moravianism in Antigua,
around 1820, had been imbued with missionary zeal and instruction: "When I
found out that I was a great sinner, I was very sorely grieved, and very much
frightened. I used to pray God to pardon my sins for Christ's sake, and forgive
me for every thing I had done amiss; and when I went home to my work, I always thought about what I had heard from the missionaries, and wished to be
good that I might go to heaven" (83).[8] Tellingly, the *History* does not spell out
what Moira Ferguson has recently revealed: that Prince converted to Moravianism in order to marry the free black widower Daniel James, since "slaves
could not marry in the Anglican Church" (*Nine* 50). The badge of social respectability seems to have been important to Prince in 1820 — perhaps as much
for the leverage that a legally and religiously sanctioned liaison with a free man
of color would grant her toward personal liberty as for its intrinsic value. A
decade later, reconstructing her experience in the home of the Secretary of the
Anti-Slavery Society, she might have omitted the detail of her desire to marry
in order to appear chaste and demure rather than libidinous and sly. She would
have been well aware that "the Antislavery Society . . . won public support by
detailing atrocities and portraying female slaves as pure, Christ-like victims and
martyrs in one of their major organs of propaganda, the *Anti-Slavery Reporter*"
(Ferguson, *History* 4). In actuality, most slavewomen did not conform to the

sentimentalized virginal figure put forth by the abolitionists. Indeed, the conditions of slavery proscribed chastity in those slaves who would have chosen it. Still, controversy and outrage enshrouded Prince and her *History* when readers learned that, in addition to forcible heterosexual molestation and homosexual transgressions she suffered as a slave, Prince had openly flouted London's religious and social mores through both prostitution and a long-term affair with a white lover, a Captain Abbott.[9] Nevertheless, in spite of the verbal restrictions placed on her by abolitionist editors, Prince, as an authoritative and autonomous narrator, triumphs over the domineering Methodist Society. The narrative posture she adopted disarmed both her "friends" and her oppressors. For just as Pringle's Methodist Society used her life story to advance its abolitionist and theological projects, Prince, in order to advance her legal case for personal emancipation, subverted the Methodists' interest, no doubt formulating her recollections very carefully. The barbarous maltreatment she had suffered throughout her life in no way diminished the value she placed on her freedom.

That Mary Prince, through oral testimony, could so manipulate, so effect a text that she could not herself inscribe, even to surreptitiously excoriating and signifying on the very person transcribing that narrative, elucidates the ironic discrepancy between whites' doubt of African intelligence and reality. Prince's mastery over Strickland demonstrates the failure of the slaveocracy to achieve its greatest goal: psychological dominance over blacks through the deprivation of knowledge. Ironically, Prince's mastery also unmasks abolitionists' own breaches of faith by implying that evangelists zealously proliferated slave literature to tout their own virtue and magnanimity. By thus controlling her *History,* Prince proves her conviction, like Douglass's a decade later, that "the power to use language to change the minds of others is the greatest power that an individual can exert" (Andrews, "Narrating" 26).

In the end, it is clear that Mary Prince executed those strategies she could in order to emerge in her dictated narrative as a persona of integrity and credibility, rather than as a victim literally with no self to speak of.[10] If her rejection of Christianity casts doubts on Frey and Wood's premise "that religious change was everywhere the product of a reciprocal process rather than of conversion by confrontation," her *History* resolutely supports their conclusion "that the spiritual and material lives of enslaved people were inextricably linked" (xii). Both representing the black woman self as autonomous and moral and confirming the integration of the sacred and the temporal would become key goals of her free African American namesake as well. *Nancy* Prince, however, went into the West Indies for reasons far different from those that had earlier taken

Mary Prince from Bermuda to Antigua. As an antebellum American Baptist missionary, Nancy Prince apparently traveled abroad in the 1840s for the same reasons that other missionaries went into "uncivilized" areas: throughout the nineteenth century, the Foreign Mission Convention of Baptists consistently included among its "Principles and Tenets" the precept that "The National Baptist Convention stands for the evangelization of all lands in general; Africa, the West Indies and Latin America in particular" (qtd. in Coan 31). Like other American missionaries, Prince apparently assumed that because the "natives" were not yet "saved," they were doomed to eternal damnation unless Christians intervened. Unlike her associates, though, Nancy Prince plainly differed from those white Christians who equated blackness and bondage with naïveté and primitivism and ironically read their ability to capture the "savages" as proof of blacks' need for salvation. In fact, Nancy Prince's *Narrative* suggests that she had suffered too much racial discrimination in America and had witnessed too much of Christian imperiousness in dictating morality and legislating hegemony to accept standard missionary dogma without sharply comprehending its colonialist proclivity. Though Mary Prince and Nancy Prince represent different nations and caste and class systems, their sentimentalized life narratives indicate that both women were social dissidents.

Whereas Maria Stewart's *Productions* describes her involuntary expulsion from Boston and the spiritual autobiographies of Jarena Lee and Zilpha Elaw chronicle the itinerant travels of African American ministers who probably would not have left their homes had they not felt required to by God, the narrative of Nancy Gardner Prince demonstrates that the missionary was never fully satisfied with her "place" in America. Her *Narrative* is rich with accounts of travels she made throughout America, Europe, and the West Indies. Before detailing any of her own experiences, the narrator admires the advantages that travel offers to others. While "travel," on one hand, was the means by which her enslaved ancestors had arrived in America, on the other hand it had also enabled them to gain their freedom. Prince recounts the story of one of her stepfathers, Money Vose, who had been "stolen from Africa" but through "travel" had secured his escape, with a companion, from a slave ship in a New England seaport. The narrator's poetic recollection of the fugitive's story foreshadows the esteem she places on mobility and the independence it yields: "I have heard my father describe the beautiful moon-light night when they two launched their bodies into the deep, for liberty" (6). The girl's own traveling days began in her adolescence, when she trekked around America's northeastern coast as an indentured servant. Besides journeying to secure a livelihood for herself, she also found jobs for her siblings that required them to travel. Thus, for Prince travel became associated with economic survival, if also with division of the family. Cheryl Fish has argued that Prince suffered "a sense of displacement, articulated textually as a dialectic between physical or masculinized strength and an infirm or feminized body that maintains an empowered spirit. . . . she valorizes a kind of mobility connected to usefulness and productive work in order to distance herself from her mother, whom she associated with the nomadic wandering of the Jew" (482). Her mother had borne many children, for which Nancy dutifully provided care. The early pages of the *Narrative* document the places to which the Gardner children were sent, or displaced, for work and sustenance and forecast not only the narrator's high regard for the power mobility generates but, more boldly, her later reproach that a newly liberated nation would force any portion of its denizenry into so poor a predicament.

The rhetoric of the initial portions of Prince's *Narrative* anticipates the critique of patriarchy that distinguishes its latter half. An extended report of the deleterious effects of poverty and disruption on her family forms the first explicit description of the author's journeys. Made long before her professional work with the Baptists, the trips definitively portend the Christian missions that Prince would later undertake. In the highly novelized account, Prince narrates her arduous journey, by foot and sleigh, in February 1816 from Salem, Massachusetts, to Boston to save her elder sister Silvia from moral and sacred ruin. Silvia, lured into a house headed by "the mother of harlots," figures as a damsel in distress, the seduction novel's deluded maiden, and the narrator herself, at seventeen, as a valiant and virtuous rescuer. This vignette offers several significant challenges to traditional sentimental literary principles, particularly with respect to class and gender. Analyzing this episode, Frances Smith Foster observes that Prince revises the conventional portrayals of men and women in seduction novels: first, "the seducer is not a smooth-talking unscrupulous man" who degrades an innocent maid but a whorehouse madame, and second, the *femme fatale* (the madame) seduces not a man, but another woman (86). As Foster cogently argues, with these reversals Prince expressly asserts the respectability of African American women like herself and, more important, calls all Christian women to act charitably, not censoriously, toward their "less fortunate sisters" (86). Casting herself as the intrepid conqueror forms a third revision of the convention. In taking on this masculine role, Prince suggests that the most admirable quality in a woman is not frailty but fearlessness; feminine respectability need not preclude a woman's exertion of physical as well as moral strength. Unlike Lee and Elaw, who frequently depict themselves as sick with either their own sinfulness or their opponents' and as healed only by providence, Prince boastfully portrays herself as her sister's spiritual savior and narrowly escapes blasphemy by proclaiming herself armed with might, right, and divinity in her achieving feat. In illustrating the immoral consequences of economic poverty, Prince advocates serviceable educational and vocational training for all women while also urging white (women) readers to recognize black women's capacity for virtue; at the same time, she spurs her female readers to resist the patriarchal mandate that they be fragile and helpless.

Nancy Prince's sentimentalization of the episode revises the object of critique in traditional seduction and sentimental novels. While Foster regards the "mother of harlots" as an "evil one . . . who deliberately creates a perverse family," it seems to me that Prince uses domestic imagery and scriptural allusion to analyze the lucrative potential that prostitution proffered Silvia and the madame for self-sufficiency. For the older woman offers an economic resistance when she and the narrator physically struggle over Silvia: "she owes me, she cannot go" (14). Rather than implying that her sister—and the madame, too—falters due to religious contumacy or moral bankruptcy, Prince asserts that Silvia's prostitution derives from the same impoverishment that forced both sisters to leave their unsteady mother. Indeed, in further defiance of nineteenth-century sentimental and domestic ideologies, Prince indicates that their mother's instability developed *because of* her marriages—and her subsequent loss of her several husbands to slavery, desertion, and death. So, while patriarchal religion—or, the Christianized republic—sanctioned those marriages because they endorsed the true womanhood ideal, it offered no assistance when each husband in his turn left Prince's mother with several children but with no resources to maintain them or herself. Furthermore, it is ironic that Money Vose, the husband whose escape story had moved and inspired Prince, physically (and perhaps sexually as well) abused Nancy and Silvia. Reporting Silvia's moral decline, Prince laments: "To have heard of her death, would not have been so painful to me, as we loved each other very much, and more particularly, as our step-father was not very kind to us. When little girls, she used to cry about it, and we used to say, when we were large enough we would go away" (12). Reflecting later on her relationship with her then-deceased sister, the mature author writes: "Even now . . . her soul is precious; she was very dear to me; she was five years older than myself, and often protected me from the blows of an unkind step-father" (15). Such statements bring to mind Lora Romero's cogent contention that early women sentimentalists "were women who found in the antipatriarchal analysis of the family at the heart of domesticity a compelling language for describing women's second-class status and for imagining ways . . . of improving it" (20). In a bold move for the time, Prince's midcentury appropriation of sentimentalism does not promote the racialized ideals of (white) true womanhood and free black family integrity so popular in her day; instead, it overtly challenges readers to grieve for mothers and daughters who are dependent on men and who are poorly skilled as workers; Prince's narrative bolsters her counsel that autonomous travel can provide sacred *and* psychic salvation.

Circumstances like those affecting her mother and sister led Nancy Gardner Prince to seize every opportunity to leave the United States she could and to contrive opportunities when they did not come knocking. Rather than wait for divine providence to light her way, Prince seized her first opportunity to travel outside of the country when Nero Prince proposed to her, according to the *Narrative*. Her marriage in 1824 relieved her of familial duties and she accompanied Prince to St. Petersburg, Russia, where he served in the czar's courts. In depicting her experiences in Russia, Prince offers an oblique critique of her native country. While living abroad, she reports, she observed that one's class mattered more than one's ethnicity or nationality: she notes, "there was no prejudice against color; there were there all cast[e]s, and the people of all nations, each in their place" (23). In August 1833, after nine years of consistently being treated as an equal by the Russians, she had returned to the United States when her husband, traveling separately, died on the eve of his departure from Europe. Thereafter, she dedicated her life to Christian benevolent activities in the United States and elsewhere; arguably, she participated in international missionary work as much for the opportunities it offered her for travel as for her altruism.

Eight years after her husband's death, Nancy Prince, a poor but proud widow of forty-one years, traveled from Boston to Jamaica. Just before she left, she met "the Rev. Mr. Ingraham, who had spent seven years there," she writes. "He told me that the moral condition of the people was very bad, and needed labor aside from any thing else" (43–44). By the end of Prince's account of her two missions in the West Indies, however, it seems that "the bad people" Ingraham refers to are not so much the Afro-Jamaicans as, more aptly, the white church officials who are engaged in missionary work there. The latter group was, in Prince's estimation, either disgracefully "deluded" or "full of deceit and lies" (62). The *Narrative* shows how Prince allied herself with other diasporic blacks rather than associate herself with the immoral and imperialist white missionaries. While Nancy Prince went with her fellow missionaries ostensibly to save slaves like Mary Prince from sinfulness and slavery, she soon concluded that the group actually in need of "civilization" were the Western whites, not the Jamaican "heathens."

To illustrate her joyful anticipation of her sacred work in Jamaica, Nancy Prince cites John 4:35, which states: "Lift up your eyes, and look upon the fields; for they are white already to harvest."[11] In her paraphrase of this verse, Prince accentuates the New Testament's landscape trope, exclaiming, "A field of usefulness seemed spread out before me" (43). Significantly, her revision elides the word "white" out of the Gospel's visual image. While citing a text that other Christians would undoubtedly recognize, she alters the perception of her individual religious mission, dissociating it from that of her racist white Christian colleagues and transforming it into an affirmation of African selfhood and salvation. The landscape of Christianity in the United States, by contrast, had already proved infertile and unyielding: the first reference to her Jamaican mission appears in a paragraph that follows an account of her failed attempt to establish in Boston an "asylum" for orphans like that she "had had the privilege of assisting in forming . . . for such a purpose in St. Petersburg" (41–42). In Russia, "where children of all classes have the privilege of instruction" (36), the Princes had also boarded and cared for several school children (26, 38). Back in the United States, however, the narrator, herself a widowed boarder dependent on others' generosity, reports that she "found many a poor little orphan destitute and afflicted, and on account of color shut out from all the asylums for poor children" (41). Predictably, then, after three months of assisting only eight children in Boston, "the committee was dispensed with, and for want of money our society [and orphanage] fell through" (42). So by the time Prince decides to journey to Jamaica, she is destitute and dispirited. Not surprisingly, she links her own poverty *and* want of funds to alleviate the poverty of others to a racist, classist nation that was indifferent to the needs of the disenfranchised.

Prince's benevolent activities consistently involved children. Her dedication suggests that she had, in part, inherited the Revolutionary-era notion of republican motherhood, which was, in Romero's phrase, "the precursor of domesticity" (14). Perhaps she chose childcare because it was acceptable—indeed, *expected*—"professional" work for women, even (or especially) women who were not mothers or did not own their own homes. Conversely, though, detailing her efforts to institutionalize childcare in an orphanage, Prince insists that she was more an administrator and an authority figure than the stereotypical domestic worker or displaced mammy. She thereby underscores the fluidity of women's affiliation with the home and the conflicted identity of the mythic true woman. Moreover, Prince implies that her work with African American youths could have made a vital contribution to New England society had it been philanthropically supported. Furthermore, the sometimes sardonic tone of the *Narrative* overtly violates the sentimental norm. Instead of consistently describing her charity activities in ways that would elicit readers' sympathy and emulation, Prince seems as determined to elicit scorn for institutions that were neglectful of the weak as she is to arouse pity for the abandoned. For example, the narrator identifies the work of the Garrisonian abolitionists she supports as "the amelioration of the *nominally free* colored people of these States, and the emancipation of the slaves in other States" (42, italics added); the phrase "nominally free" gibes at the obstacles impeding northern African Americans' pursuit of happiness. She observes the missionaries' neglect of the Jamaican children's education when she mourns, "I am sorry to say that the meeting house is more like a play house than a place of worship" (47). In caustic terms, she chides one minister for his dereliction of duty, asserting that "something must be done for the elevation of the children, and it is for that I labor" (47). On the whole, her opinionated representation of the fate of powerless Africans across the diaspora links her more closely to later authors like Jane Addams and Ida Wells Barnett than to her famously prodomestic contemporaries, including Catherine Beecher and Louisa Alcott.

Nancy Prince's embittered attitude toward Christianity is evident in her condemnation of her missionary colleagues, especially in her descriptions of her relations with other missionaries during her stint in the West Indies. The narrator does not reject Christianity by repudiating its tenets or renouncing her faith; rather, she rejects other (white) Christians for the prejudices that they exhibit in their interactions with Africans. For example, upon her arrival in the West Indies, she assists the "class-leader" with whom she lodges until the leader's teaching method offends her (46). When the leader threatens that the Society will not pay her, Prince righteously reports, "I spoke to her of the necessity of being born of the spirit of God before we become members of the church of Christ, and I told her I was sorry to see the people blinded in such a way"(46). The dispute soon goes on to involve the Society's administrator, whom Prince staunchly stands up to. She "talked with him an hour," during which she "told the minister that I did not come here to be guided by a poor foolish woman"

(47, 46). Whereas traditional sentimental writers embrace and espouse Christian ideals, Prince's *Narrative* renounces false piety and spiritedly uses church leaders to illustrate such sinfulness.

Prince undercuts the significance of her missionary work by writing a travelogue rather than a formulaic spiritual autobiography. However, the *Narrative* closes with several pages of divine adulation that form a paean to God. She includes such exaltations as, "Truly the promises of God are given for our encouragement; they are yea and amen, in Christ Jesus; they are a covert from the storm, a shelter from the heat, a sure retreat for the weary and way worn traveller [*sic*]" (86). Arguably, the laudations filling its latter pages transform the whole of the *Narrative* from a travel book to a spiritual autobiography, perhaps in the same way that the religious recollections Stewart adds to her 1879 *Meditations* transform her 1835 *Productions* from jeremiad to spiritual autobiography. But even in her laudations Prince highlights her life as a traveler and never explicitly names herself as a missionary. For example, her last paragraph begins with a prayer for pilgrims: "O Father, fearful indeed is this world's pilgrimage, when the soul has learned that all its sounds are echoes, all its sights are shadows. But lo! a cloud opens, a face serene and hopeful looks forth" (87–88). Thus, in spite of a conclusion that overtly glorifies God in ways unprecedented in the *Narrative,* Prince's omission of the free and frequent divine adulation that characterizes the spiritual autobiographies of other African American women of her era places greater emphasis on the temporal rather than the spiritual. Although the autobiography reconstructs her experiences as a Protestant missionary, Prince nonetheless underscores the secularness rather than the religiousness of the life she spent spreading the Gospel.

While the travelogue structure of her autobiography certainly does not disavow her piety, it does indicate Prince's authorial preference for the secular form over the sacred. She gives no reasons for her preference beyond her tacit expression that she hopes to gain financially from the publication of her book, a wish she states in the book's preface. Using the secular genre, she could rhetorically divorce herself from association with the likes of James W. Willmarth, a chauvinistic clergyman of the post-Reconstruction period; she also offers an implicit resistance to the American Missionary Association's various social transgressions, including sexism, classism, colonialism, and racism. In her article "Introduction: Protestantism and Its Discontents in the Eighteenth and Nineteenth Centuries," Mary De Jong exposes the gender and religious chauvinism of many male Protestants. She cites James Willmarth's essay titled

"Woman's Work in the Church," which was written for the *Baptist Quarterly Review* in October 1888. As De Jong notes, Willmarth asserted

> that God intended women to be assistants, not leaders. Therefore American women who taught overseas must be "careful to make no wrong impressions upon the native mind as to woman's proper work." Missionaries to "highly impressible and imitative" black women in the American South should not thoughtlessly assume public teaching roles, lest they give occasion to "a burlesque in ebony of man's work undertaken by women, shocking and ridiculous." Dutiful missionaries would not encourage freedwomen in political activity, for "what every race imperatively needs is saintly womanhood, not female politicians and orators." (De Jong 262)

The protofeminist *Life and Travels* attests to its author's rejection of Willmarth's brand of Baptist "benevolence." Willmarth's discourse is indicative of social and political mores that were operative in Prince's era, which she was able to escape by leaving the United States; traveling provided Prince with a legitimate, indeed revered means of earning a living, enabling others, and eluding oppression, and writing about those travels enabled her to expose such imperialism while sustaining herself.

Rejecting Sentimentalism

The *Narrative* plainly shows that Prince's optimism about a more autonomous life for herself and other Africans propelled her out of the United States. In addition, she specifies her goals in going to Jamaica when she says, "I hoped that I might aid, in some small degree, to raise up and encourage the emancipated inhabitants, and teach the young children to read and work, to fear God, and put their trust in the Saviour" (45). Notably, this articulation of a desire to participate in the political and social reconstruction of a newly freed people, especially its youth, precedes any allusion she makes to the Good News.

Moreover, Prince's justifications for traveling abroad fall midway between those of two dissimilar travelers from different time periods, a prominent sixteenth-century British lawyer named Richard Hakluyt and June Jordan, the contemporary radical African American feminist poet. In 1585, Hakluyt became interested in colonization in the Americas. Apprehensive about his prospective intercourse with the New World's indigenous peoples, he drew a list of his "Inducements to the Liking of the Voyage Intended towards Virginia," enumerating as his first and second reasons: "1. The glory of God by planting of religion among those infidels [and] 2. The increase of the force of the Christians" (qtd. in Mancall 34). After identifying some thirty additional "inducements" to immigration, Hakluyt further reasoned that

> The ends of this voyage are these:
>
> 1. To plant Christian religion.
> 2. To trafficke.
> 3. To conquer.
>
> Or, to doe all three.
>
> To plant Christian religion without conquest will bee hard. Trafficke easily followeth conquest: conquest is not easie. Trafficke without conquest seemeth possible, and not uneasie. What is to be done, is the question. (qtd. in Mancall 39)

Hakluyt and his compatriots apparently soon determined what should be done in the settling of America, for "[a]pproximately 160,000 English people went to the British mainland colonies during the seventeenth century, the vast majority (116,000) traveling to the Chesapeake region; another 190,000 migrated to the West Indies" (Mancall 24).

Three hundred years later, in 1982, Jordan joined the thousands of her compatriots who that year traveled to the West Indies, where she wrote a "Report from the Bahamas." This report eerily echoes Hakluyt's 1585 list of incentives for venturing overseas. For, although she is a black woman herself, Jordan admits feeling a vexed kinship with indigenous black women, compelling her to attempt to justify her presence in the West Indies. She has to repeatedly reassure herself that she has come there for rejuvenation. Moreover, Hakluyt's absorption with the twin tropes of conquest and "trafficke" reemerge in the contemporary author's travelogue when, buying Bahamian souvenirs for family back in Brooklyn, Jordan realizes that

> No matter that these other Black women incessantly weave words and flowers into the straw hats and bags piled beside them on the burning dusty street. No matter that these other Black women must work their sense of beauty into these things that we [tourists] will take away as cheaply as we dare, or they will do without food.
> . . . I notice the fixed relations between these other Black women and myself. They sell and I buy or I don't. They risk not eating. I risk going broke on my first vacation afternoon.

We are not particularly women anymore; we are parties to a transaction
designed to set us against each other. (40 – 41)

Jordan's discourse is characteristic of her age as well: it is candid, soul searching,
and confessional, scrutinizing her postcolonial condition as a black, middle-
class, female traveler. Similarly, Hakluyt's prose style is representative of texts
that were written during the Age of Reason: it is pragmatic, "measured," precise, and, like Jordan's candid, even as he deludes himself into a false morality
and into a rationalization to assuage his fear that after all he is not Christ's devout, but Mammon's.

For Nancy Prince's discourse to be representative of her era, it must evoke the
rhetoric of sentimentality. After all, the first edition of her travelogue was published in 1850, the same year that the *National Era* serialized *Uncle Tom's Cabin;*
the second edition appeared in 1853, the year after Stowe's best-seller was bound
in a single volume. The rhetoric of sentimentalism, as *Uncle Tom's Cabin* makes
so plain, could not be distinguished in antebellum America from the rhetoric
of evangelicalism or of domesticity. But despite Prince's exquisitely sympathetic
condition as a poor, pious, black, and often ill woman, she chose not to exploit
the rhetorical conventions and literary tropes of sentimentalism. Rather, as I
have already noted, she constructs her autobiographical self as dauntless and
self-reliant. As Jordan's literary precursor, she also shows a heightened consciousness about being an African *American* woman among other women of
African descent. Although Prince's *Narrative* antedates Jordan's "Report from
the Bahamas" by more than one hundred years, it provides as much insight
as Jordan's work into the complex "contrary instincts" that colonization occasioned in African American women travelers.[12]

Embedded in Prince's *Narrative* is the entire *The West Indies,* the pamphlet
guidebook that she had published in 1841. It describes her missions to Jamaica
in the winter of 1840 and the spring of 1842. These missions followed the typical pattern of other early Afro-Protestant missions that were commenced to
convert Africans around the world to Christianity. As Sylvia Jacobs concludes
in her survey of "The Historical Role of Afro-Americans in American Missionary Efforts in Africa," "black American missionaries [from 1810 to] 1960
had various motives for African mission work (besides the obvious desire to
Christianize Africans), including a feeling of duty, a chance to combine colonization with missionizing, a desire to prove [blacks'] capabilities, and an impulse from both individuals and institutions for the educational development of
the continent" (24 – 25). Prince's account of her first mission confirms Jacobs'
findings and speaks to the devotion of African American missionaries to the

Christian mission movement, despite the racism within it. With characteristic incisiveness, for example, she observes that among the five thousand members in attendance at the Jamaican Baptist Missionary meetings in May 1841, "there was but one colored minister on the platform" (48). In addition, her report on the meeting's black caucus implicitly contrasts white Christians' apathy with their black counterparts' commitment. She remarks that "the colored people give more readily," and adds, "The resolutions that were offered were unanimously accepted, and every thing was done in love and harmony" (49). Ethnic pride emerges in such passages as much as does Christian charity.

On the other hand, Prince's *Narrative* aligns her with European Americans in a central way: cultural imperialism is also present in the autobiography. In her work on nineteenth-century American women travel writers, both black and white, Mary Suzanne Schriber highlights their nationalism to contend that

> they wrote to promote the superiority and the manifest destiny of American political and spiritual values, for which the travel book was a fit form. . . . American travelers of either gender judged American life superior to any other, whether in religion or in morality, particularly as they expressed themselves on the topics of the American family; the treatment of women; the work ethic; the system of commerce; and, above all, the American system of government. (xxii)

For all of her fierce anger at the atrocities of antebellum slavery in the American South and at the pervasive race and gender discrimination across the ostensibly free North, Prince's *Narrative* nonetheless inscribes a colonialist arrogance comparable to that displayed by her white colleagues in the nascent mission movement.

In a long paragraph preceding her recollections of her first voyage, Prince reflects on her antislavery activities prior to sailing for Jamaica. Contemplative and pious, it is marked by a grave dramatic linguistic and rhetorical disruption:

> These meetings [with Garrisonian abolitionists] I attended with much pleasure, until a contention broke out among themselves; but much remains to be done; possibly I may not see so clearly as some, for the weight of prejudice has again oppressed me, and were it not for the promises of God, one's heart would fail, for He made man in his own image, in the image of God, created he him, male and female, that they should have dominion over the fish of the sea, the fowl of the air. . . . This power did God give man, that thus far should he go and no farther; but man has disobeyed

his Maker, and become vain in his imagination, and their foolish hearts
are darkened. We gather from this, that God has in all ages of the world
punished every nation and people for their sins. The sins of my beloved
country are not hid from his notice; his all seeing eye sees and knows the
secrets of all hearts; the angels that kept not their first estate but left their
own habitations, he hath reserved in everlasting chains unto the great day.
(42–43)

In this plaintive paragraph, Prince moves from the infamous feud in the Garrison machine to an oblique but barbed comment on the North's proscription
of blacks' educational opportunities ("I may not see so clearly as some . . . "),
then to the ballast of race and gender oppression. As if the schism that broke
out among the abolitionists inspires her own sudden break with a rigid linear
chronologizing, Prince shifts to present tense, indicative mood. But this moment of linguistic spontaneity is short-lived, and the next clause deferentially
proclaims the narrator devout, and stops short of naming herself as the "one"
whose "heart would fail." Turning then to the Genesis account of creation,
Prince's exegesis applies a Scriptural conceit to excoriate white/patriarchal supremacy. The use of the first person plural in "*We* gather from this, that God
has in all ages of the world punished every nation" amplifies her singular stern
voice to render it millennialistic. Similarly, the final sentence resounds with the
jeremiadic timbre of earlier African American evangelical rebels like Maria
Stewart and her mentor David Walker. Also like these revolutionaries, the missionary exhibits a complex double consciousness—and an acrid irony—when
she characterizes America as her "beloved country" but tropes on slaveholders
as (fallen) "angels," the word "chains" in the final clause underscoring her
double entendre. The ensuing paragraph begins understatedly: "My mind, after the emancipation in the West Indies, was bent upon going to Jamaica" (43).
So although her subsequent list of her professional goals in going abroad does
not include a desire to escape American apathy and (or about) oppression, it is
plain that her disappointment with the failure of her philanthropic efforts and
with the ideological debates dividing America's abolitionist sects made the
dream of meaningful work among other free(d) Africans very appealing.

The passage cited above significantly foreshadows Prince's millennialism,
which also emerges later in the only passage that, purportedly, represents
without deviation the speech of an Afro-Jamaican. Prince writes: "A poor old
woman, speaking of [natural] calamities to me, thus expressed herself: 'Not so
bad now as in the time of slavery; then God spoke very loud to *Bucker,* (the

white people,) to let us go. Thank God, ever since that they give us up, we go pray, and we have it not so bad like as before'" (66–67). Prince is eager to insinuate her superior class status relative to the ex-slavewoman's; her "unmediated" representation of the dialect in which the "other" woman speaks apparently serves to remind readers that, though impoverished and aging herself, the American missionary nonetheless affects some social, political, and economic advantage over her "native informant." Yet Prince follows her account of the woman's unexpurgated pronouncement with a comment clearly designed to illustrate not her difference from the Jamaican elder but rather their similitude, leveled as the two women ultimately are by race and class oppression. Acerbic and jeremiadic at once, Prince invokes Moses's masterful words in Deuteronomy to recommend "this poor woman's remark to the fair sons and daughters of America, the land of the pilgrims. 'Then God spoke very loud.' May these words be engraved on the post of every door in this land of New England" (67). Furthermore, this recollection is set amid a section of the 1853 edition of the *Narrative* that purports to describe flora and fauna, not people or social institutions. She reiterates the elderly Jamaican woman's words in the context of natural disasters—the catastrophic hurricanes and deluges that recur in West Indian history—to ironize and exoticize the woman, thus depicting her more as a natural object than a human being. However, Prince does privilege the woman's shrewd inference over her own mere corroboration: it is the Jamaican eyewitness, not the American "I-witness," who initially remarks upon the wrath and the Word of God as they are manifest in the insuperable. So, while Prince condescends to the woman as her inferior—the woman is depicted as simple, uncultivated, and crude—Prince also attests to the woman's superiority over her as one who is faithful, fearless, and prophetic. Prince, in short, shows herself as both the colonizer and the colonized.

Carla Peterson has convincingly argued that "Prince ultimately remained an outsider to Jamaican culture, perceived by many as a mere curious observer. . . . Indeed, Prince's narrative progressively enacts a shift in power relations as she increasingly positions the Jamaicans as subalterns whose consciousness she must retrieve and for whom she must speak, and as her cultural enterprise transforms them into native Others in need of racial uplift" (92). To be sure, Prince's ambivalence toward and anxiety about representing West Indians and her missionary efforts among them disrupts her rhetorical equilibrium and exposes a conflict she shares with other African Americans who find themselves, as June Jordan grieves, "parties to a transaction designed to set [them] against each other." Quite ironically, Prince's missionary *Narrative* verifies Hakluyt's seventeenth-century perception, for she realizes that, in spite of—and because of—the fact that she is an African American among "other" Africans in the diaspora, "To plant Christian religion without conquest will bee hard." Her remarkable response to this realization is to represent herself as something different than "Other." She forecasts her modern descendant, the self-scrutinizing figure in Ntozake Shange's *for colored girls who have considered suicide*, who scorns maudlin African identity in plaintive words: "i cdnt stand it / i cdnt stand bein sorry & colored at the same time / it's so redundant in the modern world" (43). Over a century before, Prince refused to conform to her own era's pathetic, commonplace images of (black) womanhood.[13] The *Narrative* repeatedly states her disdain for subservience, asserting in the preface, "There are many benevolent societies for the support of Widows, but I am desirous not to avail myself of them, so long as I can support myself by my own endeavors" (3). The *Narrative* declares her determination to establish a unique discursive otherness, a rhetorical condition of African American womanness devoid of pathos and lamentation.

To suggest her personal superiority over pejorative stereotypes of Africans, Prince avoids sentimentalized portraits of black Jamaicans and occasionally aligns herself with the recently emancipated slave population. The *Narrative* celebrates their extraordinary achievements in the face of monstrous obstructions erected by their previous condition of servitude. Although Prince reconstructs only the direct discourse of the Afro-Jamaican ex-slavewoman cited above, she records some other conversations indirectly or in paraphrase. Perhaps the most fascinating of these is the "transcription" of an exchange between the narrator and a neoteric freedman. It is especially noteworthy that while the anecdote might have been reconstructed sentimentally (the narrator confesses that her "heart sickens" when she remembers the man's recollections of slave life) in order to elicit readers' sorrowful censure of slavery, it is recast rather with curtness and derision. The dialogue involves Prince and "a respectable looking man" who overtakes her on horseback; riding together from St. Andrew's Mountain, they discuss the current conditions of Afro-Jamaican life. Using no quotation marks, Prince implies that she has flawlessly recorded the exchange; for example, she writes, "He asked me many questions, such as where I came from? Why I came to that Isle? Where had I lived, &c. . . . I asked him why the colored people did not hire for themselves? We would be very glad to, he replied, but our money is taken from us so fast that we cannot" (54). Prince indicates the ex-slave's propriety by noting his "respectable" appearance and formal discourse; this she further uses to corroborate her own virtue and discernment:

neither of these persons of African descent—each on horseback—conforms to white stereotypes of blacks as unkempt, unpropertied, ignorant, or graceless. The final sentence of the paragraph significantly combines a pithy assertion by the Jamaican with an appositive that manifests the narrator's acrid concurrence: "the Macroon hunters take all—this is a nickname they give the missionaries and the class-leaders—a cutting sarcasm this!" (54). This conclusion, like Prince's reiteration of the elderly ex-slavewoman's prophecy, asserts the Jamaican's and the American's *mutually* bitter critique of mercenary "Christians." Yet the episode featuring the freedman strikingly lacks the ambivalence of the other anecdote: in place of the condescension Prince displays toward the elderly woman, the narrator expresses admiration for the man's decorum, his sovereignty (Prince implies that he owns the horse on which he rides), his esteem of autonomy and education (explicit in their conversation as well as in the linguistic structure of his reported speech), and finally for his open critique of white missionaries, which she shares.

By demonstrating that other blacks besides herself are no more anomalous than she and are nearly as autonomous as she is, Prince validates both her own self-sufficiency and the former slaves' assiduity. In this way, she exposes the psychic and rhetorical problem of declaring the very people she has gone abroad to "save" as self-reliant. At one point, she reflects on their autonomy, writing, "Thus it may be hoped that they are not the stupid set of beings they have been called; here *surely we see industry;* they are enterprising and quick in their perceptions, determined to possess themselves, and to possess property besides, and quite able to take care of themselves" (50). And speaking to an assembly of "more than two hundred" Jamaicans, she overtly contrasts their situation with that of African Americans. Her brief reconstruction of her address, again in slippery indirect discourse, succinctly lambasts American arrogance (such as the *Narrative* itself elsewhere exhibits!) and proclaims her own estimation of African diligence and perspicacity: "I told them we had heard in America that you are lazy, and that emancipation has been of no benefit to you; I wish to inform myself of the truth respecting you, and give a true account on my return" (50). Having verified the industry and independence of the freed West Indians, Prince reinforces the evangelicalism of her abolitionist message that American slavery ought similarly to be abolished: "Where are their apologists, if they are found wanting in the strict morals that Christians ought to practice? Who kindly says, forgive them when they err. . . . Yet their present state is blissful, compared to slavery" (53). So even though she insists that emancipation in the British colonies actually amounts to *de facto* slavery—she notes "the same spirit of cruelty is opposed to them that held them for centuries in bondage" (53)—Prince passionately argues Afro-Jamaican "native" intelligence, or motherwit, and cultural pride as authentic.

Prince's narrativized account of astute, self-directed Jamaican converts runs contrary to the trope of the servile and self-abnegating Uncle Tom proliferated in the same year by Stowe. Indeed, the trope of the beaten and martyred slave adroitly served as a metonymy of the American antebellum slave narrative tradition, which was at its peak in the early 1850s when its generic conventions were grossly exploited by Northern abolitionists. Although this symbol trivialized the barbarity of actual slave experience, it was added to sentimentalism's stock entourage, alongside the seduced daughter, the homeless orphan, the abject mother, and so on. Such figures of sentimental literature precisely constitute, according to *A Narrative of the Life and Travels of Mrs. Nancy Prince*, the dangers and circumscriptions that genre presented to early African American women writers. For them to engage a sentimental aesthetics was to risk nullifying the very power sentimentalism promised because they would be required to rescind their position as subject and objectify themselves, conflating their oppressed life experiences into hyperbole and melodrama. Prince's portrait of the freed West Indians exposes the vanquished slave stereotype as a fabrication—yet that disclosure risks compromising the missionary's justification for missionary work. Ultimately, then, the rejection of sentimentalism in *A Narrative of the Life and Travels of Mrs. Nancy Prince* develops from twin authorial impulses: Prince's desire to redeem and revise (white-engendered) images of African American womanhood and her corresponding, if sometimes conflicting, desire to recast African recalcitrance as diasporic independence.

While we cannot authenticate the sanctity of the narrator of *The History of Mary Prince*, that ex-slavewoman, like Nancy Prince in *A Narrative*, also used sacred Christian ideals as a means of attaining personal secular goals. Or rather she tried to: Prince apparently aligned herself with Thomas Pringle and the Anti-Slavery Society primarily because she thought the liaison would lead to her emancipation, but ultimately it did not. As Jenny Sharpe documents, Mary Prince "was legally a slave until August 1, 1835, when Parliament passed the Emancipation Act ending slavery in the colonies" (38). Of course, dictated slave narratives like Mary Prince's do not allow us unmediated access to the mind of the slave because their amanuenses had a vested interest in portraying slave women as good Christians. The truth value whites attributed to Prince's testimony depended upon the demonstration by Christian abolitionists that she was a decent Christian woman; thus, "her narrative authority was linked to her sexuality," her virtue (Sharpe 32). Christianity, then, yielded not "eternal life" for black women of the slave era but rather the circumscription of their mortal lives and worldly choices. In the Schomburg Library edition of Prince's *History*, William Andrews remarks on the slave woman's astonishing endurance of the sadistic tortures she suffered. However, Andrews continues, "She had her breaking point . . . and when she reached it, her willingness to live by the stoic Christian's code gave out" (xxx). In other words, at that critical juncture in her life and in the *History*, Mary Prince rejects Christianity. Nancy Prince's ostensible mission to "Christianize" Afro-Jamaicans fails in precisely the same manner that Mary Prince's Christian faith abandons her when Mary Prince realizes the inability of Christianity to save her from her earthly torments. A "nominally free" black person living in the United States, Nancy Prince reaches her own breaking point, and her solution to her religious and social dilemma was to declare her independence from American Christianity by leaving the United States every chance she got.

FOUR

Slavery's Sinners: Mattie J. Jackson

"Our joy that we were permitted to mingle together our earthly bliss in glorious strains of freedom was indescribable."

MATTIE JACKSON

The theology that Mattie Jackson espouses is, like that of Maria Stewart, a theology of survival, of resistance and defiance. Unlike the orphaned Stewart, who brilliantly made her way in the world without parents and indeed almost always alone, Jackson lived with her mother, her younger siblings, and often an extended family of relatives and other slaves. Her theology is inspired by her family's escape from slavery or their endurance of the institution through the combined forces of faith in divine love and providential intervention, self-love, active resistance to injustice, and political liaisons with like-minded Christians. Jackson's narrative concludes, like Nancy Prince's, with a definitive statement of her Christian values and those she would have her readers cultivate. Even more than the spiritual autobiographies of her free- and northern-born elders, Jackson's enumerates the sins of slavery and identifies all Americans as sinners, for all who suffer under slavery—whether they personally endure its lashes or merely tolerate, if not maintain, its continuance—are tainted by it. Thus, Jackson preaches a theology cultivated to effect national healing through Christianized Reconstruction.

One of the most remarkable full-length antebellum slavewomen's narratives is the dictated *Memoir of Old Elizabeth, a Coloured Woman*, which first appeared in 1863, then was reissued by Philadelphia Quakers in 1884 as the *Memoir of Old Elizabeth, a Coloured Evangelist*. This little pamphlet of only nineteen pages reconstructs the life of its ninety-seven-year-old subject. Clearly, the transcriber of Elizabeth's story selected only a few incidents from the thousands Elizabeth experienced to privilege those that indisputably establish Elizabeth's piety and religious power. That she spent the first thirty years of her life in bondage holds little importance for the amanuensis, even though Elizabeth apparently dictated her story in the middle of a civil war fought in large measure over the question of slavery.

Published just three years after the *Memoir of Old Elizabeth*, Mattie J. Jackson's dictated narrative is a document that is radically different from its predecessor. Whereas the *Memoir of Old Elizabeth* cryptically avoids disclosing significant details about its amanuensis (his or her gender, ethnicity, class, age, or any other distinguishing characteristics are not revealed) or even its subject, including her full name, *The Story of Mattie J. Jackson* meticulously identifies the subject and her immediate and extended families, including the later wife of her mother's second husband, who "wrote and arranged" Jackson's 1866 autobiography. This crucial difference between Elizabeth's spiritual autobiography and Mattie's story derives partly from the two women's divergent attitudes toward their enslavement, as inscribed in their respective narratives. The episode related in greatest detail in Elizabeth's memoir is the reconstruction of a beating she suffered in 1784, when she was eight years old; the story covers little more than a single page of the narrative. Its focus is less on her trauma than on the divine protection her mother, sorrowfully advising that Elizabeth "had 'nobody in the wide world to look to but God'" (4), had encouraged her to seek. Even more textually dramatic, the incident that was probably most significant to the slavewoman, her manumission at age thirty, is recast in the space of one scant paragraph. Obviously, then, the *Memoir* is not as concerned with portraying Elizabeth as a slave, which she was for a third of her long life, as it is with emphasizing her sacred experiences as sinner, convert, and finally itinerant preacher. Mattie Jackson, in contrast, dictates her *Story* as a nineteen-year-old woman who had recently escaped from slavery, so it is not surprising that her narrative almost exclusively details her life in bondage in the 1850s and 1860s. In fact, while the *Memoir of Old Elizabeth* minimizes the relevance of its narrator's class and caste in strict adherence to the conventions of the classic conversion narrative, *The Story of Mattie J. Jackson* is a representative slave narrative.

Maria Stewart, Jarena Lee, Zilpha Elaw, and Nancy Prince, though they all were free, wrote about issues germane to slavery, especially about its abolition. Each of these authors wrote her autobiography from a luxurious position that enabled her to make the issue of slavery peripheral rather than central to her text. While the spiritual narrative by definition forswears the temporal to revere the eternal, these holy women's writings exhibit grief for slavery without ever representing their respective subjects as enslaved. Even Stewart's orations did not exclusively address slavery, though they were performed as part of Boston's nascent abolitionist lecture circuit, then printed in William Lloyd Garrison's freedom paper, *The Liberator*. Stewart perorated equally about the needs and concerns of free blacks in the North as about the exigency of ending slavery at the South. In fact, in Stewart's *Productions*, as in the other holy women's narratives, the struggle to abolish slavery becomes only one of the many struggles these authors enjoin all African Americans to engage.

In *The Story of Mattie J. Jackson* slavery figures as absolutely the most crucial concern in the subject's life, describing not only how Jackson lived in bondage, but also, and more important, how she escaped slavery and learned, as Toni Morrison puts it, "how it felt to wake up at dawn and *decide* what to do with the day" (*Beloved* 95). Although in this chapter I argue that Jackson's ostensibly secular narrative can and should also be read as a spiritual autobiography, it differs from the spiritual autobiographies of the earlier black holy women I study in this book by virtue of its inescapable reconstruction of the sins of slavery and the sinners who executed them. Furthermore, Jackson and Dr. L. S. Thompson, her amanuensis, manipulate conventions of the antebellum fugitive slave-woman's autobiography in their joint construction of a postbellum narrative.[1] Blending these conventions with elements of the traditional spiritual autobiography, together the former bondwoman and her amanuensis construct a narrative that implicitly calls for the conversion of postemancipation America from the sin of slavery and the slavery of sin to a national Christian salvation and Reconstruction.[2]

Jackson and Thompson's Christian purpose is unmistakable. It requires them to address disparate audiences simultaneously, for a major dissimilarity between the secular slave narrative and the religious conversion narrative is manifested in the distinct audiences associated with each genre. Other African Americans are the chief audience for a black-authored conversion narrative whereas whites are the targets of slave narratives (McKay, "Nineteenth-Century" 140). While both antebellum and postbellum slave narratives largely appeal to whites to endorse and sustain African American prosperity, a black narrator's conversion story mainly urges blacks to look past temporal concerns (such as white people) to God for divine succor and eternal life. As transcribed by Thompson, *The Story of Mattie J. Jackson* tacitly argues that the personal religious conversion of all Americans, white and black, and the collective national practice of Christian principles will yield not only an intolerance of (and thus an aversion to the reinstitutionalization of) slavery but will also secure for postbellum African Americans the secular and sacred investment of whites in their every endeavor.

Jackson's Autobiography and the Slave Narrative Tradition

The Story of Mattie J. Jackson briefly describes the lives of Jackson and her mother as slavewomen in St. Louis in the two decades before the end of the Civil War.[3] Having established by tracing her patrilineage that she is the descendant of forebears who "possessed a large share of confidence" (5), Jackson shows herself to be the valiant and defiant elder daughter of the preacher Westly Jackson and Ellen Turner Jackson. Although Ellen's first two husbands escape to freedom without her and she fails in her own initial attempts to escape, Ellen has the good fortune to remain within close proximity to her four children (unlike other slave mothers whose offspring were often sold away from them). Endowed with her mother's fortitude and perseverance, Mattie twice resists brutal maltreatment from the slaveholders who "own" her and seeks the intervention of Union soldiers at the arsenal in St. Louis. When Ellen and her children are kidnapped by a rebel slaver posing as a Union captain, first Mattie, then her sister, and finally Ellen and her young son all escape to the North. In the text's penultimate chapter, Mattie and her brother are invited by Ellen's second husband to his residence in Lawrence, Massachusetts, where Mattie meets her stepmother, who eventually transcribes her *Story*.

Although Jackson's narrative ends with an essay entitled "Christianity," her preface makes only one cursory allusion to religion or spirituality. The final sentence of the preface reads: "May God give [Mattie] grace and speed her on her way" (4). Instead of introducing Jackson as a young Christian, as one might expect of a conventional spiritual autobiography, the preface illustrates what Robert Stepto has called the pregeneric myth of African American literature: in Jackson's postbellum autobiography, as in virtually every antebellum slave narrative, the ex-slave's desire and quest for freedom from slavery is inextricably bound up with her desire and quest for literacy. Although Jackson had escaped from slavery and slavery had been judicially abolished by the time she published her narrative, *The Story of Mattie J. Jackson* nonetheless bears out both Stepto's contention and Linda Kerber's report that "urban African Americans quickly narrowed the [literacy] gap between the races after the Civil War" (*Intellectual History* 237), for most of the text describes Mattie's fervent desire for freedom and literacy. Furthermore, as consistent with postbellum autobiography, the narrative emphasis of *The Story* is less on the skills Jackson lacks than on those she virtuously pursues. Instead of depicting Mattie as an illiterate slave girl, her text casts her as an admirable, earnest student.

Jackson's preface consists of two parts. The first is a brief statement in first-person singular, presumably like the whole dictated by Jackson, which declares her two-fold purpose. She proposes, first, "to gain the sympathy of the earnest friends of those who have been bound down by a dominant race in circumstances over which they had no control—a butt of ridicule and a mark of oppression" (3). Second, she urges sympathetic whites "to buy my little book to aid me in obtaining an education, that I may be enabled to do some good in behalf of the elevation of my emancipated brothers and sisters" (3). An appended "Note" forms the second part of the preface.[4] It attests to the "high moral character" sustained by "Miss Jackson" and further petitions "all the aid of our kind friends" by asserting that those who know Jackson personally have already assessed Jackson's character as "highly worthy" (4) and so have been inspired to assist her "as far [as] their limited means will allow" (3).[5] The preface does not portray Jackson as a woman of particular Christian piety or zeal, thus stopping short of aligning her with such traditional conversion narrators as Lee and Elaw. However, it does blend the critique of slavery and the pregeneric myth of the quest for literacy of the antebellum slave narrative with the postbellum narrative's proud declaration of the ex-slave's worthiness and intelligence. Combined with an expression of commitment to black racial uplift, these elements convey Jackson's sense of her duty to "bear some humble part in removing doubts indulged by the prejudices against the natural genius and talent of our race" (5).

The narrative proper begins with Jackson's account of her ancestors, traced through her fore*fathers* to an African great grandfather (5–6). This succinct patrilineage, and the amanuensis's testimonial in the preface to *The Story,* are among the numerous conventions of slave narratives outlined by James Olney in "'I Was Born': Slave Narratives, Their Status as Autobiography and as Literature" (153). Though he is not altogether persuasive in his contention that the "rigidly fixed form" of the slave narrative renders it a poor imitation of autobiography, Olney's outline of the major conventions of slave narratives is thorough and valuable. Of the rhetorical devices and tropes he cites, Jackson's narrative features nearly all of them, making it typical. Yet *The Story* departs from the formulae in an important way. An account of an ex-slave's parentage often involves a white father, as Olney aptly observes. But when the narrator is a woman, the ex-slave is more likely to esteem her *matrilineage* than to esteem male ancestors of either race. To be sure, once Jackson introduces her mother, Ellen Turner is as predominant a figure in *The Story of Mattie J. Jackson* as is Mattie Jackson herself. Jackson's recollections of the men in her mother's life— her husbands, sons, even slaveholders—elucidate the narrator's commitment to detailing the lives of members of the various communities to which she belongs. More significantly, Ellen, as a frequent analogue for her daughter-narrator, illuminates Mattie's determination to extol her mother's remarkable achievements, to esteem and tell of her mother's extraordinary life.

Not surprisingly, the slave daughter's tribute to her mother's aggrieved yet victorious life is narrated in exceedingly sentimental terms. This portrait reverses the representation of the mother as a failed—though unfallen—woman in *A Narrative of the Life and Travels of Mrs. Nancy Prince*. In that autobiography, Prince reconstructs her mother's life in sentimental rhetoric for two significant reasons. First, Prince uses her mother's pathetic situation as a deserted wife and the mother of children she cannot feed, clothe, or protect to provoke readers' empathy and ire. She also uses her mother's situation to mobilize readers toward the reconstitution of those systems that have prohibited her mother's autonomous social advancement and made her a dysfunctional rather than a "republican" mother. Second, Prince takes pains to distinguish her mother's personal shortcomings (and the social and political failures they signify) from her own progress and success. As I have argued in chapter 3, Prince resoundingly rejects sentimentalism's victimization of African American women, especially for herself. In *The Story of Mattie J. Jackson,* Jackson and Thompson deploy sentimental strategies to demonstrate not only Ellen Turner's victimization by the slaveocracy but also her triumph over it by surmounting its obstacles to her own and her family's happiness. In "Why Daughters Die," Nancy Armstrong analyzes conjugal contracts in sentimental literature and concludes, "Whenever marriage outside a group threatens that group's ties to the country of its origins, daughters tend to become problematic" (10). Prince's *Narrative* constitutes a daughter's reflection on the problems that arose in America from marriages between her African ancestors and their spouses of disparate African groups. In other words, the childless narrator traces her own and her sister Silvia's material problems in the United States to the domestic conflicts her mother suffered in more than one marriage to a captured African. Prince's *Narrative* first appeared only sixteen years before Jackson's *Story*. That momentous interim wrought such change, however, that in Jackson's *Story* the daughter celebrates the ascendancy of her (fore)parents'—Prince's descendants'—marriages. Despite the "peculiarity" of slavery, her mother, thrice married, did not go mad as Prince's had, and none of Turner's grown daughters strayed or died.

In narrating her own and her mother's life, Jackson specifically relates many forms of physical violence perpetrated against slavewomen and thus makes a sentimental case against slavery. *The Story* alternately depicts Ellen as pathetic victim of and fearless resister to violence. Interestingly, though Ellen and Mattie are much abused as women, the narrative does not report that either suffered sexual violence, again aligning Jackson with the antebellum tradition. With the notable exception of Harriet Jacobs's *Incidents in the Life of a Slave Girl*, female slave narratives differ from the narratives of male slaves in that the latter perfunctorily portray slavewomen as victims of sexual abuse by lecherous slavers. For as Frances Smith Foster asserts, "When slave women tell their stories . . . they barely mention sexual experiences and never present rape or seduction as the most profound aspect of their existence. . . . Though they wrote to witness slavery's atrocities, they also wrote to celebrate their hard won escape from that system and their fitness for freedom's potential blessings" ("In Respect" 67). In other words, when slavewomen who were abused narrated their stories, they emphasized other parts of their lives, chiefly their survival, as paramount over that abuse. In this regard, Jackson is no exception. Furthermore, this emphasis on survival corresponds to the rhetorical decisions made respectively by Jarena Lee and Zilpha Elaw in their spiritual autobiographies; the two women underscore their achievements as ministers by documenting the resistance that was mounted against their ministries.[6]

Jackson also describes her mother's grievous loss of three husbands. Both Westly Jackson (Ellen's husband of five years and father of her three daughters) and George Brown (Ellen's husband of four years and father of her two sons) escape from slavery specifically when they believe their manhood challenged by their respective slavemasters. Ellen becomes estranged from her third husband, identified by Mattie only as "Mr. Adams," when Ellen and her children are abducted by slavers literally in the dead of night on the eve of their wedding. Eventually, they do marry. Jackson reports that although "We were gone [from him] two years and four months," Ellen and Adams "were married in a week after our return" (33).[7] By that time, both were legally free. While still enslaved, Ellen's greatest sorrow results from the deaths of two of her children. *The Story* uses sentimental rhetoric to depict these deaths. Her daughter Sarah Ann dies as an infant and a son dies at age two because a barbarous slave mistress, Mrs. Lewis, had required Ellen to keep the boy confined in a box as "it would take too much time to attend to him" (12). Drawing on the same sentimental mode that *The History of Mary Prince* uses, Jackson's *Story* exposes the monstrous slave mistress who is brutalized by the very institution that she endorses and sustains. Jackson explains that Mrs. Lewis was, for example, "constantly pulling our ears, snapping us with her thimble, rapping us on the head and sides of it" (10). In addition, because the villainous Mrs. Lewis denied Ellen time to nurture her son, Mattie's brother

> was two years old and never walked. His limbs were perfectly paralyzed for want of exercise. We now saw him gradually failing, but [were] not allowed to render him due attention. Even the morning he died [Ellen] was compelled to attend to her usual work. She watched over him for three months by night and attended to her domestic affairs by day. The night previous to his death we were aware he could not survive through the approaching day, but it made no impression on my mistress until she saw his life fast ebbing away, then she put on a sad countenance for fear of being exposed. . . . When she found he was dead she ordered grave clothes to be brought and gave my mother time to bury him. O that morning, that solemn morning. It appears to me that when that little spirit departed [it was] as though all heaven rejoiced and angels veiled their faces. (12)

Several sentimental tropes emerge in this passage, the desecrated child foremost among them. Because of the implicit textual link between sentimentality and Christianity, the boy is imaged as a Christ-like child martyr. His family appears to be exclusively female, as intimated by the domestic setting, and they are stymied in their efforts to save him. The women's watch over the child's last "dark night," though divinely sanctioned, the narrative suggests, proves futile; they are powerless over the evil forces—social, natural, or human, and political—that prey on them. Ellen's neglect of her son through the interference of her slave mistress and his consequent death reveal the perversion of the slave plantation as a domestic setting. In other words, Jackson's brother's death illustrates how slavery adulterates the home, which in sentimental literature is a place where children are nurtured rather than destroyed. As the "mother" who presides over the plantation and its inhabitants, Mrs. Lewis ultimately fails in her domestic responsibilities because of her callousness and treachery. Furthermore, Jackson's description of her brother's death is replete with Christian iconography. References to the death and resurrection of Christ, to the "little spirit" of the deceased, to the notion of "heaven" and divine rejoicing in the restoration of the dead to heaven, and to angels, who are apparently shamed by their eyewitness of this perfidious murder, figure throughout this passage. Layered one after the other, this catalog of sentimental tropes demands action from a readership that shares a common sense of Christian benevolence and social justice.

Furthermore, through this episode, *The Story of Mattie J. Jackson* passionately exalts the primacy of motherhood, a theme pervasive in nineteenth-century black women's autobiographies, largely to counter myths of black women's alleged bestiality. In the religious memoirs of free-born Zilpha Elaw, for example, the death of her mother causes the narrator lifelong, persistent grief. In her words, she often felt "bitterly, the loss of my mother, whose earthly remains had long since been consigned to the house appointed for all living, and her spirit meet for the inheritance of the saints in light, in which I hope to meet her at the right hand of God" (59). Slavewomen's narratives appropriated the representation of the figure of the dead mother from sentimentalism and Christian evangelicalism to argue that the sanctity of motherhood was not predetermined by caste, class, region, or race. As Foster has observed, slave women's narratives in particular consistently include "the stories of women who survived slavery and prospered in freedom. And more often than not, these women are [the narrators'] mothers or grandmothers" ("In Respect" 69). Although Jackson has no children of her own at the time of her dictation, she asserts the primacy of maternity and maintains the dignity of slave motherhood by telling Ellen's story. Jackson's testimony oddly reinforces the association of women and domesticity fostered by the cult of true womanhood, although white readers would not have supposed black women to qualify as "true women." By sentimentally depicting the deaths of Ellen's children, Jackson and Thompson point readers, who would have been well versed in what Jane Tompkins calls "sentimental power,"[8] to slavery's perversion of the mother-child bond and, more radically, to the slave mother's capacity to love and feel, to her "soulfulness." This same sentimental rhetoric was deployed by Harriet Jacobs in *Incidents in the Life of a Slave Girl, Written by Herself* and by the renowned abolitionist Reverend H. A. Mattison, who served as the amanuensis-editor of the dictated slave narrative *Louisa Picquet, The Octoroon.* Published in 1861, both texts sentimentally evoke nineteenth-century notions of women's essential vulnerability to condemn another aspect of the southern slave system: the psycho-sexual victimization of slavewomen. By delicately but deliberately probing the subject of sex, Jacobs and Mattison draw attention to the rampant abuse of African American women, especially black women ensnared in involuntary servitude. Although Jackson's

Story does not describe any slavewomen as sexually abused, the sentimental reconstruction of Ellen's mother-suffering effectively exploits the same precepts as other antebellum slavewomen's autobiographies.

But *The Story of Mattie J. Jackson* defies neat and facile generic categorization as sentimental literature. Its portrait of Ellen is complex and multidimensional, and the rhetorical representation of her other features, such as her impressive physical and mental fortitude, is strikingly devoid of sentimentality. Just as the spiritual autobiographies of Lee and Elaw both appropriate the figure of the invalid holy woman *and* undercut that figure with accounts of the narrators' stamina and vigor, Jackson's depiction of her mother shows that victimization need not preclude the exertion of female tenacity, pluck, quick perception, and prayer. Ironically, black holy women's autobiographies highlight the pathos implicit in the sheer necessity of these women's needing such skills and faculties in order to survive. Despite the romantically arresting image of Ellen's aborted attempt to escape with two small girls (she fasts in order to feed them but is discovered because she "had become so weary that she was compelled to leave our package of clothing on the way" [10]) Jackson proudly proclaims her mother's strength. Though she can do nothing to thwart the emotional and psychological traumas she experienced after the desertion of her spouses and the deaths of her children, Ellen often uses her body, her mind, and even her culinary skills to resist the physical violence perpetrated against her. For example, after reporting that the slaveholding Lewises use a cowhide to inflict severe corporal punishment on their slaves for even slight offenses, Jackson notes Ellen's desperate resourcefulness: "As they stinted us for food my mother roasted the cowhide" (10). Moreover, Mattie represents her own physical defiance as the legacy of her mother. Recounting an especially brutal beating, *The Story* describes how mother and daughter discouraged Mr. Lewis together: "I struggled mightily, and stood him a good test for a while, but he was fast conquering me when my mother came. He was aware my mother could usually defend herself against one man, and both of us would overpower him, so . . . he took his carriage and drove away" (16). The image of two (black) women resisting a (white) man hardly conforms to sentimental conventions. Indeed, it risks compromising Jackson's appropriation of the tenets of sentimental literature that she engages to effect social change.

Even more compelling than Ellen's physical strength is her absolute faith in the natural right of all human beings to control their own lives. Ellen's first two husbands leave her not only with her blessing, but also with her encouragement and assistance; apparently, she urged all slaves, both those on the plantation and

slaves in general, to escape. Ellen held an unwavering belief in one's natural
right to freedom, which was the source of her "runaway tongue," to borrow
Harryette Mullen's phrase; her outspokenness was her greatest gift to Mattie.
For example, though she must have known she would be punished for an "in-
correct" response, when Mr. Lewis searches Ellen's room and finds a picture
of Abraham Lincoln hanging there, Jackson says, "He asked her what she was
doing with old Lincoln's picture." Ellen offers an unabashed reply to his query:
"She replied it was there because she liked it" (14). Besides obviously defying
slavery through the telling of her story, Jackson uses the "resistant orality" that
her mother had instilled in her to sass and to tattle.[9] As Harryette Mullen
asserts about a similar situation that occurs in another narrative in which a
daughter dictates the story of her mother's life in bondage, "The mother's
subjectivity is underscored by her daughter's oral account" (248). That is, when
unjustly treated, Jackson assumes an authority denied her by the slaveocracy,
and asserts her voice to rebut or expose her oppressors; she thereby aligns herself with the tradition of nineteenth-century African American women, whose
narratives exhibit their self-esteem and self-love. And although *The Story of
Mattie J. Jackson* is a self-effacing narrative in that someone other than Mattie
Jackson is cast as its central figure for fully the first third of its pages (and even
for many pages thereafter), it replaces that figure with Jackson herself at a
significant narrative moment.[10] After Jackson reconstructs the scene in which
Lewis beats Mattie but later drives away in his carriage when he becomes convinced he cannot defeat both Ellen and Mattie, *The Story* shifts its dramatic
focus and reprioritizes its cast. The brutality of the beating—or perhaps more
precisely, the injustice of it together with its brutality—causes Jackson to have
an epiphany and brings about a new rhetorical order in the text.

This particular incident is further noteworthy for its striking similarity to a
well-known sentimental scene in the 1845 *Narrative of the Life of Frederick
Douglass, an American Slave,* a scene that also reorders that text's rhetorical pri-
orities. Specifically, Douglass, at the moment of his resolution never again to be
disciplined by the slavebreaker Covey, receives a critical head wound, and this
blow to the head becomes a metaphor for the intellectual change and evolving
consciousness Douglass later experiences during the rest of his enslavement.[11]
Jackson also suffers a head injury that marks a change in her attitude and
"consciousness." Just as the confrontation between Douglass and Covey ensues
from Covey's distrust of him (based in part on Douglass's past tricksterliness
and efforts to escape), Jackson's habitual outspokenness and intractability
ostensibly provoke her slavemistress's wrath one fateful day: "One morning I

entered Mrs. Lewis' room, and she was in a room adjoining, complaining of something I had neglected. Mr. L. then enquired if I had done my work. I told him I had. She then flew into a rage and told [her husband] I was saucy, and to strike me, and he immediately gave me a severe blow with a stick of wood, which inflicted a deep wound upon my head. The blood ran over my clothing, which gave me a frightful appearance" (16). Then, like Douglass, Jackson, drenched in blood, walks to town after this incident to seek redress and retribution from a presumably greater authority, the Union Army. But while Douglass's hypermasculine *Narrative* depicts him as a solitary hero, Jackson's *Story* carefully documents her transformation as a communal act: both Mattie and Ellen play a part in the daughter's victory.[12] In addition, before she leaves the scene of her injury, Mattie, like her father and stepfather before her, entreats Ellen's consent: "I then went to my mother and told her I was going away. She bid me go, and added 'May the Lord help you'" (16). Mattie realizes that Ellen represents those persons—the slaves left behind on the plantation—who will be most directly affected by her absence, and her Christian morality and domestic responsibility require her to beg permission before she leaves.

The Story of Mattie J. Jackson concludes with a section that definitively locates it in the spiritual narrative tradition. Like the *Narrative of Frederick Douglass*, it ends with an essay on Christianity and confirms that the two texts' parallel episodes and tropes are not coincidental. The final appended sections asserting the former slave's Christian faith problematizes Stepto's theory of the pregeneric black myth by linking a third element—religion, specifically Christianity—to freedom and literacy as components of the quintessential quest in African American literature. After all, from their earliest arrival in chains in the New World, Africans forged a theology of survival, crafting a syncretic religion from sacred African and European Christian elements that was rooted in their faith in spiritual egalitarianism even when the slaveocracy denied them equality in any forum. In neither slave narrative is this final section on Christianity linear or chronological; their respective stories both effectively end after the preceding chapter. Accentuating this "departure," Jackson's autobiography desists in its use of the first-person singular pronoun. Douglass's, on the other hand, maintains it. In fact, William Andrews uses Douglass's "Appendix" to read the entire *Narrative* as an American jeremiad. To this end, Andrews aptly cites the reconstruction of Douglass's personal "ritual of socialization," his obviation of the distinction between the secular and the sacred evolution of America as the site of divine fulfillment, his adaptations of such spiritual autobiographical conventions as the conversion experience and the testimonial, and most operatively, Douglass's self-appointed role as jeremiah as evidence of the jeremiadic elements in Douglass's *Narrative* (*To Tell* 124–27). Before Douglass's text of 1845, at least one African American woman writer had already perfected this genre: Maria Stewart fiercely and unflinchingly prophesied the end of American civilization if race persecution persisted in her 1835 *Productions*, as I related in chapter 1. Unlike Stewart and Douglass, however, Jackson is not a sacred or even a social prophet. Her concluding section lacks the common elements of a jeremiad precisely because all personal aspects of the narrator are essentially erased. It does not assert the strident tone or the nationalistic rhetoric of the jeremiad, in which an impassioned I-witness pariah-narrator exhorts and judges a religiously and politically recalcitrant nation. *The Story* prefers to luxuriate tranquilly in the glory of the wonders of the Word rather than to forecast a doomed future on earth and in the hereafter for transgressors. Douglass commences his appendix by explaining that he intends for it to correct any misapprehension readers may have about the religious propriety of the *Narrative* or about his personal Christian faith; the future minister, who, as David Blight notes, underwent a religious conversion in 1831 and in 1839 became "a licensed preacher in the African Methodist Episcopal Zion Church" in New Bedford, Massachusetts (148), writes, "I find, since reading over the foregoing Narrative that I have, in several instances, spoken in such a tone and manner, respecting religion, as may possibly lead those unacquainted with my religious views to suppose me an opponent of all religion" (Douglass, *Narrative* 121). While no comparable statement introduces the final chapter of *The Story of Mattie J. Jackson*, "Christianity" seems intended to serve a function like Douglass's "Appendix." Although not a jeremiad, it nonetheless produces an effect similar to Douglass's final statement by encouraging a rereading of the entire *Story* as a spiritual autobiography.

Jackson's Story and the Spiritual Autobiography Tradition

The Story of Mattie J. Jackson resists being read as a traditional spiritual autobiography because it does not incorporate either of the two most common conventions of that genre. First, it never overtly calls readers to conversion; not even its final chapter seeks to proselytize for Christianity in an explicit fashion. Second, it does not describe the religious conversion of its subject. Because the narrative implies that Jackson becomes a saved Christian sometime during the period that it chronicles, its failure to delineate her conversion experience seems further to insinuate its assessment of that experience as relatively insignificant.

However, various other factors cumulatively make it clear that *The Story of Mattie J. Jackson* is a spiritual autobiography. First, Jackson tangentially notes that she is the daughter of Christian parents. She describes Westly as an inspired minister: "My father was not educated, but was a preacher, and administered the Word of God according to the dictation and revelation of the spirit" (8). *The Story* also portrays Mattie's mother as devout: "But through all her trials and deprivations her trust and confidence was in Him who rescued his faithful followers from the fiery furnace and the lion's den, and led Moses through the Red Sea. Her trust and confidence was in Jesus. She relied on His precious promises, and ever found Him a present help in every time of need" (7). While Christian parents do not necessarily denote a Christian child, it seems likely that in so closely knit a family as Jackson's parents and child would share sacred beliefs and practices. In any case, Jackson's textual decision to depict her parents as Christian people significantly links her to the spiritual autobiographical tradition. Moreover, in detailing Jackson's escape from slavery, the narrative reports that Mattie "boarded" the Underground Railroad outside a neighborhood church; that she is able to secure the Lewises' permission to attend the church without arousing their suspicion suggests that she sought such permission with some regularity. Jackson's decision to designate the church as the point of her departure from chattel slavery signifies the importance she attaches to that site. *The Story* also confirms the piety of its subject with its incorporation of meticulously selected Scripture; although the corroboration of biblical authority is commonplace in nineteenth-century American discourse, its occasional yet precise application paradoxically yields an added dimension of authorial/spiritual sincerity in Jackson's case.

The final section of *The Story of Mattie J. Jackson*, the essay entitled "Christianity," argues, among other things, for the superiority of Christian values and beliefs over more academic thought systems, such as literature and philosophy. Perhaps this, too, constitutes another generic convention. *A Narrative of the Life and Travels of Mrs. Nancy Prince, Written by Herself*, for example, closes with several pages of nonlinear paragraphs, all testifying that "truly the promises of God are given for our encouragement" (86). Indeed, Prince's conclusion authenticates what her *Life* has demonstrated: the reconstruction of her experiences as a Baptist missionary, though secularized by protracted descriptions of the exotic locales to which she has traveled in this capacity, establishes that Prince is a devout and faithful Christian. When similar testimony is appended to the narrative of a woman who is only *presumably* Christian (especially if one only infers that she is because her parents are), then the cultural and rhetorical work of the testimony function differently. Jackson's appendix cannot corroborate her Christian devotion because *The Story* has not definitively proclaimed her devout; the project of the final chapter becomes to establish her piety. Since the credibility of such a final claim would depend greatly on the foundation laid in the narrative proper, seemingly banal details like Westly Jackson's ministry and Mattie's worship habits take on considerable importance when the conclusion verifies Mattie's faith.

Perhaps the most dramatic illustration of the ecclesiastical properties of Jackson's narrative is its careful documentation of the tragic effects of slavery on both African *and* European Americans. *The Story* fiercely condemns the violence against Mattie Jackson and her family throughout its pages, but its reconstruction of an incident of violence *sans* slaves comprises its most austere castigation of the "peculiar" institution. While the discourse in which the episode is recapitulated is not overtly evangelical, the subtext signifies the deleterious effects of sin. Specifically, the "Summary" of *The Story of Mattie J. Jackson* describes the torture and sadistic murder of Jackson's slaveholder's brother, Benjamin Lewis, by "his former friends, the guerrillas" of the rebel South (37). It reads: "For pretending Unionism they placed him on a table and threatened to dissect him alive if he did not tell them where he kept his gold. He immediately informed them. They then stood him against the house and fired over his head. From that, they changed his position by turning him upside down, and raising him two feet from the floor, letting him dash his head against the floor until his skull was fractured, after which he lingered awhile and finally died" (38). Ironically, the reconstruction of Benjamin Lewis's brutal death calls to mind the many scenes of torment narrated in *The History of Mary Prince*. Whereas the 1831 West Indian narrative delineates atrocities perpetrated against enslaved people of African descent, the African American slave narrative testifies as well to the horrific acts that slaveholders visit upon each other. Both Prince and Jackson suggest that divine punishment for the sins of slavery must be borne by all members of a polity that tolerates slavery. More than any other detail in the narrative, this episode depicts the Christian concept that an uncharitable, unprincipled people can execute only evil and destruction.

The description of Benjamin Lewis's vicious death that appears in Jackson's "Summary" further places the responsibility for the demise or the salvation of all members of a nation onto the members of that nation. Thus, *The Story of Mattie J. Jackson* may also seem to constitute an American jeremiad in the tradition of Maria Stewart's *Productions*. Yet, in revising the rhetorical purpose of the whole of Jackson's autobiography from former slavewoman's narrative to unorthodox spiritual autobiography, "Christianity," the final section of *The Story*, does not recast Jackson's autobiography as jeremiad, unlike the final section of Douglass's 1845 *Narrative*. Jackson's *Story* does parallel Douglass's *Narrative*, however, in that the appendix of each text seems designed to function as compensation for a potentially offensive narrative posture. Douglass admits to having written his slave autobiography in a "tone and manner" that perhaps appear anti-Christian. Jackson and her amanuensis, Thompson, apparently share this concern, for "Christianity" seems intended to reassure readers whose good faith in Jackson might be challenged by various rhetorical elements of her narrative. In the nineteenth century, an assertion of spirituality in an otherwise secular document would seem merely prudent, besides (especially in a document by or about a woman). If Nancy Prince, whose Christian piety would presumably have been established by the fact of her profession alone, hoped to ensure the financial success of her *Narrative* by appending an overt statement of devotion to an already elaborate account of her diligence and zeal as a missionary, then Jackson and Thompson in all likelihood also reasoned that a declaration of religious ardor could only enhance the earning power of *The Story* for the education of an anonymous ex-slavegirl.

But what exactly about the "tone and manner" of *The Story of Mattie J. Jackson* might have made Jackson and Thompson fear that the text would alienate its audience? What might have rendered their project suspect? Perhaps it is its *unsentimental* demand for social and political equity. For the clearest chord in *The Story of Mattie J. Jackson* is that which reverberates with satisfaction that justice—divine and economic, blind and sweet—ultimately prevails over the Lewises' cruelty. Despite its often heavy appropriation of conventional sentimentality, which cultivates pity in place of self-righteousness, ultimately the decisive arrangement of Jackson's *Story* illuminates an unmistakable sense of gratification at the denouement of slavery for slaveowners. But to indulge one's feeling of justification is perhaps to act uncharitably; it is to demonstrate a lack of the common sense of benevolence. To give even the appearance of rejoicing in another person's distress, no matter its source, is to seem cruel and unsympathetic. To believe one's self righteously capable of ascertaining what another merits or deserves is to usurp divine authority; it is to blaspheme God. In seeming to adopt a sometimes smug, judgmental posture, then, *The Story of Mattie J. Jackson* risks alienating its readership, who were used to abiding by the rules of sentimentalism. If by its "Summary" it has vexed readers' perception of

Jackson's virtue, then *The Story* requires a Christian ending both to restore readers' confidence in Mattie's virtue and to reassert her true submissiveness.

The composite portrait of Mattie Jackson and Ellen Adams may offend some readers because of the considerable risks taken in the reconstruction of Jackson's story. For example, with her meticulous demonstrations of the insouciance of the slaveocracy with regard to black familial love, Jackson risks imaging the thrice-wed Ellen Turner Jackson Brown Adams as unchaste or promiscuous, when in actuality Ellen believed herself to be twice widowed. *The Story* also risks the condemnation of Ellen as "unwomanly" as opposed to self-loving for her open resistance to physical violence in an era dominated by the ideology of true womanhood.

Perhaps Jackson and Thompson's most consequential risk is the adoption of a rather "unfeminine" narrative style. Just as Jackson and Thompson express satisfaction with the Lewises' eventual just desserts, they insist (before "Christianity") on a discursive style that privileges the inherent authority of black women to engage or reject hegemonic discourse. In fact, *The Story* privileges heteroglossia more definitively than do other nineteenth-century black women spiritual narratives.[13] Maria Stewart's *Productions* and Jarena Lee's *Religious Experience and Journal,* for example, generally do not inscribe multiple voices. Instead, the relative absence of voices besides the narrators' own betrays the authors' anxiety about self-assertion and about women's right to resistant discourse, despite their conviction of having been called by God to sacred endeavors. Conversely, Zilpha Elaw reserves direct, allegedly unmediated discourse for a sensational moment in her *Memoirs,* inscribing her dying sister's chilling prediction, "My dear sister, I am going to hell" (72). Moreover, the confident deployment of heteroglossia in Jackson's *Story* exceeds the manipulation of tricksterly doublespeak in the *Memoir of Old Elizabeth,* the itinerant minister's autobiography cited at the beginning of this chapter. The "coloured evangelist" so adeptly narrates her life that her memoir is characterized by a reproach of clerical chauvinism (emanating dually from the evangelist and her amanuensis), as well as by the singular whisper of a critique of secular slavery and racial discrimination (of which the amanuensis seems unaware). Thus, poised between African American women's antebellum and postbellum narrative traditions, Jackson's testimonial of her life, together with Thompson's "arrangement" of it, offers an unprecedented assertion of the primacy of black women's multivocality and discursively disclaims the limitations of a prescribed "feminine" rhetoric. The embedded discourse includes numerous passages from Scripture or popular music of the day, from a few lines to whole hymns, as in,

"My mistress indulged some hopes [of Secessionist triumph] till the victory at New Orleans, when she heard the famous Union song sang [*sic*] to the tune of Yankee Doodle:

> The Rebels swore that New Orleans never should be taken,
> But if the Yankees came so near they should not save their bacon.
> That's the way they blustered when they thought they were so handy,
> But Farragut steamed up one day and gave them Doodle Dandy. (14)[14]

Besides song lyrics, Jackson also boldly provides the direct discourse of some of her autobiography's key players, as when she describes Lewis's brother beating a hoisted slave on his own plantation, an event she likely did not witness. According to Jackson, he would extend his victims, fastened to a beam with their hands and feet tied, and "inflict from fifty to three hundred lashes, laying their flesh entirely open, then bathe their quivering wounds with brine, and, through his nose, in a slow rebel tone he would tell them 'You'd better walk a fair chalk line or else I'll give yer twice as much'" (37).

In "Style and Content in the Rhetoric of Early Afro-American Feminists," Karlyn Campbell identifies nineteenth-century women's discourse that does *not* contain the stylistic markers of what she calls "feminine" rhetoric. She finds the characteristics of "unfeminine" discourse to include blunt elocution; deductive structure; an "authoritative, at times, even sarcastic" tone; plainly stated claims; literal analogies and few but bitter metaphors; and an impersonal form of address, with rare use of the pronoun "I." In short, "unfeminine" rhetoric contains nothing "to indicate that it was [engaged] by a woman" (441).[15] While *The Story of Mattie J. Jackson*, as a woman's personal narrative, certainly divulges the gender of its subject, its rhetorical style features several of the other traits of "unfeminine"—or masculinized—discourse and compellingly does so at the risk of appearing unchristian.

Among the rhetorical devices listed by Campbell that Jackson and Thompson employ with peril is the "authoritative . . . even sarcastic tone." For *The Story* is replete with sarcasm and dramatic and verbal irony, often engaged to accentuate or to moderate the sentimentality or pathos of a particular incident. The momentary mistrust of sentimental power in this case is not unlike that which pervades *A Narrative of the Life and Travels of Mrs. Nancy Prince*. Prince always—and Jackson and Thompson sometimes—seems wary of arousing excessive emotion in her readers, as if too much pity for a black woman's plight could retard practical action on her behalf. For example, a single lengthy paragraph plaintively reconstructs memories of three sorrowful moments in Jackson's life: first, her imprisonment with her mother and younger siblings after Ellen's unsuccessful attempt to escape; second, "one severe contest Mr. Lewis had with my mother," in which "for some slight offence . . . Mr. L. came in and rashly felled her to the floor with his fist"; and third, another slave girl's nightly flogging by cowhide to train her to awaken early to attend the master's children (10). In the same paragraph, the melancholic tone is undercut with humor or satire. An incisive illustration lies in Jackson's straight-faced observation, as I cited earlier, of her mother's roasting the very cowhide with which slaves were beaten. The sentence succeeding Jackson's comment sustains the irony: "It was rather poor picking, but it was the last cowhide my mother ever had an opportunity to cook while we remained in his family. Mr. L. soon moved about six miles from the city" (10). This rhetoric parallels Frederick Douglass's, who had, as Andrews has shown, first used the negative expressive as "a way to recontextualize baldly factual assertives about the past so that the reader could be shown not just the incident or what the incident signified but how to *feel* about the incident" (*To Tell* 103). Thus, *The Story* reveals the masculinized quality of Jackson's discourse as well as her endeavor to control both the image that sentimental readers developed of African American women and the facile validation of their own humanity such sentimentality provided them.

Similarly, Jackson and Thompson abstain from "feminine" rhetoric by using sarcasm to complain about a "traitor" who informed against her family when "King Whiskey fired up his brain one evening, and out popped the secret" (18). Sarcasm informs another amusing metaphor Jackson uses when her attempt to embark on the Underground Railroad briefly seems foiled: "It appeared as if my mistress used every possible exertion to delay me from church, and I concluded that her old cloven-footed companion had impressed his intentions on her mind" (27). Such witticisms present relatively minor risk for Jackson, but other instances of her unfeminine discourse potentially erode, or even destroy, her credibility and create the need for a final chapter that authenticates her piety. Two very serious instances involve Jackson's "owner," Lewis. For beating Mattie so mercilessly on the day that she walks covered in blood to the Union Arsenal, Lewis is "immediately arrested" and given "one hundred lashes with the cow-hide, so that [the Unionists] might identify him by a scarred back" (18). Then for reneging on an oath to the Union General regarding the humane treatment of his slaves, Lewis is later fined $3,000. Jackson's decision to provide these details and Thompson's resolution to inscribe them in *The Story* evidence the women's collective interest in promulgating their mutual faith that divine (and economic) justice prevails over the sins that ensue from slavery, which in itself is a sin. In general, their selection of detail for the narrative affirms their commitment to providing a factual eyewitness account of bound life. Yet the reconstruction of Lewis's punishment is problematized by an expressive statement: "My mother had the pleasure of washing his stained clothes, otherwise it would not have been known" that he had been whipped (18). For it acknowledges a black woman's joy in a white man's comeuppance, and its appearance in the narrative indicates that Ellen told others of her detection. While neither Ellen's "pleasure" nor her disclosure constitutes a "sin," they also do not, strictly speaking, conform to orthodox Christian behavior—though, arguably, the disclosure does serve as an act of dutiful Christian witnessing of divine punishment enacted through the medium of the Union army. The deployment of sentimental tropes throughout the narrative indicates that Jackson and Thompson envision a readership familiar with sentimental literature. Such readers, especially the women among them, would have aspired to leading Christian lives. The detail about Ellen's laundering Lewis's shirt, then, forms a rhetorical risk. In including this incident, Jackson risks compromising the sanctified images of herself, Ellen, and even Thompson that *The Story* needs to maintain for white Christian readers if it is to fulfill its proclaimed project.

A second instance of unfeminine rhetoric, which also involves Lewis, is similarly problematic. In the "Summary," in the paragraph following her description of his brother's murder, Jackson confesses to stealing from Lewis: "When I made my escape from slavery I was in a query how I was to raise funds to bear my expenses. I finally came to the conclusion that as the laborer was worthy of his hire, I thought my wages should come from my master's pocket. Accordingly I took twenty-five dollars" (38). Here again Jackson parallels Douglass, for like his *Narrative, The Story of Mattie J. Jackson* "announces that truth to the self takes priority over what the white reader may think is either probable or politic to introduce into discourse" (Andrews, *To Tell* 103). Moreover, in establishing the primacy of economic justice, Jackson and Thompson disregard "feminine" rhetoric to insist on a black woman's innate authority to choose to exact economic justice for herself and to inscribe that choice as discourse and as text. One way of reading the effect of Jackson's true confession is not as a repudiation of Christian virtue but as a revision or expansion of it so that the confession entails a demand for justice, perhaps especially economic justice, that human beings themselves must assume the responsibility for extracting. Arguably, for Jackson and Thompson Christian virtue necessitates such a demand.[16] Less than sympathetic readers, no matter how sentimental they are, could read Jackson's confession as a validation of the myth of an essential black depravity.

With its representation of Jackson's pecuniary audacity, *The Story of Mattie J. Jackson* recalls *The Narrative of William Wells Brown, a Fugitive Slave* (1847), in which Brown, a former slave, unabashedly tells how he tricked a free black man into taking a beating intended for Brown himself. After Brown "accidentally" spilled wine on a slave trader, his master "gave [him] a note to carry to the jailer, and a dollar in money to give to him" (49). The narrator, noting that he was "determined not to be whipped," hires a free black man, who was new to the city, to deliver the note in his stead. For his favor the free black man earned not only fifty cents but also a severe beating. Brown concludes his recounting of this incident by avowing, "Had I entertained the same views or [*sic*] right and wrong which I do now, I am sure I should never have practised [*sic*] the deception upon that poor fellow which I did . . . and I heartily desire that it may be at some time or other in my power to make him amends for his vicarious sufferings in my behalf" (51).

Like Brown, Jackson and Thompson may be read as effectively daring the (white) reader to challenge the propriety of the material (and the rhetorical) gesture. In addition, *The Story* echoes Brown's antebellum *Narrative* in appending an afterthought to Jackson's confession: "After I was safe and had learned to write, I sent him a nice letter, thanking him for his kindness to me in time of need. I have never received any answer to it" (38). While there is no apparent reason to suspect its earnestness, the passage is undercut by a certain faux naïveté.[17] Undoubtedly, Jackson did write to Lewis after her escape, and no doubt her letter was "nice" and did "thank him for his kindness." One wonders, though, how sincerely so savvy a woman as Jackson expected the reply she reports she did not get. If Jackson's real act constituted an effort to sell her master on the idea that she genuinely appreciated his "kindness," then perhaps she and Thompson, following African American tricksters like Brown, here try to "sell" readers of *The Story* an image of Jackson as a courteous lady instead of an errant thief.[18] An assertion about the moral that Brown appends to his confession, written by contemporary scholar G. Thomas Couser, also applies cogently to the ironic reconstruction of Jackson's trespass and subsequent reflection: "This gesture, which by itself might seem to undermine the sincerity of the narrative, may be part of a strategy that implies the reader's responsibility for honest communication, for if the reader is constructed here as a master to be 'sold' when the narrator's feelings might be unacceptable, then the very form tests the reader's readiness to accept an uncensored narrative" (*Altered* 134). In other words, Jackson may include tales of her theft and subsequent letter of gratitude to challenge the good faith of her sentimental readers. Their Christian values and compassion ideally prepare them for the act of forgiveness. Jackson asks forgiveness not for herself for pilfering, but instead for Lewis's sins, such as his unchristian "possession" of chattel slaves and his denial of the slave girl's birthright to freedom. Jackson's reconstruction of the episode with its ironic reversals of fortune is "unfeminine" in every way.

The Story of Mattie J. Jackson is indeed a narrative that "tests" readers' amenability to accepting the discursive authority of a nineteenth-century black woman. Thompson's identification of herself on the title page as "Formerly Mrs. Schuyler" as well as "Dr. L. S. Thompson" indicates her supposition of a degree of (at least local) renown among blacks and whites that will validate her text. Indeed, the narrator observes at one point that her physician "step-mother was continually crowded with friends and customers without [racial] distinction" (35). Thompson thus asserts herself as having transcended the anonymity that Jackson still has. Her claim to the authority requisite for the transcription and, more significantly, the interpretation of another black woman's life seems partly to lie in her own self-image. By projecting herself as professionally adroit and locally prominent, Thompson tacitly explains her assumption of a traditionally male role, the rhetor. Thus, *The Story* is intended as much for men as for women, for the educated and elite (as the figure of the amanuensis seemingly illustrates), and for the scholarly and socially aspirant (such as Jackson herself embodies).[19]

In this manner Jackson and Thompson thus join the African American women's spiritual autobiography tradition. The amanuensis-author and her narrator-subject may signal different socioeconomic classes, but their purposes, like their synchronous "voices," derive from their common race, religion, and gender and converge for a common sacred good. Together they embrace and subvert one of the nation's guiding ideals, created in Jeffersonian America: the belief that "a reciprocal relationship between an informed people and a virtuous people" renders literacy—and its deployment through Christianized texts—a moral obligation (Kerber, *Intellectual History* 238). As disenfranchised black women, their individual lives could only be improved by the success of their unified call for the eradication of the enduring sins occasioned by slavery, such as the savage death of Benjamin Lewis, in the aftermath of the nation's abolition of the sin of slavery. By figuring sin itself as a "peculiar institution" that enslaves blacks and whites alike, Jackson and Thompson obliquely argue for a national conversion to Christian principles as an integral component of Reconstruction. Here, Virginia Brereton's notion of surface and submerged plots in women's conversion literature illuminates an interesting difference between Jackson's text and other black holy women's narratives. Brereton defines a surface plot as one that reconstructs a woman's transition from sinfulness to "complete acquiescence to God's will" (28). The submerged plot, palimpsestically (and perhaps also unwittingly) layered "beneath" the surface plot, reveals that "the outcome of conversion" includes a rhetorical release of the energy required to act subversively by proclaiming God. The submerged plots of other early black women's spiritual autobiographies, such as Lee's *Religious Experience and Journal* and Elaw's *Memoirs*, express a feminist resistance to racial and religious oppression and to patriarchal obstructions to their work as sanctified women.[20] Inversely, Jackson's secular slave narrative, as transcribed by her female amanuensis, excoriates race and gender oppression in its surface plot while its submerged plot comprises a call to salvation through Christian conversion.

If their subtle call is to be acknowledged and heeded, then Jackson and Thompson cannot afford to alienate readers. Their use of sentimentalism repeatedly asks readers to strive to become more than voyeurs, to put themselves in Jackson's place, to feel what she has experienced—not as *she* lived through the horrors of slavery, but rather as they themselves would experience it in her place. *The Story* often solicits white readers' sorrow and the "right" action that is its natural result. Saidiya Hartman has argued that in important respects empathy confounds sentimental literature's efforts to enkindle white identification with the enslaved "because in making the slave's suffering [one's] own, [one] begins to feel for [one's self] rather than for those for whom this exercise in imagination is presumably designed to reach" (19). However, this is precisely Jackson's project: she urges readers' imaginative leap into a life of "white" bondage instead of black bondage, asking white (women) readers to "imagine" themselves as personally impacted by slavery as either slaves or slavers. If Jackson's reconstruction of the ways the Union Army's beating disciplines her "owner" for his violence against slaves should offend white readers or cast Christian doubt on her story as an impious indulgence, then the depiction of the murder of Benjamin Lewis functions as the compensation for that breach of religious (and narrative) etiquette. What happens to one Lewis is represented as justice served, but though Jackson describes the other Lewis as "a more severe slave master than the one who owned me" (37), his death is nonetheless interpreted as horrific and unwarranted. Consequently, the episode figures significantly as the dominant incident of the narrative's "Summary," and elicits sympathy for its (white) eye-witnesses (i.e., Benjamin's "wife and another distinguished lady" [38]) and (black) I-witnesses (i.e., his slaves). The episode induces anxiety about the potential and the actual effects of slavery as an American institution.

Most important, it engenders an admiration for Jackson and Thompson as two African American women who, although they had been victimized by slavery, were still capable of portraying with compassion the demise of a savage white master whom they clearly perceive to be also victimized by slavery. Such admiration does much to redeem the narrator and amanuensis from critical condemnation and to endow *The Story of Mattie J. Jackson* with discursive authority.

In the early days of emancipation, Dr. L. S. Thompson labored ardently to rectify the excruciating antebellum reality of white control over black texts, which was true even in the cases of such extraordinarily able authors as Frederick Douglass and William Wells Brown. As Jackson's amanuensis, Thompson authorizes *The Story of Mattie J. Jackson* without white authentication. She proclaims her allegiance to her subject and to herself as greater than her narrative duty to readers and, fashioning her narrative after antebellum fugitive slave writers like Douglass, Brown, and Jacobs, boldly declares Jackson's lived experiences in bondage superior to her readers' sacred and secular truths.

In the final analysis, however, Thompson's exegesis fails—and admits that it fails—"to tell a free story."[21] Because *The Story* never depicts Mattie Jackson as wholly illiterate, it leaves open the possibility that she will one day be able to inscribe her own text. Moreover, it concludes with the assurance that she *will* do so: "When I complete my education, if my life is spared, I shall endeavor to publish further details of our history in another volume from my own pen" (38). At the outset, the narrative takes as its premise the "promise" of her education; by beseeching its readers to contribute to her formal academic training, the autobiography ascertains its dependence on a portrait of Jackson as naturally intelligent and educable. So intermittent details include Mattie and Ellen poring over newspapers, piecing together, to the envy of their unlearned slave-mistress, bits of war news; Ellen and Westly's lost love letters after Westly's escape to Chicago; Mattie's own letter to Lewis after the war. With these references, Jackson's pledge—couched prudently, distinctively in "feminine" rhetoric with its conditional clause, its use of the plural pronoun "our" and collective subjectivity, and its promise not to succeed but to essay—is credible.

But Jackson's pledge is problematized by another, protracted passage in *The Story* in which her amanuensis disrupts the narrative's syntax and chronology by changing its mood from the indicative to the subjunctive, then, to the imperative: "I would advise all, young, middle aged or old, in a free country to learn to read and write. If this little book should fall into hands of one deficient of the important knowledge of writing, I hope they will remember the old maxim:—'Never too old to learn.' Manage your own secrets, and divulge them by the silent language of your own pen" (29). Plainly, the passage does not overtly state that had Jackson authored her own narrative, it would have been substantially different from that "written and arranged" by Thompson (or that when she does write her own story, as she subsequently pledges, it will differ from Thompson's version); it does not posit a dialogic of difference between the autobiography's amanuensis and its subject. But the trope of surreptitiousness that ironically permeates the quoted passage does suggest the extent to which Jackson feels herself yet bound, only enslaved differently by her illiteracy. Indeed, by constructing a figure of a "reader" who is "deficient of the important knowledge of writing," and thus as dependent on literate others for access to her story as she is for her narration of it, Jackson (as both textual persona and actual subject) overtly problematizes her relationship to Thompson. In short, *The Story* implies that even when an ex-slave narrator and an amanuensis are analogously oppressed by hegemonic intolerance of blackness and of femaleness, they may still be affected differently according to their respective class and caste. *The Story* maintains that without literacy (a manifestation of one's class), one can never truly become an "ex"-slave.

Accordingly, Jackson's "new" maxim—"Manage your own secrets, and divulge them by the silent language of your own pen"—accentuates the dialectic of identity that inspires Jackson's and Thompson's shared commitment to securing education and opportunity for recently freed African Americans. In this way, Jackson's *Story* characterizes illiteracy and material dependence as two more egregious sins issuing from the sin of slavery of which reconstructed America must repent. And it brilliantly illuminates the sense of crisis that John Beverley underscores in his discussion of the dictated narrative, the *testimonio*, an autobiographical act in which "an urgency to communicate, a problem of repression" is implicated in the very act of narration (94). By hinting at the pathos of confinement and subjugation, Jackson's *Story* sentimentally contends that the need for a slave pass has only ostensibly passed with the abolition of slavery. *The Story of Mattie J. Jackson* persuasively argues that as long as Jackson and former slaves like her must seek autonomy by means of a "slave pass"—that is, through any text that signifies the social, civil, political, economic, and educational restrictions against its bearer[22]—then the sins of slavery and the nation's enslavement to sin remain unrepented and unforgiven. Jackson's *Story*, then, advances the tradition of African American women's spiritual autobiographies with its appropriation of sentimentalism, as it voices the sacred and secular concerns of black holy women amid the institutions that restrict them.

FIVE

Thunderous Daughter:
Julia Foote

While the folk idiom "son of thunder" was used to designate the
booming voiced, fiery preacher, the origin of the term may also be
related to "Shango," the West African god of thunder and lightning,
whose symbol was the axe.

C. ERIC LINCOLN AND LAWRENCE MAMIYA,
The Black Church in the African American Experience

Julia Foote's theology follows that of her nineteenth-century holy foremothers'
in that it espouses black women's defiance against sin, generally manifest as
verbal protest. Foote is very specific about her theology of defiance: African
American women, she insists, must be careful that in fighting oppression and
refusing to submit to its diverse and powerful forces they do not unwittingly
forsake God. More than any of the other women examined in this book, Foote
images God as a loving, protective Father—a figure of far greater importance
than biological mothers. The passion with which Foote draws this contrast
nearly surprises, for their mothers are invariably the sole means by which black
women learn what Harryette Mullen calls "resistant orality," their saving grace.
Exalting God the Father, figures of blessed children, and a series of surrogate
holy mothers, Foote's autobiography transforms defiant verbality into a matrifocal theology that teaches how to honor the sacred through sass.

Nineteenth-century African American women autobiographers, especially
former slaves, almost invariably feature a black female analogue for themselves
at the center of their narratives; this other black woman is often among the narrator's blood-kin, most frequently her mother or grandmother. Perhaps more
than any other extant nineteenth-century African American autobiography,
that of Mattie Jackson, the former slave discussed in chapter 4, illustrates this

phenomenon, for *The Story of Mattie J. Jackson* is as much an account of the life of Ellen Turner Jackson Brown Adams as it is of the life of her daughter Mattie. While another slavewoman's conversion narrative, the *Memoir of Old Elizabeth*, generically attends to the narrator's bond with God rather than with other mortals, it isolates Elizabeth's mother as the closest of her immediate family members. In the earlier spiritual writings of freeborn Maria Stewart, Jarena Lee, Zilpha Elaw, and Nancy Prince, the narrators' representations of their relationships with their mothers are similarly subordinated to more detailed accounts of the authors' lives as divinely chosen women. Both the *Productions of Mrs. Maria W. Stewart* and Elaw's ministerial *Memoirs* divulge at the outset that each narrator was orphaned very early in life, so neither narrative can depict a mother-daughter relationship beyond expressions of loss and longing.[1] Conversely, Nancy Prince loves but eventually leaves her mother, a woman she portrays as distracted by failed marriages and numerous children. By contrast, the *Religious Experience and Journal of Mrs. Jarena Lee* indicates that Lee's mother reared the itinerant minister's sons while she traveled and that, though they were often involuntarily estranged from each other for many consecutive years, the two women nonetheless enjoyed a loving and nurturing intimacy.

Whereas these narratives written or dictated by early nineteenth-century African American women esteem a black maternal figure to propose a matrifocal theology, the spiritual autobiography of Julia Foote, born in Schenectady, New York, in 1823 to slaves who had purchased their own freedom, does not. Instead of idolizing either her mother or an ideal bond with her mother, *A Brand Plucked from the Fire* defines the mother-daughter dyad as one suffused with tension and conflict. Although she ultimately describes her mother as "sainted," for most of the 1879 narrative Foote implies that her mother is a poor parent whose evangelical shortcomings contribute to her young daughter's periods of theological delinquency. This characterization is especially startling, not only because it diverges from the tradition to which Foote's text belongs, but also because *A Brand* begins with a veneration of the narrator's mother as a survivor of slavery. Foote's spiritual narrative departs from autobiographies by other slavewomen, who extol their mothers' valor and devotion largely by appropriating, then racially transforming what Elizabeth Ammons has called the "mother-savior" by applying this ideal to a black woman. This sentimentalized figure (and the revised concept of republican motherhood from which it emerges), while "already a highly politicized concept when Harriet Beecher Stowe wrote *Uncle Tom's Cabin*," is rooted in Stowe's ideology of "the right kind of mothering," that "provide[d] children with love and . . . [taught] them to internalize the values of hard work, integrity, and the avoidance of evil" (Ammons 160). *A Brand Plucked from the Fire* measures its central mother figure against this trope of motherhood and finds her wanting. Foote depicts her mother with great complexity: she is figured as a flawed human being, sometimes laudable for teaching her daughter to love and assert herself, other times culpable for failing to teach her daughter to put God before humanity. The spiritual auto-biographer consistently asserts Christianized maternal values, and, ironically, ardently embraces the very trope of the sentimentalized pious mother that she cannot locate in her biological mother as she reconstructs her search for devout surrogate mothers.

Foote and the Tradition of Verbal Resistance

In "Runaway Tongue," her invaluable essay on African American women's verbal resistance, Harryette Mullen analyzes nineteenth-century black women writers' amalgamation of two opposing literary traditions: the (European American) women's sentimental tradition of submission to patriarchal author-ity and the black, particularly the black male slave, protest tradition, which fea-tures the slave's resistance to oppression and the slave's quest for corporeal and ideological freedom (245). According to Mullen, nineteenth-century African American women's reconciliation of these traditions is concentrated chiefly in the "grafting [of] literacy onto orality" as a way of including the voices and ex-periences of black/enslaved women who were generally prohibited by illiteracy from writing their lives. Their stories, Mullen cogently argues, often consist of their spoken instructions to their daughters to resist hegemonic tyranny; in other words, one black women's literary tradition entails the representation of "resistant orality, or verbal self-defense, which included speech acts variously labeled sassy or saucy, impudent, impertinent, or insolent" (245). By inscribing her mother's speech acts, often in the form of novelized dialogue or indirect dis-course in *A Brand Plucked from the Fire*, Foote joins this distinctive tradition of African American women's writing and honors her mother's life and memory. Her entire autobiography pays tribute to the legacy of her mother's resistant orality, for in many ways the narrative itself constitutes the daughter's speak-ing up and out against domination and subjugation. Foote ambivalently reports her mother's oral expressions, however. The vexed bond between the narrator and her mother inversely parallels that between Harriet Jacobs's slave narrator, Linda Brent, and her grandmother Martha in *Incidents in the Life of a Slave Girl*. When Linda seduces a white neighbor to thwart the sexual advances of her "master," "Aunt Martha" espouses true woman ideology and denounces Linda's resulting pregnancy as profligate. In the case of Foote and her mother, the opposite operates: it is the younger woman who reproves the elder's unholy acts. *A Brand* ambiguously represents Foote's mother as the wellspring of her daughter's self-affirming verbal power and as an antagonist who sometimes separates Foote from true piety.

Regarding black women's chastity, Foote's narrator is unlike Jacobs's Aunt Martha in that the former is indisputably an "impudent woman [who] refuses to be modestly silent" (Mullen 246) about the sexual persecution of slave-women. After the conventional autobiographical opening, "I was born," Foote shifts attention from herself to her mother, at once narrating what may well be the mother's most profound memory: a beating by her "owner" for refusing slave concubinage:

> She had one very cruel master and mistress. This man, whom she was obliged to call master, tied her up and whipped her because she refused to submit herself to him, and reported his conduct to her mistress. After the whipping, he himself washed her quivering back with strong salt water. At the expiration of a week she was sent to change her clothing, which stuck fast to her back. Her mistress, seeing that she could not remove it, took hold of the rough tow-linen under-garment and pulled it off over her head with a jerk, which took the skin with it, leaving her back all raw and sore. (166)[2]

This incident conforms to stock sentimentalism; it narrates what Laura Doyle has called "the most common sentimental plot[:] that in which a humble heroine's virtue is assailed by an evil-intentioned man (often of a higher class/race) but is usually preserved as well as displayed by her physical expressions of sentiment" (167). And it produces the codified effect that Doyle contends sentimentalism ultimately yields: a redefinition of *nobility* such that it transcends race and class hierarchies and argues for a "common"—shared and humble—sense of Christian virtue (176). In addition, like accounts in the *History of Mary Prince* and *The Story of Mattie J. Jackson*, Foote's (mother's) reconstructed memory represents the literary tradition that exposes slavery's physical and psychosexual dominance. Emphatically, the incident actually records *two* generations of resistant orality, two women's speech acts against the violation of a slave-woman: Foote's and her mother's. The mother is beaten as much for her disclosure to her slave mistress of her master's proposition as for her noncompliance with his wishes. A first speech act, her spoken denial of the master, compels a second, her divulgence. The consequences of the second act of resistant orality are severe and manifold. The slavewoman suffers the master's animosity both because she has refused him and because she has exposed him to his wife. Then she apparently suffers the mistress's wrath for that same "betrayal." The incident demonstrates Foote's mother's paradoxical position: though she lacks hegemonic power or even access to it, the slavers ironically perceive her as equally assailable and treacherous. Moreover, Foote's decision to reconstruct and broadcast the incident, especially at the very inception of her autobiography, reveals her commitment not only to exposing but also to celebrating her mother's survival and to proving her mother's story notable precisely for the slavewoman's determination to name and condemn the inhumanity she endured.

Furthermore, by beginning her autobiography with these details of her mother's sexual defenselessness and corporal punishment, Foote sets the foundation for distinctions that the author subsequently makes between her mother's life and her own. Foote depicts her mother as a woman who orally resisted physical maltreatment, although she ultimately failed to protect herself, in order to prepare readers for a narrative account of her own efforts to engage resistant orality, thus providing readers with a point of comparison. That is, having narrated the abuse her mother suffers, Foote obliquely juxtaposes instances of her own suffering with this incident and portrays herself as having learned her mother's discursive skill even in those instances where her own verbal self-defense proves as ineffectual as her mother's. In addition, because Foote does not live as a slave and so does not suffer as one, the representation of the incident from her mother's life in bondage also serves as a basis for the material distinctions between slavewomen's and free black women's lives. And because *A Brand Plucked from the Fire* enumerates Foote's labors as an itinerant minister, the initial recollection further suggests that the narrative will clarify differences in the lives of sexually vulnerable black women and sexually chaste ones.[3]

Ironically, the autobiography demonstrates that the slave mother's plight anticipates her preacher-daughter's plight. For just as the mother's exteriorized sexuality and the slaveocracy's socially sanctioned contempt for her as sexual chattel render her, in Mullen's phrase, "paradoxically both vulnerable and threatening" (246), the daughter's interiorized repressed sexuality and her ministerial chastity (she is a widow at the time she pens *A Brand*) likewise render her simultaneously powerless and powerful. Moreover, in further violation of idealized motherhood and its corollary mythical domesticity, the mother's mode of resistance eventually leads her daughter away from her and from home. For Foote revises the object of her verbal resistance—and that of African American women generally—so that in defying oppression and refusing to submit to its forces, she does not and they do not inadvertently forsake submission to God. Although Foote never again alludes to her mother's life as a slave after the first paragraph, her narrative maintains its duality by depicting Foote's mother as impiously bound to temporal, mortal concerns while the narrator pursues the "sweet soul rest" of salvation (163).

Her Mother's Good Daughter

On the whole, *A Brand Plucked from the Fire* illustrates Foote's careful adherence to her mother's lessons in resistant orality, but chapters 1 through 11 of the spiritual narrative also demonstrate that, as a young girl, Foote occasionally resists even her mother. Implicit in black women's practice of resistant orality is their faith in exposé, a conviction that uncovering—or in nineteenth-century terms, unveiling—the illicit behavior of an oppressor will cause him or her to cease the behavior; *A Brand Plucked from the Fire* is an exposé that exercises this faith. One clear project of the autobiography is to narrate Foote's mother's story; indeed, Foote's life constitutes a quest for the righting/writing of her mother's victimization. The daughter holds faithful to this objective and also to her certitude that she possesses an innate authority as well as a divinely endowed authority to uncover sacred truths. Her fidelity is so strong that she exempts not even her mother from among the persons and institutions that her narrative unmasks.

One of the chief ways that *A Brand Plucked from the Fire* establishes the daughter's learning of her mother's lessons is through the repeated and ironic invocation of the nineteenth-century child as uncorrupted, innocent, and pure—in other words, as inherently salvific. Although the opening chapter closes with the narrator's memory of once being "stupidly drunk" as a child (168), for most of the autobiography children are regarded as sacred creatures.[4] Specifically, the trope of the Christ-like child consists of a diminutive, often invalid or dying child who has the capacity to convert numerous unregenerate souls to Christianity. Akin to the noble slave and the true woman, the holy child mediates between this world and the next. As Jane Tompkins has noted, the figure of the child functions fundamentally as a pure sacrifice for the religious salvation of many, analogous to Christ's own sacrifice for humankind, to espouse a philosophy at once evangelical and ideological (*Sensational* 128). The figure of the child primarily functions as a symbol of sorrow; like virtually all sentimental tropes, its chief work is to arouse sympathy and to stimulate reform in order to establish what Karen Sánchez-Eppler calls a "bodily bond" between authors and readers. Especially through both the depiction and the manipulation of tears, sobs, gasps, and faints, sentimental literature calls readers to express concern for literary figures and to express anguish about their own souls. Foote implicitly compares her narrative self with the figure of the holy child as incarnated in Eva St. Clare, the child evangelist of Stowe's *Uncle Tom's Cabin*. The effectiveness of the trope as it is embodied in Little Eva lies in the evocation of the ideals chastity, femaleness, whiteness, natural sanctity, wealth, frailty ensuing from illness, and premature death.

Like other African American sentimentalists, Foote deploys sentimentalism particularly to produce a child figure that transcends race and class hierarchies but she leaves its recuperative and redemptive powers intact. In *The Story of Mattie J. Jackson,* for example, Jackson reconstructs her baby brother's death by paralysis and neglect. The child is ultimately martyred, and yet his death reforms no one in the narrative, Jackson implies, for the monstrous slave mistress responsible for his death only feigns bereavement (and notably does not affect remorse). Yet her inclusion of this grotesque tragedy demonstrates her faith that the figure *can* redeem the unsaved among her readers and move readers of all persuasions into action. Foote, however, modifies the figure of the child in rather *unsentimental* ways. Her survival, even more than self-sacrifice or death, constitutes a revolutionary act for a black child, especially a black girl child. Given societal indifference to the plight of black children, Foote revises the figure to emphasize the *recovery* from childhood incidents and illnesses instead of the capitulation to them. A similar transformation in black invalid women occurs in the spiritual autobiographies of Jarena Lee and Zilpha Elaw: while the frail, ill white woman signifies pathos and elicits sympathy, her black counterpart's endurance garners respect and inspires emulation. As she tells of her maturation, Foote's narrator indicates that her power to do God's work depends on her ability to triumph over the adversities present in her life rather than her death.

A Brand Plucked from the Fire both implores parents to practice Christianity for their children's sake and emphatically encourages adults to revere the natural spirituality of children by accepting the decree in Isaiah 11:6 that "a little child shall lead them." Thus, Foote asserts a paradox: children are naturally pious, but their goodness depends on their parents' devotion. She inscribes the two positions throughout her autobiography. For example, in chapter 1 she reveals her ambivalence toward her own parents as Christian stewards. She initially implies that, as slaves, they are more sinned against than sinners: besides narrating the sexual exploitation of her mother, she mourns her father's "hardships in slavery, the worst of which was his constant exposure to all sorts of weather" (166). Then, deploying the sentimental tropes of the "fallen" mother and the imperiled infant, she writes, using a double entendre, about her parents' turn from sin toward salvation: "One night, as they were on their way home from a dance, they came to a stream of water, which . . . had risen and carried away the log crossing. In their endeavor to ford the stream, my mother made a misstep, and came very nearly being drowned, with her babe in her arms. This nearly fatal accident made such an impression upon their minds that they said, 'We will go to no more dances'" (166 – 67). Despite the discrimination they afterward brooked in New York's racially mixed churches, and though they were poorly led by listless spiritual guides, Foote reports that they nonetheless "continued to attend to the ordinances of God" (167).

However, the rest of the short chapter criticizes their religious practices and charges her parents and the local clergy with intemperance because, at funerals, weddings, and other communal events, they "would imbibe as freely as any one" (167). From this generalization, which situates Foote squarely in the Reconstruction-era women's temperance movement, the narrator recalls how her parents' debauchery precipitated her own intoxication at the tender age of five. Noting that after this episode in her life "sickness unto death followed, but [her] life was spared," she deems herself "like 'a brand plucked from the fire'" (168). But rather than end the chapter with this rhetorical flourish, Foote sentimentally transforms it into a sermon on the intersection of domesticity and religiosity: "Dear reader, have you innocent children, given you from the hand of God? Children, whose purity rouses all that is holy and good in your nature? Do not, I pray, give to these little ones of God the accursed cup which will send them down to misery and death. Listen to the voice of conscience, the woes of the drunkard" (168). Thus, the conclusion of the first chapter significantly looks back to antebellum sentimentalists' morality guides and instruction tracts written for earnest Christian parents. Among these is Stowe's essay, "Children," which decries the deleterious effects that a corruptive society—especially its lax parentage—can have on children. Stowe writes, "The hardened heart of the worldly man is unlocked by the guileless tones and simple caresses of his son; but he repays it in time, by imparting to his boy all the crooked tricks and callous maxims which have undone himself" (81–82). Stowe elsewhere argues famously and passionately against masculinist economics and patriarchal values; here the crucial juxtaposition between parents and children specifies the father-son relationship. By implying that worldliness more than maleness has hardened the father's heart, and claiming that a son (as well as a daughter) can possess "guileless tones and simple caresses," Stowe argues that gender is irrelevant in moral matters, that either parent might impart to tender offspring "all the crooked tricks and callous maxims" that lead toward degeneracy.

Foote's second chapter emphasizes children's sanctity, for it recalls the author not as a five-year-old inebriate but as an eight-year-old incipient religious convert. Within only days of a "big meeting"—probably a camp meeting or revival—in her parents' church, a grizzled minister teaches her to pray, arousing her confidence in him by regarding her with unfamiliar earnestness and by praying with and for her. Foote uses the minister as an exemplum for readers who are parents, observing that he inspired her mother to take her daughter's salvation more seriously: "After [he and another minister] had gone, my mother talked with me about my soul more than she ever had before, and told me that this preacher was a good man . . . and that, if I were a good girl, and said my prayers, I would go to heaven" (169). Then immediately she affirms the effect of her mother's love, remarking, "This gave me great comfort." In the next sentence, however, she introduces a surrogate mother—one of several to whom she defers in the narrative—and this particular model of Christian duty is a white neighbor: "A white woman, who came to our house to sew, taught me the Lord's prayer. No tongue can tell the joy that filled my poor heart when I could repeat, 'Our Father, which art in heaven.' It has always seemed to me that I was converted at this time" (169). Thus she at once posits the racelessness and the reverence of parental piety.

Chapter 2 effectively portrays young Julia as a child predisposed to Christian virtue and instruction (the narrator recounts in later chapters other events that developed her gradual conversion).[5] In addition, the chapter combines the quest for spiritual rectitude with the quest for literacy and links the religious theme of the narrative to a sharp aside on contemporary African American education. Declaring her training deficient because she lived where "there were no schools where colored children were allowed" (170), Foote further asserts that "children of the present time . . . cannot realize my joy at being able to say the entire alphabet when I was nine years old" (170).[6] The conjoined themes of spirituality and literacy form the basis for the sermon that ends chapter 2. For just as she concludes the first chapter by shifting from a linear account of her life to direct(ive) discourse, she explicitly addresses "Dear children" at the end of her second chapter, exhorting them, "You have nothing to fear, dear children; come right to Jesus" (170). Moreover, she provides the precise means by which a child might convert. Invoking the biblical stories of Adam and Eve and the Ten

Commandments, clearly regarding them as staples of religious fare for youth, she meditates on the image of the child Christ as "obedient to his earthly parents" and of an older "dear, loving Jesus, who, when on earth, took little children in his arms, and blessed them" (170). Finally, anticipating chapter 30, forthrightly titled "How to Obtain Sanctification," Foote concludes her exhortation with a prayer that she says children should repeat verbatim. Thus, in the second chapter of her autobiography, Foote establishes herself as an extraordinarily devout child who has matured into an authority on the conversion of children.

Chapters 3 and 4 detail her experiences as an indentured servant and reiterate the idea that children possess a natural sensitivity that predisposes them to piety, and they close with similar meditations on the souls of children and their parents. Moreover, they cast Foote herself as a religious prodigy. Deploying several major sentimental tropes (including the holy child, the converted invalid, and the death of a Christian), she recalls her precocious wonder at age ten about the state of the soul of her employer's gentle brother, "who was dying of consumption" (171). To accentuate her sensitivity and the sympathy it engendered, she remembers, "I used to stand, with tears in my eyes, and watch him as he slowly moved across the fields, leaning against the fence to rest himself by the way. I heard them say he could not live much longer, and that worried me dreadfully." She further novelizes the incident by having the two figures speak without mediation: "I stepped up to him and said, 'Mr. John, do you say your prayers?' and then I began to cry. He looked at me for a moment, then took my hand in his and said: 'Sometimes I pray; do you?'" When John Prime dies happily, the narrator recalls, "I heard them say he died very happy, and had gone to heaven. Oh, how my little heart leaped for joy" (171). Within the space of a few short sentences, Foote appropriates from European American women's literature a classic sentimental scene, complete with cues to spur the proper responses in readers, in this case, tears of both sorrow and joy. By supplanting Little Eva with the image of her girl-child self, she revises the relationship between her mother and the enslavers with which her autobiography begins. Unlike most other autobiographies by blacks in the wake of the Reconstruction, she does not overtly petition for equal rights for African Americans; *A Brand Plucked from the Fire* implicitly demonstrates blacks' readiness for civil rights and social equity by asserting their humanity through the example of a child's extraordinary healing powers.

The subsequent reconstruction of the execution of one of her childhood teachers similarly evidences the author's delicate feelings and impressionability and suggests that her sensitivity to evil is as profound as her sensitivity to virtue, for the narrator reports, "Such a night! Never since that day have I heard of a person being hung, but a shudder runs through my whole frame, and a trembling seizes me" (174). Foote inscribes a liberal theology, linking a religious principle to an ideological one to condemn capital punishment: "Oh, what a barbarous thing is the taking of human life, even though it be 'a life for a life,' as many believe God commands" (174). Thus, early in her spiritual narrative, Foote represents herself as divinely chosen from childhood and as authorized in adulthood to instruct about evangelical matters. Foote's child self cares deeply for the salvation of adults, especially her immediate family, in accordance with Sánchez-Eppler's assertion that "the Christian child . . . should not merely conform to proper domestic norms but even becomes responsible for the familial perpetuation of those norms. Thus, the first lesson in honoring father and mother lies in ensuring that they behave as Christian parents might" ("Raising Empires" 413). Furthermore, by detailing her acute response to sensationalized situations, she discursively challenges the long-lived myth of black women as insensate creatures, thus arguing for African American holy women's capacity for modesty and piety alike. To underwrite her spiritual and feminine authority, she draws on the Scriptures directly and indirectly and addresses without hesitation readers she designates in accordance with their domestic roles, including "dear children," "Parents," and "Christian men."

Foote sustains the characterization of the narrator as a divinely inspired and protected child throughout the early chapters. After verifying her innate sense of justice and righteousness, she explores those themes further by reconstructing a crucial incident that casts her girl self as the victim of an unfeeling employer (depicted as a variation of the antebellum monstrous slave mistress). Specifically, chapter 5, titled "An Undeserved Whipping," narrates the occasion on which Foote is accused of stealing poundcakes that her employer has baked for guests. Foote emotionally identifies Mrs. Prime as "a cripple" (171) who "had treated me as though I were their [i.e., Mr. and Mrs. Prime's] child" (176). Despite her insistence that she "was entirely innocent of the crime laid to my charge" (175), Foote is nonetheless beaten with a rawhide and pressed to confess. Rather than accede, the narrator, as well trained by her mother in material defiance as in oral, acts in much the same way as Mattie Jackson's mother, who similarly resists oppression by taking a cowhide into her own hands. Foote writes: "I carried the rawhide out to the wood pile, took the axe, and cut it up into small pieces, which I threw away, determined not to be whipped with that thing again" (176). Afterward, perhaps frightened by her own audacity, she walks "a long, lonely road" to her family's home, where her mother lovingly accepts her innocence but uncharacteristically does "not say very much about it." Ultimately, Foote says, her mother "sent me back with them, very much against my will" (176). In later years, the verbally resistant mother reveals that "she talked very sharply to the Primes when [Julia] was not by" (176). The incident unites mother and daughter, but Foote asserts that the Primes' mistrust in her and their physical abuse retarded the development of her childhood godliness, whereas confidence in her goodness and their belief that she had not stolen the cakes, on the other hand, would have enhanced her piety.

This brief but significant chapter reinforces the roles that evangelical domesticity conventionally assigned to parents and children. The narrator's fear of Mrs. Prime during the initial confrontation about the cakes highlights children's requisite submission to authority. Her visceral response ensues in part from Mrs. Prime's departure from the matron's prescribed role: "She, who had always been so kind and *motherly*, frightened me so by her looks and action that I trembled so violently I could not speak. . . . The dear Lord alone knows how my little heart ached" (175, italics added). Similarly, the sentimentalized child's natural meekness and socially dictated powerlessness are emphasized when the narrator cannot prove that the culprit she suspects (another child servant) is in fact guilty. Moreover, Foote clarifies the psychological fragility she suffered: the experience occasions a memory of John Van Paten, her executed teacher, and the girl wishes to die as he did. This sinful idea precipitates a visit from Satan, whom she reports "came to me and told me to go to the barn and hang myself" (175). Only the appearance of the cake-stealing boy saves her. First, the boy mocks her, which provokes her wrath. Then, after she lunges at him, "he [eluded her] grasp and ran away, laughing" (175). Apparently presuming that her rage was so great that she would have hurt him had he not escaped her, the narrator interprets the escape as the "second time" that providence intervenes to save her from "a dreadful sin" (the first time was when she was rescued, like St. Augustine, from drunkenness at age five). Thus, Foote declares herself divinely protected.

Furthermore, the reflective adult narrator implies that Mrs. Prime's unwarranted suspicion of a virtuous girl and her violation of her social duty to treat her employee decently and, most important, her Christian duty to act as her indentured servant's surrogate mother very nearly result in the commission of an unpardonable sin, suicide. As it is, Mrs. Prime's reprehensible actions throughout the episode constitute a breach of the tenets of standard nineteenth-century resources like *The Mother Book,* in which Lydia Maria Child stipulates that "the first rule, and the most important of all, in education, is, that a mother govern her own feelings, and keep her heart and conscience pure" (244). For Mrs. Prime indulges in pride and ire—two of the Seven Deadly Sins that John Bunyan cautions against in *Pilgrim's Progress*, the exemplary precursor for Methodist spiritual autobiographies like Foote's. Mrs. Prime's indulgence in sin induces in her young charge a fear and distrust of adults, to whom she should ideally look for spiritual guidance. She diminishes the girl's self-esteem and faith in righteousness when she fails to accept her word (and consequently authorizes the actual unpunished culprit to continue to sin); she humiliates the child by beating her; she disturbs the girl's peace of mind and indirectly causes her nightmares, which predispose her to seeing a vision of Satan and the evil this vision prophesies. Mrs. Prime can be considered ultimately responsible for the narrator's angry and violent attack on the supposed thief, obliquely condoned by the beating the girl herself received. Foote instructively indicates that Mrs. Prime's most grievous offense embodies all her other offenses: her collective sins undermine the narrator's Christian faith and encourage not religious devotion but degeneracy. As Foote concludes, "The experience of that last year made me quite a hardened sinner" (176). Thus, she juxtaposes Mrs. Prime's transgressions as surrogate mother figure with her biological mother's more charitable responses. She demonstrates her mother's benevolent and comforting acceptance of the child's credibility. Even asserting that "my mother sent me back with them, very much against my will," she maintains the image of her mother as nurturing and judicious: she sends Julia back because, "the Primes being an old and influential family, they were able to send [her] to a country school, where [she] was well treated by both teacher and scholars" (171). On the whole, the narrator esteems her mother's conformity to true matronly virtue and maternal responsibility.

However, in chapter 6 the narrator reasserts her ambivalence toward her mother in a solemn condemnation of her maternal guidance. Now an adolescent and no longer an indentured servant, the narrator is reunited with her immediate family, whom she describes as active African Methodist Episcopal Christians living in Albany, New York. Among them, she becomes more devout and "began to see such a beauty in religion that I resolved to serve God whatever might happen" (177). But as an adolescent she finds herself still tempted by the "pomps and vanities of this world" (177). Her mother, attentive to her daughter's ecclesiastical and social "needs," gives the girl additional domestic responsibilities, including the care of her younger siblings, which, despite her own search for surrogate mothers, she ironically pronounces "a thing which I did not at all relish." When the mother's endeavors to teach Julia to cease "barter[ing] the things of the kingdom for the fooleries of the world" prove unsuccessful, she disciplines her severely for secular activities. After an unauthorized excursion to the theater, for example, the daughter is punished so that she "never had any desire to go again" (177). Furthermore, as good, pious parents, the Footes forbid dancing (perhaps a consequence of the near-death experience in which the mother and one of the children nearly drown). When the narrator goes dancing in spite of the parents' opposition, she believes "the hand of God" literally comes upon her, drawing her away from sin: "I was so frightened that I fell," she writes (178). Unable to withstand the "loud . . . demonic laughter" that she incurs from the others at the dance, though, she dances again, and again providence discourages her and protects her from great peril:

> Being shamed into it, I did try it again, but I had taken only a few steps, when I was seized with a smoldering sensation, and felt the same heavy grasp upon my arm, and in my ears a voice kept saying, "Repent! Repent!" I immediately left the floor and sank into a seat. The company gathered around me, but not with mocking laughter as before; an invisible presence seemed to fill the place. The dance broke up, all leaving very quietly. Thus was I again "plucked as a brand from the burning." (178)

Although this visitation does not conclude the chapter, it sets up Foote's now formulaic chapter ending: inclusive theology addressed to an inscribed readership; a meditation on the religious state of an individual or group; a prayer or appeal; finally, a call to conversion or sacred conscientiousness. Moreover, the exhortation at the end of each chapter invariably disrupts the linearity of the autobiography.[7] Chapter 6 departs from this structure by returning to the chronology; it describes a period Foote spent "in an agony of prayer" (179). This reflective time ends when, at her mother's insistence, she attends a party where she "engaged in all the sports of the evening, and soon my conviction for sin wore away, and foolish amusements took its place" (179). Foote implies that heeding her mother's irreverent counsel leads her astray from spiritual reflection. She concludes the chapter with the admonition that mothers especially must be careful not to cause "the eternal destruction of . . . daughter[s]" (179). In this way, Foote undercuts the earlier portrayal of her mother as dutiful and upright.

Reconstructing her psychosocial development, Foote asserts her allegiance and submission to her parents, and she depicts them as worthy of her trust and deference. Maintaining the ambivalence toward parents that underscores all of

A Brand Plucked from the Fire, however, Foote sometimes implies that her mother or both of her parents are inconsistently devout and so do not always merit obedience. She uses chapter 10, marked in the original text by a chiasmus (*X*), to place her narrative within an African American narrative tradition in which the tenth chapter functions as a critical turning point in the subject's life.[8] Pointedly entitled "Disobedience, But Happy Results," Foote's tenth chapter signals the narrator's acquiescence to personal, interior authority: "Finally, I did something I never had done before: I deliberately disobeyed my mother" (186). The insubordination follows days of mourning after her mother denies her permission to visit religious elders who have urged the "young believer" to seek sanctification (also called *holiness*).[9] Specifically, this meant freeing one's self from sin, purifying one's self of the human predisposition to sinfulness. In addition, nineteenth-century believers in spiritual sanctification contended that only God had the power to endow human beings with purity and divinity; thus, sanctification was unpopular among Methodist offshoots like Foote's parents' AME church, though early sanctioned by the Wesleyan sect from which it originated. Foote observes that her mother's refusal depresses her, admitting, "To have my mother refuse my request so peremptorily made me very sorrowful for many days" (185).

Foote's decision to ignore her parents' disapproval and visit the elders against their wishes attests to her conviction that sanctification is a sacred gift. Although she is already more than fifteen years old at this point, she clings to the image of herself as a child evangelist and justifies her defiance and the distress she suffers by contending, "But truly, God does make his *little ones* ministering angels—sending them forth on missions of love and mercy" (186, italics added). Moreover, she relates her ambivalence toward maternal figures by accentuating her regard for one of "the two old saints" who inspires her sanctification. Designating this woman as a "dear old mother in Israel" sent specifically by God to her (186), she introduces another mother figure. This "pilgrim" serves as the young woman's spiritual mentor, and at the sight of her Foote rejoices, "my heart seemed to melt within me, so unexpected, and yet so much desired was her visit" (186). Three women, then—Foote's biological mother, Mrs. Prime, and the religious elder—all signal her early regard for women, her desire for a strong, central maternal figure from whom she could extract ecclesiastical, moral, and social counsel, and, most important, the matrifocal theology she would espouse as an itinerant minister. In subsequent chapters, Foote transforms her pursuit of maternal figures to an interest in "spiritual sisters" and memorializes her intimacy with women like the frail elder daughter of a

Mrs. Riley and later Sister Johnson; these two holy women serve as her traveling companions. But the narrative representation of the three influential women of her youth denotes Foote's search for maternal protection; the spiritual autobiographer recalls that the three women fulfilled that need to varying degrees of satisfaction for her child-self.

Furthermore, by naming the three "mothers" of her early life, Foote places *A Brand Plucked from the Fire* among the tradition of nineteenth-century African American women's spiritual narratives in which autobiographical disclosure of other black holy women's lives reveals the authors' closeness with sister Christians and their commitment to inscribing a collective identity. Jarena Lee and Zilpha Elaw, for example, both describe close relationships with holy women, black and white, whom they encountered as they traveled the ministerial circuit. Traveling across New England and the mid-Atlantic states during the same years, as William Andrews has written, Lee and Elaw "happily shar[ed] at least one pulpit" together (*Sisters* 3). Elaw identifies dozens of women, not all of them holy, who influenced her ministry in some way—from prostitutes she met in "houses of ill fame" (105) to a Cape Cod woman of "vanity and haughtiness" (116) to "an extensive circle of young ladies who were constant attendants upon [her] ministry" (119). The spiritual accounts of women of this tradition consistently demonstrate that the rhetorical representation of other African American women's lives in one's narrative is an effective and a revered way of validating and telling about one's own life. Her brave self-assertion aside, Foote's attention to the three women who nurtured her indicates her desire to project a collective identity.

The Father's Good Daughter

Foote's reliance on verbal resistance increased as she aged and encountered greater forces of oppression, so *A Brand Plucked from the Fire* offers a corresponding increase in the deployment of resistant orality as a rhetorical trope. However, in it Foote transforms the figure of the child who both sasses and saves (or saves through sass) into the figure of a married minister who must zealously resist her spouse and the clergymen who would impede her evangelism. In 1841, at age eighteen, Julia married George Foote, an unsanctified sailor about whom she had great "anxiety lest the devil should steal away the good seed out of his heart" (190). When she sets up a class-meeting in the Boston house where they board after wedding, the tremendous interest she excites in sanctification in her audience leads her to conclude that "it was not the voice of man that had bidden me go out from the land of my nativity and from my kin-dred, but the voice of my dear Lord" (192). Shortly after this revelation, though disparaged by many as espousing a "foolish doctrine" (193), she begins to evan-gelize especially about sanctification. Before long, George Foote protests her ministry, ironically inciting her to defy him by provoking her to speak out against his efforts to silence the word of God.

Although her essay "Runaway Tongue" offers a useful context in which to read Foote's autobiography, Harryette Mullen misreads a crucial feature of the spiritual autobiographies of Julia Foote and other nineteenth-century black holy women. Mullen contends that literacy inspired the authors to replace sass with a less "sinful" speech and that, having renounced sass, they supplanted it with "a visionary literacy based on emotionally charged religious experi-ence that confirms the truth of the Bible and empowers them as speakers and writers. As God's chosen spokespersons, Jarena Lee, Zilpha Elaw, and Julia Foote—through their acquisition of spiritually driven literacy and personal communication with God by means of visionary experience—purify their 'impudent' tongues of the 'sinful' speech in which . . . they had indulged as in-dentured servant girls" (256–57). While I agree that these holy women repre-sent their revelations as evidence of their divine authority, it seems to me that they renounce sass specifically to reveal their self-love and their obeisance to the will of God. Instead of repudiating her impudent tongue, as Mullen argues, *A Brand Plucked from the Fire* indicates that Foote consciously cultivated it. Af-ter chapter 10 Foote must represent her narrator as having matured beyond the image of the child evangelist; so she must transform the image of her narrator from the impertinent but inspired girl who chops the whip and chases boys into a woman through whom the Word of God continues to emanate. As a woman who endorses the doctrine of holiness and later as a woman who ministers, however, Foote faces severe opposition, especially from male ministers. Endur-ing this opposition necessitates sass: her adversaries are so hostile that God em-powers her with verbal skill—insolence—precisely so as to confront them. In-deed, the narrator implies that her most insolent speech acts are significations that God is speaking through her. In her "Threshing Sermon," for example, Foote ominously promises, "There are many instances of the successful appli-cation of the Gospel flail, by which means the devil is threshed out of sinners. With the help of God, I am resolved, O sinner, to try what effect the smart strokes of this threshing instrument will produce on thy unhumbled soul" (223).

At the same time, however, she comes to realize that true charity consists in exercising particular care as His spokeswoman. Acknowledging that some "people had been to me in such an unchristianlike spirit that I had spoken to and about them in rather an incautious manner," Foote learns not to give up her insolence but to speak clearly and fearlessly, "to maintain that purity of lips and life which the Gospel required" (192). Like Lee and Elaw, whose autobiographies also sanction holiness doctrine, Foote revises her discourse to challenge other professed Christians, but she claims to modify it under God's guidance; thus, she becomes more rather than less "offensive," according to social standards for true women. And she finds herself facing the same paradox that her spiritual predecessors also faced: the more she yields to divine authority, the more her society considers her an intractable woman. The "purity" of speech she cultivates sends her astray of the patriarchal code set for submissive women, ironically requiring her to defend herself verbally all the more.

Foote uses resistant orality continually in responding to the controversy surrounding the doctrine of holiness. This doctrine, which refers to the third of the three stages of Christian salvation—after repentance, the acknowledgment of one's sinfulness, and justification, the divine forgiveness of one's past sins—wrought great controversy because its followers believed only God authorizes the power to preach. Consequently, sanctified women who perceived themselves called to preach did not feel bound by church law, which, as a patriarchal institution, barred women's preaching. As Bettye Collier-Thomas asserts, "Belief in the doctrine of holiness empowered [women] to set aside denominational law and practice and to repudiate elements of the polity that inveighed against their freedom to preach" (17). Foote apparently belonged to those holiness believers who cautiously claimed that holiness simply enabled sanctified persons to resist sin more effectively (Brereton 64), for *A Brand Plucked from the Fire* testifies that sanctification diminishes one's interest in sin and makes sin not impossible but improbable. Foote earnestly clarifies her position: "Do not misunderstand me. I am not teaching absolute perfection, for that belongs to God alone. Nor do I mean a state of angelic or Adamic perfection, but Christian perfection—an extinction of every temper contrary to love" (232). The idea of a state of grace on earth, however, proved too theologically impertinent for many of Foote's associates.

Conspicuous for their emotionally vehement worship service, their belief in divine visions and visitations, and their experiences of glossolalia, devotees of holiness doctrine were frequently disdained by other Protestants as primitive, specious, ill-educated, hyperactive, indecent, and hysterical. Not surprisingly, the controversy around holiness, particularly in the AME Zion church, to which Foote belonged, routinely fell along gender lines—though not along racial lines. Men especially were loath to be associated with the movement. In the *Memoir of Old Elizabeth*, the holiness-practicing narrator recalls an embittering interview with another minister, one who "confessed [he] did not believe in revelation, [saying,] 'You think you have these things by revelation, but there has been no such thing as revelation since Christ's ascension.'" Elizabeth does not blench: "I asked him where the apostle John got his revelation while he was in the Isle of Patmos. With this, he rose up and left me, and I said in my spirit, get thee behind me Satan" (18). Two fundamental challenges posed by holiness women to the male-dominated AME church are identified by Jean Humez. First, whereas men regarded formal seminary training as requisite credentials for preaching, women ministers tended to declare an authentic call by God as the most profound license to interpret Scripture. (One thinks, for instance, of Anne Hutchinson.) And second, whereas men of the church were prone to spilling secular concerns over into ecclesiastical matters, women ministers vehemently critiqued—or orally resisted—what they considered to be an "increasing wordiness" in the church, and complained of its growing secularity (Humez 140). Moreover, as Humez also notes, it was the very physical and linguistic manifestations of holiness spirituality and divine ordination, of which male clergy were skeptical, that holy women regarded as both the sources of their authority and the proof of their authenticity as God's representatives (138).

Foote's clash with other Christians begins long before she first feels called to preach, as her adolescent struggle with her parents signifies; after publicly declaring herself sanctified, the narrator drolly observes, "Many of them fought holiness with more zeal and vigor than they did sin" (187). She uses sarcasm to reconstruct one of the first visits she receives upon sanctification at about age fifteen. Foote's reconstruction of the incident demonstrates her practice of her mother's lessons in verbal self-defense in order to fulfill her Father's work. She begins chapter II, willfully titled "A Religion as Old as the Bible," thusly: "The pastor of our church visited me one day, to talk to me about my 'new religion,' as he called it. I took my Bible and read many of my choice passages to him, such as—'Come and hear, all ye that fear God, and *I will declare* what he hath done for my soul'" (188, italics added). When the minister leaves, frustrated by his inability to reform her, she "involuntarily burst forth into praises: 'My soul is full of *glory inspiring my tongue,* / Could I meet with angels *I would sing* them a song'"(188, italics added). This vignette illustrates the author's manipulation of resistant verbality, transforming it into a matrifocal theology of both oral and textual discourse, and attests to her clever maternalization of sacred texts the minister would presumably sanction, including the Scripture she cites and the hymn she sings.

Foote's greatest trials come predictably with her acceptance of God's call to her to preach, so it is in defense of her divine ordination that she most passionately applies her mother's teachings. If the whole of *A Brand Plucked from the Fire* constitutes an exposé in which Foote engages a matrilineal resistant discourse to divulge the uncharitable practices of supposedly Christian forces, then her pastor, Mr. Beman (whom she never honors by calling "Reverend"), and the entire AME Zion Church Conference are unsheathed by her pen. For his part, Beman's sexism motivates him to excommunicate Foote, ostensibly for impiety, but actually for insubordination. Detailing her excommunication and the recourse she attempts with the AME Conference, chapter 19 deploys acrimonious observation and open invective as well as sentimental rhetoric. First, she cloaks her budding ministry under the veil of domesticity, accentuating its site in the homes of church members who are ultimately threatened themselves with excommunication. In addition, she belittles her work as "feeble efforts" blessed by the Lord (205). On the whole, the portrait that emerges shows her a humble woman persecuted by powerful, pretentious, and self-serving men. The rhetoric inspires pathos as she details the psychological torment and character defamation she endured—*until*, perhaps, she writes of her sassy rejoinder to the excommunication committee's dismissal. Foote writes, "When I reached the door, I turned and said: 'I now shake off the dust of my feet as a witness against you. See to it that this meeting does not rise in judgment against you'" (206). Drawing righteousness from her conviction that God protects her, she tells the council, "I fear God more than man" (206); her use of "man" resonates with gender specificity. Foote further risks compromising her ambiguously sentimentalized account when, reporting Beman's bogus explanation about Foote's leaving his church, the harassed narrator unflinchingly insists, "Mr. Beman told an actual falsehood." With rhetorical flourish, Foote then signifies on the secular-minded church patriarchy by incorporating into her spiritual autobiography a personal parody of the discourse of the nation's most respected secular authority, the Supreme Court. She concludes the chapter about her "Public Effort" with a derisive allusion to the Court's Dred Scott decision: "Even ministers of Christ did not feel that women had any rights which they were bound to respect" (207). Foote's statement is reminiscent of the opinion of Chief Justice Roger B. Taney, whose vitriolic response to the 1857 case of the Missouri slave included the famous contention that the Negro "had no rights which the white man was bound to respect." The secular reference underlines Foote's un-mitigated verbal resistance to religious patriarchal oppression. Her equation of sexist men with racist whites demonstrates her faith that verbal resistance is both a divine right and a spiritual obligation, the inscription of which in her autobiography forms a defiant theology. With this faith, she declares herself bound by divine authority to refuse to submit to mortal authority. Thus, Foote argues for a feminization of Christianity based on the kind of active resistance she learned as her mother's daughter and found sanctioned as a right/rite by her Father.

Foote and Her Spiritual Foremothers

The second half of *A Brand Plucked from the Fire* repeatedly demonstrates Foote's conviction that she is authorized by God to do His work in unorthodox ways, in spite—and because—of her gender. In chapter 20 (or, *XX*), titled "Women in the Gospel," for example, she adopts a protofeminist exegesis to interpret the New Testament. Echoing earlier spiritual autobiographers' am-biguous interpretations of Paul's New Testament epistles, she whimsically con-cludes, "When Paul said, 'Help those women who labor with me in the Gospel,' he certainly meant that they did more than to pour out tea" (209). When she subsequently instructs other Christian women, admonishing them, "Be not kept in bondage by those who say, 'We suffer not a woman to teach,' thus quoting Paul's words, but not rightly applying them" (227), her hermeneutics parallels Maria Stewart's. Predating Foote, in the 1830s Stewart read Paul's missives from a prowoman perspective. Whereas Foote asserts that her con-temporaries misinterpret the apostle's meaning at I Corinthians, Stewart even more brazenly proclaims in her "Farewell Address to the City of Boston" that she has as much insight as Paul does into heavenly projects for public women like herself:

St. Paul declared that it was a shame for a woman to speak in public, yet our great High Priest and Advocate did not condemn the woman for a more notorious offense than this. . . . Did St. Paul but know of our wrongs and deprivations, I presume he would make no objections to our pleading in public for our rights. Again, holy women ministered unto Christ and the apostles; and women of refinement in all ages, more or less, have had a voice in moral, religious and political subjects. Again; why the Almighty hath imparted unto me the power of speaking thus, I cannot tell. (75)

Although they are separated by over four decades, Foote and Stewart make the same argument, which is to say that the circumstances for black holy women went virtually unchanged during this time. In their respective spiritual autobiographies, the two authors image themselves as female questers confident that their evangelism is inspired and approved by God, and, consequently, that as His apostles He empowers them to speak about the role of women in the church.

As a conventional spiritual autobiography, *A Brand Plucked from the Fire* exhibits many rhetorical features common to other narratives by or about early African American holy women. Throughout *From Sin to Salvation* Virginia Brereton argues that, from its inception in America, the spiritual autobiographical tradition has been characterized by the similarities of the texts that comprise it; that is, the aesthetic value of a spiritual narrative is determined not by its imaginative departure from convention nor by an innovative or improvisational rendering of generic conventions but by a close adherence to convention. Consequently, a spiritual narrative is most rhetorically successful and most effective as a text that authenticates a religious convert's salvation when it deploys a rhetoric identical to that of other conversion narratives, invoking the very same biblical passages, descriptions of visions and revelations, and so forth as all other spiritual autobiographies. Given this factor, it is not surprising that Foote's autobiography reads very much like the spiritual narratives of her black female literary precursors. Among the most apparent similarities, Foote cites Joel 2:28 ("And it shall come to pass that I will pour out my Spirit upon all flesh; and your sons, and your daughters shall prophesy"), the Scriptural epigraph and central thesis of the *Religious Experience and Journal of Mrs. Jarena Lee*. In addition, Foote proposes a cogent argument for women in the ministry when she cites the same New Testament passage that serves as the epigraph for the *Memoir of Old Elizabeth*, that unifies one of Stewart's "Meditations," and that appears in many other narratives besides: "There is neither male nor female in Christ Jesus" (Gal. 3:28). Moreover, Stewart's "Farewell Address" impressively chronicles the contributions of holy women such as Esther, Mary Magdalene, an ancient Greek woman who delivered oracles, and a thirteenth-century woman of Bologne, who, as a twenty-six-year-old Doctor of Laws, "began publicly to expound the Institutions of Justinian" (78). Over fifty years after Stewart, Foote likewise meticulously acknowledges myriad holy women of history whom she claims as her evangelical foremothers.

Foote's chapter 20, "Women in the Gospel," parallels Stewart's "Address Delivered Before the Afric-American Female Intelligence Society of Boston."

The Afric-American Female Intelligence Society, according to Paula Giddings in *When and Where I Enter,* was one of a "proliferation of Black ladies' literary, intelligence, temperance, and moral improvement societies" developed by antebellum African American women in northern cities to pursue acculturation without succumbing to the pressure on them to conform to white American class-consciousness (49). Stewart's address to this group was quite likely an ideal opportunity for the orator to reiterate her paradoxical call to black mothers to assume the virtues of true women (especially piety and chastity), on the one hand, and to resist patriarchal restrictions on women as thinking and working citizens, on the other. But rather than reassert her radical position redefining the domestic sphere as a potential site of social and political evolution / revolution, as developed in such essays as "Religion and the Pure Principles of Morality," Stewart mysteriously falters in her address to the Female Intelligence Society. Only her final statements are gender-specific; only the last paragraph explicitly beseeches, "O woman, woman! upon you I call; for upon your exertions almost entirely depends whether the rising generation shall be any thing more than we have been or not. O woman, woman! your example is powerful, your influence great; it extends over your husbands and over your children, and throughout the circle of your acquaintance. Then let me exhort you to cultivate among yourselves a spirit of Christian love and unity, having charity one for another, without which all our goodness is as sounding brass, and as a tinkling cymbal" (62–63).

The paradox inherent in Stewart's odd reticence is indirectly addressed in Carla Peterson's essay "'Doers of the Word': Theorizing African-American Women Writers in the Antebellum North." Peterson argues that Stewart and other antebellum black women responded to their race and gender marginalization by further ostracizing themselves, partly by engaging in religious evangelicalism. Although true woman ideology required white women to cultivate chastity and sanctity, religious evangelicalism constituted one of "those socially liminal spaces created by the Second Great Awakening," spaces that, because of their public nature, were denied to middle-class white women expected to adhere to the cult of true womanhood (192).[10] Peterson rightly asserts, I think, that while their work as holy women afforded African American women a certain freedom of self-expression as well as a divinely ordained authority, it also resulted in their further marginalization from the communities of race and gender with which they might otherwise have been united (192). African American holy women autobiographers' intrepid, affirmative response to the divine call to preach often meant their estrangement from other blacks and from other women, even from other Christians, who could not be counted on to embrace women who were socially outcast for their outspokenness. Julia Foote suffered this isolation as much as any of her foremothers, to be sure. She did not always have the support of other African American women because, across the century, many of them accepted patriarchy's rule.

Just as she concludes each of the initial chapters with a brief sermon, Foote's entire autobiography becomes increasingly less chronological and more directive and didactic as it progresses. Consequently, the last few chapters reveal relatively little about Foote's later life, substituting for narrative detail her open letter to Christian women in chapter 20, "A 'Threshing' Sermon" in chapter 26, and a homily titled "Love Not the World" that serves as chapter 29. The text concludes with the overtly didactic "How to Obtain Sanctification." Thus, the latter chapters of *A Brand Plucked from the Fire* illuminate the rhetorical strategy of the whole. Similarly, they indicate that the author of this "Autobiographical Sketch" is in fact much less invested in sketching her autobiography or narrating the life of the convert than in specifying the joys of salvation and extending a call to conversion.

Fittingly, Foote meticulously narrates the major events of her childhood, for during that period especially she lived experiences that proved central to her religious development. In addition, the detailed scenes of her youth establish her connection with her mother(s) and reveal the young woman's desire for the kind of maternal and feminine nurturance she herself would come to provide for her "Christian sisters." Moreover, the images of the willful girl render plausible and more readily comprehended the later woman who initially feared divine revelation, but then stalwartly embraced her ordination. One comes to see the mother's experiences in slavery as enabling the daughter's eventual evangelical defiance; one wonders whether Foote might have succeeded as a leader among women ministers without her mother's lesson in active resistance. But although elements of *A Brand Plucked from the Fire* suggest a movement away from the rhetoric of sentimentality in the tradition of black women's spiritual autobiography, it nonetheless presents the author first as a holy child, then as an outraged and outspoken holy woman, both figures that are narrativized as lovingly protected by an omnipotent Father.

Spirit and Ecstasy

In a racist and sexist society the concept of a black woman empowered by God is doubly radical.

CLAUDIA TATE, *Domestic Allegories of Political Desire*

Batter my heart, three personed God; for you
As yet but knock, breathe, shine, and seek to mend;
That I may rise and stand, o'erthrow me, and bend
Your force, to break, blow, burn and make me new.
I, like an usurpt town, to another due,
Labor to admit you, but Oh, to no end,
Reason, your viceroy in me, me should defend,
But is captiv'd, and proves weak or untrue.
Yet dearly I love you, and would be loved fain,
But am betroth'd unto your enemy:
Divorce me, untie or break that knot again,
Take me to you, imprison me, for I
Except you enthrall me, never shall be free,
Nor ever chaste, except you ravish me.

JOHN DONNE, "Holy Sonnet XIV"

Using Donne's sonnet to conclude a discussion of nineteenth-century African
American holy women may seem very odd, yet this famous poem masterfully
illustrates the literary tradition that I address, that is, a tradition that marks the
convergence of Christianity, conversion, mysticism, transformation, and sexuality. I end this study with the suggestion that the black holy women's autobiographies analyzed in this book emerge from the traditions not only of the Christian
conversion relation and the literatures of slavery and sentimentalism, but more

specifically from a tradition that privileges ecstatic, charismatic, "enthusiastic" religious expression and power. Reading closely (albeit concisely) the sentimentalized tropes in ex-slavewomen's spiritual oral testimonies transcribed and excerpted in *God Struck Me Dead*, a small volume edited in the early twentieth century, I situate them among a silent majority—that is, among postbellum African American women whose anxiety about the emotionality and latent sexuality of certain forms of sacred expression worried the black holy women discussed in this book into a prim, cultivated silence. The words of Marianna Torgovnick pertain to my discussion with great irony. Noting that the word *primitive* "entered the English language with special reference to the Christian church" (4), Torgovnick writes: "The primitive continue[s] to be associated with heathenism, sexuality, and excess in a way that support[s] the idea that primitives [need] Western guidance and control—in short, the goals of imperialism and empire" (13). Postbellum black women's "control" over excess and their silence I trace to the grievously scarce scholarship by African American(ist) feminist scholars that attends to African American women's sacred experience. I want to urge these scholars not to conform to the academic priggishness that inhibits the study of ecstasy in its diverse manifestations in black holy women's texts.

Donne's speaker begs for religious purgation or transformation through brutal sexual violence; he desires a battering so severe that death is a possible outcome. The metaphysical poem is a genre characterized by conceits that portray death as synonymous with rest or sleep, often with the sleep that accompanies sickness; in this case death is associated with the aftermath of sexual consummation. Ironically, death functions as a Renaissance euphemism for *orgasm*. Similar imagery pervades Donne's oeuvre, but the poetic conjunction of spiritual salvation, sexual passion, and organic death as a symbol for release did not originate with him, of course. In many religions, as James Hillman asserts, "Death usually comes first as an experience of the soul, after which the body expires" (qtd. in Allinson 36). Furthermore, according to Mark Allinson, "A close examination of religious texts from all traditions makes it clear, especially in their esoteric expressions, that transformation in spiritual (or psychological) terms is often referred to as a death experience" (36). Galatians 3:20 ("I have been crucified with Christ; it is no longer I who live, but Christ who lives in me"), for example, is a fundamentally Christian text that associates death with salvation and mysticism. For Christians, to be saved is to become dead to a life of sin; the figure of the resurrected Christ symbolizes the transformation Christians seek to emulate when they are "born again."

In a secular literary tradition prior to the Renaissance, the aesthetic union of spirituality, sexuality, and mortality is the subject of Elizabethan airs like "Thoughts Make Men Sigh," in which death signifies the sex act:

Thoughts make men sigh, sighes make men sick at hart,
  sicknes consumes, consumption kills at last:
Death is the end of everie deadlie smart,
  and sweet the joy where every paine is past:
But oh the time of death too long delayed,
  where tried patience is too ill apayed.

Hope harpes on heaven, but lives in halfe a hell,
  hart thinkes of life but findes a deadly hate:
Eares hark for blis, but heares a dolefull bell,
  Eyes loke for joy, but see a wofull state:
But eyes, and eares, and hart, and hope deceaved,
  tongue tels a truth, how is the mind conceived.

Conceited thus to thinke but say no more,
  to sigh and sob till sorrow have an end:
And so to die till death may life restore,
  or carefull faith may find a constant friende:
That patience may yet in her passion prove,
  just at my death I found my life of love.

This secular lyric exemplifies a serious, melancholic contemplation of death and spiritual—and sexual—transcendence. The thoughts that make human beings sigh are synonymous with the sighs of lovemaking; that death symbolizes orgasm is clear in that it is only through death that life can be restored. In other words, only through the sex act can procreation occur. Thus, as Daniel Fischlin writes, through a series of paradoxes the poem "details the progression of afflictions that lead to death (thoughts, sighs, sickness, and consumption), and the transcendence of death through love. Again, death and sexual climax are equated, thus allowing for the ultimate reversal in which dying 'may life restore'" (13) and passion yields "conception." The "love" is regenerative and in the poem could as easily refer to Christian love as to sexual love.

Christians and seventeenth-century Western poets have not alone across time produced this kind of aesthetic representation of deep feeling, death, and transcendence. In our own day, the association of pleasure with death explicitly controls the musings of French philosopher Michel Foucault, as when he writes:

> I think that pleasure is a very difficult behavior. It's not as simple as that to enjoy one's self. And I must say that's my dream. I would like and I hope to die of an overdose of pleasure of any kind. Because I think it's really difficult and I always have the feeling that I do not feel *the* pleasure, the complete total pleasure and, for me, it's related to death. Because I think that the kind of pleasure I would consider as *the* real pleasure, would be so deep, so intense, so overwhelming that I couldn't survive it. I would die. (qtd. in hooks, 26–27)

Although not marked by the same hedonism or solipsism as Foucault, nineteenth-century Christian women of African descent, situated between Donne and Foucault, narrated autobiographies that are marked by a similar union of spirituality, sexuality, and mortality. *God Struck Me Dead*, a collection of (mostly) conversion narratives dictated by former slaves to a Fisk University graduate student, is a case in point. During the late 1920s Andrew Polk Watson interviewed one hundred elderly men and women who had lived as slaves in America before the end of the Civil War; he edited more than forty of their narratives for his master's degree in anthropology. The stories in *God Struck Me Dead* detail very private mystical experiences, but the autobiographers reconstruct these as public performances, following the Christian tradition of confessing and declaring one's self "saved." The early American Puritan relation, the genre from which later spiritual narratives evolve, required converts to stand before the religious community and "relate" their purgative, salvific encounters with the Divine. In their spiritual relations, nineteenth-century African American women used complex religious discourse to reconstruct themselves as rapt in religious ecstasy at the peak of the kind of sacred experience for which John Donne's speaker pleads in "Holy Sonnet XIV." These women draw on metaphors as provocative as Donne's to testify from what Joanne Braxton calls a "wild zone"—a discursive "space of difference" that challenges hegemonic power (73).

The religious experiences described in the conversion narratives of *God Struck Me Dead,* like earlier spiritual autobiographies by black holy women, represent a syncretic doctrine derived from African as well as European religious traditions and exhibiting characteristics of both. As Frey and Wood explain in *Come Shouting to Zion,* African Americans' "participation in evangelical meetings of various kinds initiated them into aspects of white culture and therefore served as a crucial part of the assimilative process that integrated them into the community" (122). Analyzing the comparable transformative elements of Christian conversion and African initiation in his introduction to a recent edition of Watson's work, Albert Raboteau underscores the affinity between many African initiation rituals and the major symbols of Christian conversion and regeneration. More important for my argument, Raboteau finds that "the ecstatic behavior, widely associated with revivals—such outward expression of the Spirit's inner promptings as shouting, clapping, jerking, and dancing—mirrored the singing, dancing, and drumming in ceremonies of possessive trance that regularly manifested the presence of the divine among followers of many African religions" (xxii). In addition, Frey and Wood cite documents from the First Awakening indicating that "forms of ecstatic expression [such as shouting and other vocalizations were] congruent with both African and Protestant patterns" (123). They assert that even the shout that blacks "had invented to help them reach the spiritual ecstasy of conversion also served to forge social relations" with whites (123). Frey and Wood further observe that charismatic women held leadership roles in early American evangelical movements, "in part because of the emotional nature ascribed to women" (122). Moreover, African American women's West African ancestors had revered women's participation in religious activities and divine cosmological systems, even to honoring sacred women as "diviners, religious specialists whose functions were related to that of the medium" (12–13).

Nineteenth-century black holy women's narratives retain elements of this faith and illustrate that they, like Donne, consolidated the spiritual and the temporal. The title narrative of *God Struck Me Dead* exemplifies this point. The speaker describes her conversion in the wake of her husband's death:

> When God struck me dead with his power I was living on Fourteenth Avenue. . . . I was in my house alone, and I declare unto you, when his power struck me I died. I fell out on the floor flat on my back. I could neither speak nor move, for my tongue stuck to the roof of my mouth; my jaws were locked and my limbs were stiff.
>
> In my vision I saw hell and the devil. I was crawling along a high brick wall, it seems, and it looked like I would fall into a dark, roaring pit. I looked away to the east and saw Jesus. He called to me and said, "Arise and follow me." (59)

Thus the anonymous woman describes her conversion experience as one of death, rejuvenation, and ultimately resurrection. (Tellingly, *none* of the names of the ex-slave narrators in *God Struck Me Dead* is provided.) This narrative is representative of slavewomen's accounts of conversion in *God Struck Me Dead;* like most of them, it reconstructs a mystical vision. In these visions, black female *spirituality* and black female *corporeality* merge, and the discourse itself is incarnate and erotic at once; the narrative bridges the boundaries that Alicia Ostriker has found in *Anglo-American* discourse that tend to divide spirit and flesh, the transcendent and the immanent (16–17). In diametric opposition to the often luxuriant natural setting in which she is often abruptly blinded by divine revelation (in a cotton patch, a berry patch, a cornfield or thicket, on a country road, on 14th Avenue), the black woman convert loses life in her body as she gains life in her soul. Or she might be rendered mute, her body "split open from head to foot" by rays of light or the rod of Jesus, as one woman recalls (61, 100). The autobiographical writings of free-born Rebecca Cox Jackson open with a similar recollection of religious conversion also striking for its deployment of natural phenomena to signal her "welcoming God's spirit into her soul" (Sasson 162): "In the year of 1830, July, I was wakened by thunder and lightning at the break of day and the bed which had been my resting place in time of thunder for five years was now taking [*sic*] away. . . . I expected every clap of thunder to launch my soul at the bar of God with all my sins that I had ever done" (Jackson 71). Later, recalling "A Dream of Slaughter," Jackson similarly highlights the integration of corporeal and spiritual matters. In this dream, a "robber" assaults her to the point of religious submission: "He took a lance and laid my nose open and then he cut my head on the right side, from the back to the front above my nose, and pulled the skin down. The skin and blood covered me like a veil. . . ." (94). The assailant continues until he has taken "all my bowels out and laid them on the floor by my right side." Ultimately, Jackson comprehends the religious import of the dream, for "when the lance was going through my nose it felt like a feather was going over my nose. I sat in silent prayer all the time saying these words in my mind, 'Lord Jesus, receive my spirit'" (95).

Other African American women describe their sacred metamorphoses as physical experiences that generated their spiritual rebirths throughout the interviews Watson conducted. The unnamed subject of one of the longest accounts in Watson's collection, casually labeled "Stayed With Her People after Freedom," is eighty-eight years old at the time of dictation. Her narrative opens with the subgenre's classic statement of self-assertion: "I was born in Mississippi, in Juniper County. I belonged to Major Ellison, but I was raised right here in Tennessee till I was eleven years old; then Major Ellison bought me and carried me to Mississippi. I didn't want to go. They 'zamine you just like they do a horse; they look at your teeth, and pull your eyelids back and look at your eyes, and feel you just like you was a horse" (129). The autobiographical sketch begins with the woman's characterization of slavery as a dehumanizing institution. To be sure, slavery was largely a system of labor, and the chief commodity was the laborer's body. In this particular account Watson studies the black female body as a site of bondage by gendered objectification. The narrator recounts the maltreatment of her slave child body, which is handled as if it were an animal's, literally, the body of a work horse. Numerous slave narratives attest to this sort of maltreatment as major means white slaveholders used to debase those bound by the "peculiar institution." The narrator subsequently reveals another aspect of her corporeality, saying, "Me and my sister was the brightest [in color] ones on our place" (135). This description suggests perhaps that she is a "mulatta," a factor that she says caused conflict for her in the color-hierarchal slaveocracy. In addition, Watson writes that her children are "white," inserting that bracketed word into (his version of) her story: "They had an old woman to keep the colored chillen, and I would take my chillen [white] and go down to the quarters" (135). Her children apparently embody evidence of rape.

In his transcribing, editing, and organizing of her narrative, Watson pays excessive attention to the narrator's physical appearance. The sketch emphasizes aesthetic details, in the description of the narrator's removal from a slave farm in Tennessee to one in Mississippi: "soon they took my cotton dresses and put 'em in a box, and they combed my hair, and I heard them tell me that Mr. Ellison had done come after me" (130). Many details about the slavewoman's clothing are given, notably the shift from her cotton slave garments to a particularly memorable dress, and thereby accentuate her physical and aesthetic appearance. Apparently, Watson transcribes the autobiographer's minute details, allowing her more space than almost any other autobiographer in the whole of his thesis:

> I went in the house, and they had all the glasses around there, and I just turned and looked and looked at myself 'cause I had never seen myself in a glass before. . . . The woman in there went in the trunk and got some domestic and some calico and made me a dress and some drawers and a drawer body. She went to work and made those things for me, and then she told the women . . . take them duds and give them to your sister, and you comb her head and wash her all over. And, Honey, they washed me all over and put them things on me and I was never dressed so fine in my

life. I just thought everybody was looking at me because I was dressed so fine. 'Course they wasn't paying me no mind a tall. The dress had some red in it, and some big flowers in it. I was looking at myself in the glass, and I would pull up my dress and look at my pretty, clean drawers and things, and when I went in the room where my mistress was I pulled it up again, and started looking and saying to myself, "Don't I look nice and clean under here?" and my mistress said, "You mustn't do that; that's ugly." Then I went out in the woods where there was lots of cedars thick around, and I got down there and pulled up my dress and just looked and danced and danced. (130–31)

Ironically, counter to his expressed intentions, Watson's editing demeans his subject as vain and casts suspicion on her piety and femininity. Moreover, the details play into persistent myths about blacks' alleged flamboyance and notorious love of vibrant, "loud" colors.

Watson tacitly suggests that hard on the heels of the narrator's pride is her commission of sin, lust, for the adolescent's absorption and fascination with her developing female body are treated as a kind of homoerotic lechery, a prelude to a breach of chastity. Vanity and impurity further violate the slave era's code of conduct for true (white) women, who were expected to be demure, submissive, disembodied, and *self-less*. Yet, to be sure, the detailed passage presents a profound instance of ego formation: the subject's selflessness at the reconstructed moment becomes infeasible. Indeed, the inclusion of this heavily manipulated reconstruction of an unnamed orphaned slavewoman's budding self-awareness and sexual awakening signals that Watson does not restrict "conversion" to Christian religious transformations.[1] While virtually all of the testimonies in *God Struck Me Dead* conform to the rhetorical conventions of traditional Christian conversion narratives, Watson redefines this incident in the life of a slave girl as a wholly secular occasion conspicuous first, for its emphasis on the body, especially the genitals; second, for its depiction of the slave child's indiscretion and disobedience and thus her feminine impropriety; and third, and perhaps most compellingly, for the manifest candor of her disclosure at age eighty-eight. Thus, the episode could go a long way toward reinscribing fallacies and myths about black (female) bestiality, wantonness, and primitiveness, even at historically black Fisk in the heyday just after the New Negro era.

However, read from a perspective that privileges her African American heritage and her mature piety, the same incident constitutes a powerful spiritual and jubilant episode in a slavewoman's life. Whereas the ideology of true womanhood, represented in this case by the remonstrative slave mistress, requires the slave girl's denial and repression in the name of sanctity and chastity, African American sacred culture makes different demands on her. In *Conversions and Visions*, Kimberly Rae Connor explains the reflexivity of self-affirmation and godliness for black women. She defines as conversion "any confrontation of issues of identity and culture by which a black [woman] claims a sense of self" (3), and cogently argues that "conversion signaled a connection to God and a connection to self—it was an imaginative act of transforming themselves by way of adopting a new image of themselves and of God based on characteristics they chose and knew to be real" (4). Given this, then, in the natural, fertile setting of a grove of cedars, a young slave's exultation in her clean body and in her "private" self marks an encounter with the sacred that an imperceptive interlocutor cannot discern. Just as in the title narrative, this slave girl's story of physical metamorphosis revolves around figures of both theological truth and sexual conceit. As Raboteau has astutely asserted, "Amidst a system bent on reducing them to an inferior status, the experience of conversion rooted deep within the slave converts' psyche a sense of personal value [a sense of divinely created self] and [of] individual importance that helped to ground their identity in the unimpeachable authority of almighty God" (xxv).

Of course, not all black holy women's narratives represent the female body in explicitly sexualized terms. Yet almost all of them do construct a woman's corporeality using the rhetoric of incarnational theology, the Christian tenet of "the Word made Flesh." In her introduction to *Spiritual Narratives*, a collection of early works by black women, Sue Houchins explains that many nineteenth-century African American women, like European female mystics of the medieval period, believed deeply in the union of God with humanity, as taught in essential Christian theology privileging the "embodiment" of God in the person of Christ. Houchins persuasively argues that the erotic imagery of Christian discourse is a logical conclusion of a doctrine teaching that the human body can and should express the power of the Holy Spirit (xxxii–xxxvi). In the antebellum spiritual recollections of her life as a Shaker (i.e., as a member of the Society of True Believers in Christ's Second Coming), Rebecca Jackson uses extraordinarily sensual (and often sensational) discourse, the rhetoric of salvific ecstasy, to describe the fervor of her conversion experience as she moves through the stages of conviction, justification, and redemption. In unexpurgated terms suggesting sexual orgasm, Jackson writes, "And in this moment of despair the cloud bursted, the heavens was [*sic*] clear, and the mountain was gone. My spirit was light, my heart was filled with love for God and all mankind. And the lightning, which was a moment ago the messenger of death, was now the messenger of peace, joy, and consolation. And I . . . opened the door to let the lightning in the house, for it was like sheets of glory to my soul" (72).[2] The climactic moment thus signifies Jackson's sense of union with the divine—a slight irony since Shakers exercised celibacy.

The two women's narratives from *God Struck Me Dead* similarly demonstrate the complexity of narratives incorporating the same theological precept that Houchins cites. They and the other narratives in Watson's collection have received none of the critical acclaim that John Donne has received—we will probably never even know the ex-slaves' names. Yet their narratives are just as worthy of our attention as Donne's works are even though they were dictated to a rather injudicious interlocutor (to whom we are, quite ironically, nevertheless deeply indebted). Just why it is that we know Donne's "Holy Sonnets" but not these particular holy women's stories? One chief reason for the scholarly inattention to this literature is the relatively new access we have had to the texts. Because they have been undervalued in the traditional academy, these works have been unavailable there and in those sites the academy influences. However, due to the interest of the Black Power and Black Arts movements of the 1960s in recovering "lost" black narratives, we have had renewed access to several early black women's spiritual writings for over three decades now. During this time Watson's *God Struck Me Dead* was republished for the first time since its initial 1932 appearance, and such landmark edited anthologies as *The Black Woman*, by Toni Cade, and *Sturdy Black Bridges*, by Roseann Bell and others, were produced. In the 1980s many early African American women's spiritual narratives were republished in such projects as Jean Humez's *Gifts of Power: The Writings of Rebecca Cox Jackson*, Dorothy Sterling's *We Are Your Sisters*, William Andrews's *Sisters of the Spirit*, and Henry Louis Gates's general editorship of the forty-volume Schomburg Library of Nineteenth-Century Black Women Writers series. Such dazzling productions have made Christian conversion narratives written or dictated by black holy women available to twenty-first century readers through mass publication. And it is notable that, perhaps because it emerges from the black historical and literary movements of the 1960s, African Americans have done much of this work.

Yet, for all the new publications, we would do well to heed the words of black feminist historian Darlene Hine, to whom we owe a debt of gratitude for her centrality to the extensive recovery of early black women's literature and history. She admonishes us to assess the limitations of historical scholarship and canon reformation, contending that "it is not enough simply to uncover the hidden facts, the obscure names of black foremothers." Hine calls as well for "the development of an array of analytical frameworks that allow us to understand why black women of all classes behave in certain ways and how they acquired agency" (47).

In speculating about other reasons for the scholarly silence about black women's spiritual writings, I have concluded that this silence is itself the perpetuation of a longer-lived silence: that enshrouding black women as sexual victims in America. That is, there exists a legacy of rape (including marital rape) and domestic abuse of African American women that occurred not only during slavery but throughout our history in America, and at the same time there exists a silence—and separately, a shame—about that sexual violation. For 350 years of American history, the compulsory "breeding" and concubinage of slavewomen were commonplace.[3] Alongside these degradations lay slavewomen's lack of power to select their own sexual partners (of whatever ethnicity or orientation). This legacy continues to victimize black women. For, as Paula Giddings contends, contemporary African American women's disclosure of their sexual violation and exploitation at the hands of African American men constitutes "the last taboo."

The complex feelings of shame, self-contempt, and culpability in the sexual violation of African American women are excruciatingly expressed in Harriet Jacobs's antebellum autobiography, *Incidents in the Life of a Slave Girl.* Jacobs uses the rhetoric of sentimentalism in *Incidents* as a strategy to persuade her white and northern women readers to reconsider blaming the victims of slave concubinage and unwed motherhood for sexual offenses. In the rhetoric of the seduction novel, her narrator confesses her commission of a sexual sin, the seduction of a white man she calls Sands, in order to prevent being raped by her slavemaster. Thus, *Incidents* specifies three major goals it undertakes: to expose the pervasiveness of the sexual assault of slavewomen by their "masters"; to provide incontrovertible evidence that slavewomen desired chastity but, as the "legal" property of others, they could not govern their own sexual fates; and to beseech the reader's pardon for the author's unchaste acts. I would argue, however, that the last of these goals forms an *untrue* confession—that is, I am not convinced that Jacobs sincerely asks readers to judge her relationship with Sands as unchaste. In meeting these goals, Jacobs presents her body as a site of slave infraction and fills *Incidents* with ostensible expressions of contrition to atone for what patriarchal American society would have deemed her breach of virtue. She explicitly expresses her resentment of the slave status that renders her body subject to the will of a man whose power over her is arbitrarily determined. Writing in the middle of the nineteenth century, Jacobs insists that she lost her "self-respect" and thereby challenges the myth that African American women are devoid of modesty and purity. And although telling her story requires her to confess herself a fallen woman and an unwed mother—sentimentalized figures that her (white) women readers would judge as licentious, even lascivious—she is determined to refute the untruth that black women are incapable of moral virtue.

Ironically, after the Civil War, African American women *reversed* Jacobs's and other antebellum blacks' commitment to exposing the heinous crimes perpetrated against slavewomen; instead of unveiling sexual abuse, they masked it. As I related in chapter 5, for example, the postbellum spiritual autobiographer Julia Foote opens *A Brand Plucked from the Fire* with a brief account of her mother's torment when her slavemaster sought to force her into concubinage. While Foote strenuously condemns this attempt at a black woman's sexual violation, the incident is isolated in her text both by its pithy appearance at the outset of the narrative and in the fact that it is the only instance in which she remarks on sexuality at all. Sexual dominance by white men certainly continued to plague black women after the war, but instead of documenting that tyranny, Foote turns against her mother to castigate the ex-slavewoman's maternal and religious shortcomings. Sadly, Foote is representative in her silence about sexuality.[4]

In "Black (W)holes and the Geometry of Black Female Sexuality," a profoundly insightful essay theorizing African American women's (especially lesbians') sexual agency, Evelynn Hammonds summarizes two pertinent historical phenomena that emerged at the end of the nineteenth century. Borrowing Darlene Clark Hine's conceptualization of the "culture of dissemblance," Hammonds explains that African American women developed a particular culture by which to conceal the dominant view of themselves as sexually wanton. A second historical device contrived to protect black women's sexual image is one that Hammonds borrows from Evelyn Brooks Higginbotham, namely the "politics of silence," which African American women developed to deny the myths perpetuated about them as sexual and social beings.[5] Hammonds cogently argues that both the culture of dissemblance and its twin, the politics of silence, "emerged as political strateg[ies] by black women reformers who hoped by their silence and by the promotion of proper Victorian morality to demonstrate the lie of the image of the sexually immoral black woman" (132). Moreover, she rightly concludes that these strategies only *seemed* to put forth black women's thoughts about their bodies and their sexualities while actually they shrouded them in invisibility and secrecy. Unfortunately, the force of late-nineteenth-century black women's desire to be perceived as morally upright and virtuous was so strong that it led them to police each other for "deviant" behavior, ranging from "loose" conduct to streetwalking. The urgency of the perceived need for such patrol generated anthropologist Cesare Lombrosco's *The Prostitute and the Normal Woman* (1893). This "study" of the causes and conditions of prostitution contended that the "source of [prostitutes'] passion and pathology" was located in the genitalia of poor women, which he argued were more primitively structured than affluent women's genitalia (Giddings, "Last Taboo" 419). Lombrosco's classist argument, reinforced by Social Darwinism and scientific racism, is, of course, rank with racial implications. No wonder, then, that black women became obsessed with secrecy, which resulted in their failure to name and characterize their sexualities even among and for themselves.

In further contemplating the reasons that Donne's "Holy Sonnets" are so broadly known but black holy women's narratives are not, and bearing in mind Hine's exhortation that feminist scholars should do more than identify our foremothers, I want to speculate specifically about the role of African American(ist) feminist literary critics and historians in excavating these early narratives. I am struck by a silence that seems to me to parallel the collective silence that Higginbotham analyzes in her work on late-nineteenth-century African American women reformers. I attribute this contemporary silence to an *anxiety of emotionality* that I believe derives in part from the immersion of African American women in the contemporary American academy, perhaps particularly in the discipline of English studies. Although ours is increasingly regarded as a "feminized" profession, the academy remains traditional—eurocentric, androcentric, and phallogocentric—and *secular*—disdainful and fearful at once of spiritual matters. Traditional academicians (and that term regrettably now includes some black feminist scholars) read a false dichotomy between *spiritual* and *rational*, between *religious* and *political* in religious matters, and they disparage these matters as sophistical, untenable, or specious.

In "The Uses of the Erotic," black poet Audre Lorde points to the fallacy of oppositional thinking. In her extraordinary radical way, Lorde calls attention to the indivisibility of the spiritual and the political, the sacred and the secular. Urging the contemplation of a third, too oft-neglected component, the *erotic*, that binds the other two phenomena together, Lorde writes:

we have attempted to separate the spiritual and the erotic, thereby reducing the spiritual to a world of flattened effect, a world of the ascetic who
aspires to feel nothing. But nothing could be farther from the truth. . . .
The dichotomy between the spiritual and the political is also false. . . . For
the bridge which connects them is formed by the erotic—the sensual—
those physical, emotional, and psychic expressions of what is deepest and
strongest and richest within each of us, being shared: the passions of love,
in its deepest meanings. (56)

Of course, not all scholars dismiss spiritual or erotic discussions. Indeed,
more black feminist scholars are beginning to pay unprecedented attention
to black female eroticism and sexuality—Hammonds and Hine perhaps chief
among them. Among literary critics, Hazel Carby, Wahneema Lubiano, Deborah McDowell, and Michele Wallace do this work. Scholarship on black
female sexuality in the social sciences has also been generated by Angela Davis
and bell hooks. So with this scant, though also partial, list of brave scholars,
who represent an infinitesimal fraction of the thousands of professors in this
country, we can see that work on black female sexuality *is* being done. And it
is being done in some instances at professional risk; like Hammonds, I am
painfully aware of how our at-risk status in the academy hinders this work.
As she acknowledges, "Black feminist theorists are themselves engaged in a
process of fighting to reclaim the body—the maimed immoral black female
body—which can be and still is used by others to discredit them as producers
of knowledge and as speaking subjects" (134). Ann duCille has put the matter
more candidly: "In the 1990s . . . the principal sites of exploitation are not simply the cabaret, the speakeasy, the music video, the glamour magazine; they are
also the academy, the publishing industry, the intellectual community" (qtd. in
Hammonds 135).

The personal religious faith or political identification of any individual
scholar notwithstanding, our collective scholarship generally avoids extended
discussion of the *theology* of spiritual narratives by African American holy
women. I believe that most scholars read there a literary trope with which they
are uncomfortable. Perhaps exceptionable in this regard are womanist theologians and historians of religion who have done very useful (preliminary) work
on this figure *without* stultifying their disciplines.[6] Writing this book has allowed me to study the figure of the black holy woman and to consider what I
will call the stereotype of the black church woman.[7] It seems to me that both
the specter of this stereotype and an academy-specific anxiety about "emotion-

ality" and "excess" obstruct scholarship about this figure. When feminist literary critics especially circumvent the idea of the black church woman and neglect to address the intricacies of spirituality and sexuality that she embodies in black holy women's writings, then we risk including a greater sentimentality than we perceive in the allegedly specious texts we would avoid.

Before I proceed, I would like to clarify my own location as a scholar. My work diverges from two specific groups of African American(ist) feminist scholars whose work I admire and esteem. Specifically, the first group is composed of literary critics; the members of the other are womanist religion scholars. Generally, I read the collective work of African American(ist) feminist literary historians as reconstructing the tradition from which contemporary African American women writers emerge. These scholars write revisionary history that challenges and revises the traditional andro- and eurocentric American literary canon, and as archivists or, in Frances Smith Foster's phrase, "literary anthropologists," they uncover "lost" texts by early African American women in order to demonstrate that black women have written or spoken themselves into being in America since the eighteenth century. Reading the wide range of literary genres to which early black women writers contribute, these scholars focus most closely on the social impact of their literary contribution, appraising their work for articulations of black women's collective resistance to race, gender, and material oppression.

Womanist theo-ethicists, as I interpret their work, generally espouse particular systems of thought that argue for black women's inherent morality and that describe the tenets of that moral code. These scholars also read back into black women's history to locate there early texts that illuminate precisely that African American women are moral agents in possession of religious and ethical values, to examine the essence of those values, and to enumerate the processes by which those values are individually and collectively maintained. Although they generally are not archivists themselves, these scholars contribute to the overarching black feminist scholarly project of fully chronicling black women's cultural traditions.

Influenced by the outstanding scholarship of both groups, my own work is situated between that of literary historians and that of womanist theo-ethicists. However, at this apex, instead of reading early black holy women's narratives exclusively to promote their subjects as brave social activists (as literary historians tend to do) or exemplary "nurturing" Christians (as womanist theo-ethicists tend to do),[8] my work reads the early writers as valiant and pious *theologians.* The neglect of current African American(ist) feminist scholarship to discuss the whole importance of early black women's religious writings is ironic not only in that Christianity forms a vital base for African American history, but also in that these narratives first and foremost assert a religious doctrine. Notably, neither group of feminist scholars pays full attention to the theology encoded in nineteenth-century African American women's spiritual autobiographies. Furthermore, I have contemplated exactly why it is that the excellent scholarship of early black women's texts to date is marred by its abrupt halt just at the religion line. It seems to me that literary historians tend to gloss over the theological significance in early black texts, some because of their acceptance of an academic elitism, others because of Marxist influence; both thought systems spurn religion as spurious. On the other hand, womanist theoethicists, many of whom are ordained ministers, belittle the contributions of early black women by sparsely analyzing their texts.

Both groups seem to grapple with a bogeywoman, the stereotype of the black church woman. What—or who—exactly do I mean by "the black church woman"? For me, she is a contemporary variation on the slave plantation mammy[9] as she is imagined in twentieth-century films by actors like Hattie McDaniel and Louise Beavers. In *Uncle Tom's Cabin,* she is Aunt Chloe, the compliant Christian wife of the novel's most earnest preacher, Uncle Tom. The incarnation rarely falters, by whatever name she is called: she is always obese, buxom, faithful, obedient, patient, long-suffering, whole-hearted, open-handed, nurturing, maternal, selfless, and sexless. In *Black Feminist Thought,* Patricia Hill Collins distinguishes her from her white counterpart: "'Good' white mothers are expected to deny their female sexuality and devote their attention to the moral development of their offspring. In contrast, the mammy image is one of an asexual woman, a surrogate mother in blackface devoted to the development of a white family" (72).

It is ironic that the mammy, a stereotype that connotes maternity and domesticity, is also seen as asexual since, obviously, motherhood requires that a woman engage in sexual activity. Nevertheless, the mammy is not seen as a sexual being, nor even as an actual mother (of black children), only as a surrogate mother. However, a contemporary literary variation on the mammy-churchwoman figure, Pauline Breedlove from Toni Morrison's *The Bluest Eye,* is neither chaste nor charitable. Indeed, Pauline first appears in the novel just after sexual intercourse with her husband, Cholly, the novel's villain. In subsequent chapters, Morrison describes her as hypocritical, hostile, and cruel to her own family, but where whites are concerned, she is domestic and willing to serve. Never asexual, Pauline is characterized instead as *hypersensual*—as this description of her pubescent reveries featuring a hazy savior figure illustrates:

In church especially did [her day-]dreams grow. The songs caressed her, and while she tried to hold her mind on the wages of sin, her body trembled for redemption, salvation, a mysterious rebirth that would simply happen, with no effort on her part. In none of her fantasies was she ever aggressive; she was usually idling by the river bank, or gathering berries in a field when a someone appeared, with gentle and penetrating eyes. . . . The someone had no face, no form, no voice, no odor. He was a simple Presence, an all-embracing tenderness with strength and a promise of rest. It did not matter that she had no idea of what to do or say to the Presence. . . . the Presence would know what to do. She had only to lay her head on his chest and he would lead her away to the sea, to the city, to the woods . . . forever. (90)[10]

How did the figure of the black domestic Christian woman come to be sexualized, even hypersexualized? According to Giddings, in the late nineteenth century "difference [between blacks and whites] would be characterized at its most dualistic: as binary opposition—not just in terms of race and sexuality, but of gender and class as well" ("Last" 417). And Cynthia Lyerly provocatively suggests that "perhaps Mammy was created to ease white fears of religious black women" (211).[11] Moreover, the medical profession at the turn of century separated upper-class "ladies" from lower-class/"bad" women: the former were expected not to have erotic feelings—or, if they did, to have their ungovernable sexual urges surgically eradicated through such radical gynecological procedures as clitoridectomies. As Giddings notes, such severe surgeries were necessary to sustain the diametrically opposed identities of "good" women and "bad" women, the latter invariably designated as lower class and very frequently as black ("Last" 418–19).

But if the poor were deemed as "bad," then Mammy, always economically (but never emotionally) destitute, should have been among the worst. If the poor were "bad," why didn't the poorest woman become the most morally depraved? Ironically, instead of soiling her, Mammy's poverty increased her purity and piety. Perhaps this remarkable circumstance is attributable, on the one hand, to the pertinacity of the myth of Mammy's asexuality, and on the other hand, to the overwhelming success of the class-driven campaign of the National Association of Colored Women. The NACW, also known as the black women's club movement, set the standard for African American women's social conduct throughout the end of the nineteenth century and into the twentieth, and this code was precisely the cloak of silence donned in defiance of the myth of African American women's innate licentiousness. Hine reads the intersection of anxiety about propriety and the club movement in her analysis of "the culture of dissemblance," pinpointing its institutionalization with the 1896 formation of the National Association of Colored Women. She writes, "By 1914 the NACW had a membership of 50,000, far surpassing the membership of every other protest organization of the time, including the [NAACP] and the National Urban League. . . . Not surprisingly, the primary targets of the NACW attack were the derogatory images and negative stereotypes of black women's sexuality" (44). Moreover, this attack entailed a more ardent embrace of white middle-class standards of womanly deportment than African American women had ever pursued, effecting an abnegation of racism in late-nineteenth-century black women's discourse. As Claudia Tate has noted about turn-of-the-century black female novelists, "[I]n fictionalizing their gratification of black civil impartiality, these African-American women writers of the post-Reconstruction era centered their narratives on one half of the abolitionist equation—ideal domesticity—while marginalizing, even erasing, the other half—racial subjugation—that compelled them to write" (20). For African American antebellum spiritual autobiographies like Jarena Lee's *Religious Experience and Journal* and Zilpha Elaw's ministerial *Memoirs*, or even Julia Foote's postbellum *A Brand Plucked from the Fire,* such erasure of the essential would have been absurd and infeasible.

Another, perhaps more valid response to the question of the inherent virtue versus the natural depravity of the mammy lies in a class tension that Laura Doyle persuasively argues is "internal to sentimental form itself." Doyle contends that "sentimentality reaches across race lines to create a middle-class position and sympathetic self-image, paradoxically invoking the values of the humble folk to mythologize this alliance among educated-class persons. The race-transcending class bond rests on the simultaneous romanticization and marginalization of the uneducated classes" (175). Surely class figures in *God Struck Me Dead,* considering the glaring gap between the highly educated master's student and the uneducated humble folk who shared their experiences with him. Watson's sentimental treatment of the ex-slaves he interviewed invokes their Christian values to "lift" his (elite) readers to an admiration of their (folk) survival—an irony given the condescension implicit in his gaze and gesture. On the other hand, in the case of Elaw, for example, Doyle's argument yields bizarre meanings. For Elaw's autobiography is self-authored and the author herself is explicitly proud of her early formal education. It signifies on both the resistant white reader and the class-conscious at one point by recalling an experience she had in Alexandria, Virginia: "There were some among the great folks whom curiosity induced to attend my ministry; and this formed a topic of lively interest with many of the slaveholders, who thought it surpassingly strange that a person (and a female) belonging to the same family stock with their poor debased, uneducated, coloured slaves, should come into their territories and teach the enlightened proprietors the knowledge of God" (92). Yet she had emerged from a family so poor that her father had desperately placed her into indentured servitude while she was still quite young. Years later, as a widow of only thirty-three years, Elaw again found her circumstances so reduced that she was forced to place both herself and her small daughter "in different situation[s] of servitude. . . . and remained in service until my health was so impaired that [I] was compelled to relinquish it" (85). Elaw represents the working poor and the virtues of this humble class. Yet her deployment of sentimental conventions works, as I have argued, in much the same way as Stowe's in *Uncle Tom's Cabin,* including her use of the trope of sinful death to instill terror and incite reform. Disparaged by some for her holiness practices, she nonetheless leads "love feasts," charismatic evangelical services that quite likely aroused anxiety about expressions of emotionalism in early American Methodist sects (Frey and Wood 122–23). As Frey and Wood report, "Long after shouting had become institutionalized and ritualized as part of the structure of conversion, black shouting could still incite awe and fear in whites witnessing it for the first time" (123). Elaw implies that many considered her ill-educated, primitive, hysterical, and so on, in the way of all enthusiastic, or charismatic, Christians. In other words, counter to Doyle's assertion that "black writers['] representations and in some cases endorsement of class differences among blacks fostered an ambivalent attachment to 'the folk'" (175), Elaw exemplifies one African American author who does *not* deploy sentimentality to establish class divisions among blacks. If anything, Elaw and other black holy women autobiographers appropriate sentimentalism to break down the class and race categories that divide people not from each other but from Christian salvation. Conversely, though, when Elaw depicts herself grieving her sister's death, it is indeed the conventional image of the innocent, chaste, pure, and pious sentimental heroine that she appropriates and asks readers to pity. So as a sentimentalist she invokes the values of the working (poor) class, "the humble folk" ascribing to the nobler traits of chastity and piety that characterize such classic sentimental figures of womanhood as Rowson's Charlotte Temple and Stowe's Rachel Halliday. Furthermore, while Elaw is able to write her text herself, the autobiographer has much more in common with the working class/humble poor than with the educated elite, who are conceivably Elaw's readers. Thus, she demonstrates that when poor black women deploy sentimental conventions in their representation of evangelical cultures and "enthusiastic" converts, if they are condescending in any exclusionary way at all, perhaps it is toward the willfully recalcitrant—toward those who would read their narratives and ignore the theological implications of them. Contemporary African American(ist) feminist scholars could well be included among such a resistant readership.

After Elaw, the NACW advanced ideals conjoining the discourses of sentimentality and domesticity with Protestant evangelicalism and ancient patriarchal notions of virtuous womanhood that influenced black women's behavior for decades.[12] Lucy Ann Delaney, for example, concludes her 1891 secular autobiography *From the Darkness Cometh the Light* by claiming to have "'made the best use of [her] time' in answering affirmatively the question, 'Can the negro race succeed, proportionately, as well as the whites?' [S]he rested her case in the assertion that her work had been done for the glory of God and the benefit of those 'for whom I live'" (Andrews, "Changing" 238).[13] Delaney and the other race women of the club movement religiously fostered an image of the paradigmatic Victorian woman; she was prim and proper, "straight" and narrow, chaste and benevolent—in a word, "ladylike." Nothing about this model matron vaguely resembles the stereotypical image of Mammy-in-church, or the black church woman. In conceiving the ideal of the Victorian "lady," one thinks of such images of African American post-Reconstruction "upright" womanhood as exemplified by black women like Ida B. Wells-Barnett or Anna Julia Cooper, each of whose lovely visage, erect and dignified, is well-known among academic feminists. These stylized early portraits, picturing them with soft eyes but firm jaws, have become ubiquitous—often purchasable as postcards as proof of their purchasers' liberalism and benevolence.[14] Counter to this unflinching yet unthreatening gaze, the (usually darker-skinned) churchwoman seems always rapt—ensnared, rather—in the throes of passion/The Passion. She exemplifies and *embodies* the sexual energy that is intrinsic in the religious ecstasy Donne's speaker covets in "Holy Sonnet XIV" and illustrates the spiritual release found in Christian churches, specifically some sects of Afro-Protestantism. Her expression of sacred joy and jubilation can take precisely that enigmatic and rare form of rejuvenation that the metaphysical poet prayed for when he wrote, "That I may rise and stand, o'erthrow me, and bend / Your force to break, blow, burn and make me new."

But perhaps this image of black holy women caught "wild" and "unintelligible" at the ecstatic moment is the primary reason that African American(ist) feminist scholars shy away from the spiritual autobiographies of their nineteenth-century foremothers, where narrative representations of the "inspirited" black woman abound. Again, Torgovnick's words in *Primitive Passions* pertain here with stunning irony: "Ecstasy . . . has a sexual register, of harmony and tranquility, which involves stepping outside the self and experiencing the eternal cosmos; but it also has a commonly perceived sexual register, which can be positive (a sign of *eros* or life force) or can be imagined as a state of excess, frenzy, and potential violence" (14–15). Because the academy purports to privilege "reason" over "emotion," and because this figure connotes "irrationality" and "blind faith," and because *black* feminist scholars occupy so precarious a place in the academy, too few of us are willing to attend to the autobiographies where sister-ministers of the Gospel wait for us. One apparent reason African American feminist scholars, descendants of class-privileged club women and race reformers, avoid studying the intersection of spirituality and sexuality in these nineteenth-century Christian texts is that we want further to avoid the double bind we fear we will have to confront, that we will have to choose between, on the one hand, the "academic standards of pragmatism and excellence" that have (tenuously) secured our places in the academy, and on the other hand, allegiance to a common race and gender heritage, to pass again the tiresome authenticity test as to our *"real* blackness." I wonder that we black feminist scholars do not worry that we will find ourselves in concert with traditional academic gynophobia and negrophobia that judge these narrative figures according to the fixed stereotype—as overzealous, untenable, primitive, superstitious, excessive, and emotional.

So finally this book calls for the reading of early black holy women as more than either literary figures or preachers. Our circuitous treatment of the theological accomplishments of these forebears of contemporary African American women's literature strikes me as part of an antifeminist concern that we will be mistaken as arguing for the validity of this stereotype. That is, perhaps we black feminist scholars fear that our work will be read as an attempt to legitimate and thus to authenticate the stereotype as "the genuine article." Or perhaps we worry that we ourselves will be thought to embody the stereotype, that even studying religious women taints us, renders us "too subjective," makes us as "preachy" and "primitive" as our foremothers are said to be. If the academy finds us specious, of course, it will find us superstitious as well; if we are judged uneducated, then surely we will be judged *uneducable* in turn. The specter of the stereotypical black church woman has controlled and circumscribed black feminist scholarship to an immeasurable degree—and altogether unnecessarily.

I would like to consider these two groups of scholars in greater detail. In 1987, on the eve of Oxford University Press's publication of the first reprints in the Schomburg Library of Black Women Writers Series, OUP published Hazel Carby's *Reconstructing Womanhood: The Emergence of the Afro-American Woman Novelist;* this study marked the emergence as well of a number of additional outstanding transformational analyses of early African American women's literature by prominent black feminist literary critics. They are few enough to enumerate here: Joanne Braxton's *Black Women Writing Autobiography* (1989); Claudia Tate's *Domestic Allegories of Political Desire* (1992); Ann duCille's *The Coupling Convention* and Frances Smith Foster's *Written by Herself* (1993); and Carla Peterson's *"Doers of the Word"* (1995). A recent contribution to this stellar list of African American(ist) feminist literary history might be called a crossover study; I refer to historian Nell Painter's biography *Sojourner Truth: A Life, a Symbol.* With the exception of duCille and Tate, who attend exclusively to fiction, the other scholars all address a range of genres employed by black writers, including formulaic spiritual narratives dictated or authored by nineteenth-century African American women.

In these outstanding studies, there is an undercurrent of dis-ease with the theological discourse the scholars encounter in early black women's religious writings. The distinguished scholarship of Foster's 1993 *Written by Herself* provides an example—though more recently, Foster has insisted, "Greater respect for the genius, strength, and resiliency of African American culture would allow different readings of the evangelists who published their religious experiences and . . . the scholars and the theologians who published textbooks, disciplines, and spiritual meditations" (*Minnie's* xxiv). In *Written by Herself,* Foster argues that Elaw's *Memoirs* were conceived as purposefully literary and as an extension of the minister's evangelism. She reads Elaw (and the Baptist missionary Nancy Prince) exclusively as "autobiographical precedents" (83) to the abolitionists Harriet Jacobs and Harriet Wilson, thus effectively citing Elaw's literary achievement and theological argumentation merely to contexualize Jacobs's and Wilson's secular narratives. While *Written by Herself* also analyzes Jarena Lee's spiritual autobiography, brilliantly situating Lee among other early writers, male and female, black and white, sacred and secular, its greater attention is to novelists and secular autobiographers. Like Braxton and Carby, Foster reads black holy women's writing to demonstrate their effect and impact on their social milieu and political climate and to showcase their intrepid resistance to oppression. Similarly, Peterson reads Elaw's *Memoirs* to argue for its overtly political rhetoric and achievement, celebrating Elaw's and her holy sisters' activism for social and political change. Her thesis in *"Doers of the Word"* is precisely that nineteenth-century black women writers in the American North used a variety of rhetorical strategies to effect constructive and widespread resistance to hegemonic oppression.

These scholars exhibit only minimal interest in the women's theology and theological significance. They read early black spiritual autobiographers primarily to argue that the early writers' rhetorical strategies problematized hegemonic definitions of who they were and proscriptions of what they could and should do. This is invaluable scholarship. But by ignoring or depreciating the *theology* of these women's spiritual autobiographies, contemporary scholars perpetuate the academy's proclivity toward keeping the personal and the private outside its walls, as if it *were* possible to sever the personal from the professional. To black feminist studies' celebration of the documentation of black women's political and cultural achievements, I seek to add, and to urge more scholars to add, an appreciation of the theological in their critical frameworks.

The relatively small group of African American(ist) feminist academics who label themselves "womanist theo-ethicists" claim as part of their mission a study of the tradition of writings that reconstruct African American women's religious experiences. As formulated by Katie Cannon, who is perhaps the group's best-known scholar, womanist liberation theo-ethicists "look directly to ancestral cultural material as well as relatively fixed literary forms" (29). In addition, Cannon asserts, they "have a solemn responsibility to investigate the African American women's literary tradition, by asking hard questions and pressing insistently about the responsibility of this canon of books to the . . . consistent and coherent representation of Black existence in contemporary society" (30). These scholars look to twentieth-century African American women's imaginative literature as one set of texts that present a broad spectrum of black women's experiences and of situations in which black women reveal their ethical and moral values. They use those texts, chiefly novels, to theorize who African American women are and what we respect and revere, particularly those values we hold that pertain to Afro-Protestant churches.[15]

Besides Cannon, this small group of prominent womanists includes Delores S. Williams. Cannon and Williams especially have drawn on literary texts by Zora Hurston, Alice Walker, Toni Morrison, and other writers whose stories appear in anthologies edited by black feminist scholar Mary Helen Washington (for example, *Black-Eyed Susans* and *Midnight Birds*). From these texts, they develop womanist "theo-ethics," which I deduce to be a system of integrated cultural, ecclesiastical, moral, and political values asserted and practiced by African American women. Williams argues overtly for the propriety of cross-reading contemporary novels as theological discourse in a note appended to her article "Women's Oppression and Lifeline Politics in Black Women's Religious Narratives." There she states, "In this study, the works of Zora Neale Hurston, Margaret Walker, and Alice Walker are called religious narratives because religious language, religious practices and religious issues help effect the resolution of these plots" ("Women's" 59). Other prominent self-identified womanist theo-ethicists include Cheryl Gilkes, Jacquelyn Grant, Joan Martin, Emilie Townes, and Renita Weems; each of these scholars also seems to be an ordained Afro-Protestant clergywoman. Their scholarly use of early theological narratives consists of parenthetical references cited as proof of black women's traditions of spirituality and of holistic service to others. Rather than assessing them as theologians whose primary aim is to theorize the nature of God and the relationship of God to human beings, and, inversely, the relationship of human beings to God, womanist theo-ethicists generally interpret early black holy women as theo-ethicists like themselves, indeed, as the foremothers to their academic and apostolic enterprise.

They, like literary critics, read the evangelical narratives of such nineteenth-century black holy women as Jarena Lee and Rebecca Cox Jackson as precursors to a variety of contemporary African American women's literary traditions. Yet they make only brief allusion to the autobiographers and tend to gloss over the early authors' appropriation of sentimental and evangelical discourses and of the complex rhetorical strategies they implement in the narrative reconstructions of their lives. Of course, an examination of the trajectory of black women's literature is not the primary aim of womanist ethics studies. However, insisting on the capacity of early black holy women to "nurture" others, womanist-scholars seem collectively (and sentimentally) to attempt to nurture and shield the spiritual autobiographers of the past, as if the autobiographers could not endure serious scholarly scrutiny. If my criticism is valid, this perspective constitutes a deleterious underestimation of the profundity of early African American women's writings.

Nonetheless, juxtaposed against contemporary African American(ist) feminist literary historians, these womanist theo-ethicists pay much more attention to the theological significance of early black women's religious writings.

As ordained ministers and devout Christians, these scholars generally exhibit no anxiety about the notion of Christianity—or any religion—as mere sophistry. Yet while they attend more to early black women's autobiographies as religious doctrine, both collectively and individually, perhaps they do so too cursorily to impact the disciplines of ethics, literature, or theology. Consequently, nineteenth-century narratives need to be analyzed more comprehensively if scholars and students in these disciplines are to appreciate the complexity of their texts and their influence on American life and letters since the antebellum era.

While I greatly appreciate *every* endeavor to interrogate African American women's cultural history, I find a void yet exists in scholarly investigations of early black women's spiritual autobiographies, as yet unfilled by either womanist theo-ethicists or African American(ist) literary historians. As I have speculated, I wonder that this gap does not exist in part because of African American feminist scholars' vexed relationship with the stereotype of the black church woman. There is a plethora of scholarship on this phenomenon in black feminist studies, led by the sociology of Patricia Hill Collins and the cultural criticism of Michele Wallace and bell hooks. The myths about the Mammy-in-church figure derive from those same folk who, as Gloria Wade-Gayles writes, "did not understand that in worship they called 'primitive,' we were respecting and connecting to [and] with the unseen power that governs the universe" (6). Moreover, this figure has been maligned in traditionally canonical literature and popular culture alike by African American critics as dissimilar as writers James Baldwin (in, for example, *The Amen Corner* and *If Beale Street Could Talk*)[16] and Toni Morrison (*The Bluest Eye*), and comedians Flip Wilson and Martin Lawrence.[17] As I have grappled with this problem in my research, confronting it both directly and aslant, I have realized that nineteenth-century holy women's narratives can help us to debunk the stereotype. Reading for theological rather than—or as well as—political, social, literary, or cultural significance requires attention to what early black holy women writers assert and instruct about who and how "God" is and about the kinds of relationships humans (should) have with the divine. Although the specter of the black church woman is often seen by critics as obstructing such work, the writings in question often deconstruct and demythologize her. Therefore, these women writers warrant scholarly regard as theologians and thinkers. We need never again restrict their significance to "social work" of any kind. These evangelical authors were far too radical and visionary for so narrow a relegation.

Perhaps the stereotype of the black church woman is one that we have internalized. However, when we black women declare ourselves "spiritual," we are not thereby also proclaiming ourselves fatuous and daft, self-sacrificing and sentimental, untutored or that worst of all womanly traits, "emotional." "Emotional" is one more false constriction the academy places on African American scholars, especially black *women* scholars—just as charges of the genre's use of "excessive emotion" impeded critical analyses of sentimental literature for so long. For as Sue Campbell asserts in a brilliant essay, "The Politics of Emotional Expression," in which she invokes the myths used against us: "Women who are not emotional are cold. Women who are emotional are expressing themselves in such a way as to be dismissable" (62). I have written this book in part to urge black women in the academy to recognize that class and color (but significantly not "race") divisiveness hurt us when they circumscribe our attention to ourselves as subjects of study. Charges of "sentimentality" and "emotionality" limit the expression of cultural, spiritual, and private experience; with these charges, we police each other and "at the same time, allow for the dismissal of what is significant to women about our own lives when this significance is a violation of the constraints on gender performance" (Campbell 63). The result is a loss of expressive power we cannot afford. Like Giddings, Hammonds, and others, I urge black feminist scholars, free from the restrictions that have previously bound us, especially to continue the essential work of theorizing African American women's spirituality and our sexuality. Giddings reminds us that it is because our evasion of thought and talk about sex and spirit, even among ourselves, has been so complete that "to break through the silence and traditional sense of [race, gender, and spiritual] solidarity is such a controversial act for us" ("Last" 423). Until we act controversially and courageously, African American holy women's writings will not be thoroughly explored. John Donne's works will remain in the canon, and our own sacred works will remain unknown. Until we act, each of us risks being dismissed, discounted, disregarded, disadvantaged, and disrespected. Through our efforts, then, we can raise the voices of our black foremothers to be heard by all in both their secular and their sacred glory.

NOTES

Preface

1. "The twelve were with [Jesus], as well as certain women who had been cured of evil spirits" (Luke 8:1–2).

Introduction. Sympathy and Revolution

1. Belinda won her case, and the General Court soon awarded her "an annual pension of some fifteen pounds out of the expropriated rents and profits of her former master" (Kaplan and Kaplan 244). However, after a single year of receiving the pension, she could gain only one additional year's relief; securing it required a second appeal to the legislature in 1787. Royall's mansion and slave quarters, the only remaining in the American Northeast and the place where Belinda undoubtedly lived, still stands in Medford, Massachusetts.

2. Scholars have not definitively determined that Belinda was not literate. Kaplan and Kaplan reproduce a facsimile of Belinda's second petition, which bears her "mark," thus suggesting she was illiterate. For a scholarly discussion of the fine line between dictated slave narrative and *bona fide* autobiography, see Rampersad.

3. The editors of *Root of Bitterness: Documents of the Social History of American Women* point to an explosive "spread of basic education and consequent literacy for women in the middle to late eighteenth century. The publication revolution, of which literacy was a part, was only one of the revolutions that rocked this era" (xviii). In *Nineteenth-Century Women Learn to Write*, Catherine Hobbs reports: "At the start of the nineteenth century perhaps half or more white women qualified as reading at some level, compared to men's illiteracy rate of only 25 percent. Nonetheless, by 1870 women had nearly equalled men in basic literacy, with women's illiteracy rates only one percentage point above men's 9 percent. Immigrant, Latino, Native American, and southern women remained behind them. African American women, many of them prohibited by law from reading and writing just when white women were making great strides in literacy, ended the century about where white women had begun it" (2). Hobbs also links the religious revivals of the Great Awakenings to a mid-nineteenth-century education explosion, and

emphasizes the tendency of all races and whites of all stations to exploit literacy for their own social advantage (6). For more on eighteenth-century and nineteenth-century American literacy, see Cornelius (especially on slave literacy) and Graff.

4. See Gates's account of the difficulties faced by Phillis Wheatley as chronicled in "In Her Own Write," the foreword to each text in the Schomburg Library of Nineteenth-Century Black Women Writers (vii–xxii).

5. This does not mean, of course, that blacks were uninterested in telling stories. Indeed, the black impulse for storytelling is clear in the extensive body of folk literature preserved orally since the arrival of blacks in the Americas (though not collected in written form until the 1890s).

Scholars now believe that the first black fiction published in America was Frederick Douglass's novella "The Heroic Slave."

6. Carretta argues that most eighteenth-century blacks expressed greater loyalty to England than to America, "taking advantage of the British promises of emancipation for refugee slaves of the colonial rebels. . . . Of the half-million Blacks in the thirteen colonies, the overwhelming majority of whom were slaves, approximately five thousand served the colonists' cause while tens of thousands, perhaps as many as one hundred thousand, were lost to the British, though many of those remained as slaves under Loyalist masters" (6–7).

7. For a comprehensive publication history of Gronniosaw's *Narrative*, see Potkay and Burr.

8. For more on the development of African American literary traditions, see Gates, *The Signifying Monkey*. For a discussion of the critical controversy surrounding the formation of a black *women's* literary tradition, see Henderson, "Speaking in Tongues."

9. See Andrews, *To Tell a Free Story*. See also Andrews' introduction to *African American Autobiography*, 1–7.

10. In the Revolutionary spirit, additional petitions were filed by individual and groups of white women. For instance, Esther DeBerdt Reed petitioned George Washington in a tract titled "The Sentiments of an American Woman" and published in 1780; it drew the support of 1,645 women for the Revolutionary War effort. A century before, Mary Easty, condemned to die at Salem for witchcraft, had appealed to the governor and magistrates of Massachusetts on May 20, 1692, to free other alleged witches. See Harris, 251–67.

11. The terms also suggest the age-old rape of the women of nations at war, intended as much an offense to the opposing men as to the women themselves, as well as the more recent sexual torture perpetrated especially against women during the Middle Passage and throughout antebellum slavery. For more on sexual violence in military contexts, see Susan R. Grazel, Beverly Allen, and Kristin Hoganson.

12. While the critique of early American (white) women's sentimental novels that apparently reinscribe patriarchal norms falls outside the reach of this study, I believe such scholarship to be invaluable. As Harris contends in *American Women Writers to 1800*,

"Texts that at times perpetuate dominant-culture ideologies must be studied carefully: first, because *all* women—acquiescent or radical—had to struggle with those ideologies; second, as a means of better understanding the conditions (ideological and material) under which women produced their texts; and third, because those ideologies are often subverted textually" (6).

13. See also Samuels, *Romances of the Republic*.

14. My discussion of Paine and *Common Sense* is greatly informed by Barnes's article, but our goals are not the same. Here I am more concerned than Barnes with the implications of the domestic discourse as used by some male authors in the Revolutionary era and the effects of the rampant antifeminism signified by those men's deployment of that discourse.

15. While not precisely interchangeable, domesticity and sentimentalism are conflated because they attend in similar ways to white, middle-class women's issues as well as to an ideology of "separate spheres" between men and women. For example, Romero references their close association thusly: "Traditionally, [cultural authorities] have used domesticity and its cultural offspring (denominated variously as 'sentimentalism,' 'women's fiction,' or 'the domestic novel') in order to demarcate a stable divide between a 'subversive' high cultural tradition and a 'conservative' popular cultural tradition in the United States with origins in the mid-nineteenth century" (1).

16. For another example of men's uses of American sentimentalism, see Foster's discussion of the "romantic" (i.e., sentimental) tropes of *A Narrative of the Lord's Wonderful Dealings with John Marrant, a Black* (1788), a dictated hybrid autobiography that combines conventions of the slave, conversion, and captivity narrative in a single document (*Written* 64–67).

17. For an analysis of ways that the Declaration of Independence set up reunion, see Wald.

18. Cf. Douglas, Tompkins, Gillian Brown, and Samuels.

19. One of the early American novels most enthusiastically recovered in recent years is Tabitha Tenney's *Female Quixotism*, an antisentimental novel first published in 1801. This satire spoofs Tenney's American sentimentalist contemporaries, both male and female, and also such "great" literary precursors as Cervantes. Also, Elizabeth Barstow Stoddard has recently been read as refusing to walk the sentimental Christian path laid out for European American women writers; see Croce. The first known fiction texts by African American women were published in 1859, and both *Our Nig,* a novel by Harriet E. Wilson, and "The Two Offers," a short story by Frances E. W. Harper, were sentimental fictions.

20. For more on these novels and their readerships, see Davidson. Some argue that neither novel unequivocally espouses a feminist agenda. Conversely, Ryals argues that Rowson's novel is not a sentimental text. For a reading of *Charlotte Temple* as a feminist novel that inspired antifeminist violence against both text and author, see Tompkins, "Susanna Rowson."

21. *The Power of Sympathy: or, the Triumph of Nature* is the title of the 1789 American novel by William Hill Brown that Barnes's article discusses at length. Brown implies that sympathy and sentimental texts that advocate or arouse sympathy eventually impair a society by nullifying its members' power of free will.

22. Romero explains that "the death of one or both parents or the abandonment of children is a compelling donnee for women novelists because it provides an opportunity for distinguishing between character and conduct. Only with the parent absent can the child's internalization of principle be gauged" (27). Korobkin cogently demonstrates that lawyers' *stories*, like novels, are designed "to elicit deeply emotional, personal responses" from jurors. See her *Criminal Conversations* for more on the deployment of sentimentalism in American legal cases. For an important discussion of the trope of the orphan in early American literature, including Christian conversion narratives, see Pacinky.

23. This is not to say that European American women writers did not also transform the stuff of their actual lives in fictions: feminist scholars have established that Rowson modeled Montraville, Charlotte's seducer, for example, on her own capricious spouse, and that Foster narrativized the destruction of her actual relative Elizabeth Whitman in her roman à clef chronicling the demise of protagonist Eliza Wharton.

24. Belinda's petition seems to correspond to the legal form of a complaint, the proper language of which virtually always includes a clause indicating that the plaintiff "prays" for a certain amount or kind of remuneration. Given this, the final clause "and she will ever pray" assumes even greater irony. I am grateful to Shileen Dupre for this insight.

25. My discussion of theology is informed by the definition of the term in Blair et al., eds., *The Feminist Companion to Literature in English*, 1069–71.

26. For more on the dismissal of feeling and of women as "hyperemotional," see Sue Campbell. I return to the phenomenon of religious ecstasy in the conclusion.

27. For an excellent analysis of nineteenth-century myths about the black body, see Felipe Smith.

28. Recently, several scholarly texts have appeared treating Roman Catholics in the 1800s, some paying close attention to African American nuns of the antebellum era. See, for example, Posey, Ryan, and Raboteau, *A Fire in the Bones*.

29. For more on the numbers of African American converts to Methodism during the Great Awakenings, see Campbell, *Songs of Zion* and Frey and Wood, *Come Shouting to Zion*.

30. Foster describes eighteenth-century African American spiritual narratives as also influenced by African praisesongs, citing in the former such elements of the latter as "statements of self-identity as well as historical accounts of ancestral lives and times" (64).

31. Paul Goodman's account of the tremendous progress made by African Americans in the Northeast during the early decades of the nineteenth century suggests a surge in the numbers of black readers as well as a proliferation of black-authored texts: "In Philadelphia, for example, the number of black churches grew from five to sixteen between

1813 and 1837, monuments [of] ... black devotion to Christian faith. Likewise, the number of beneficial societies throughout the country mushroomed from 11 in 1811 to 43 by 1831 and 110 by 1838. . . . Blacks had long looked to education as a key to uplifting the race, and despite white resistance, by 1837 two-thirds of the black children of Philadelphia attended public schools" (23).

32. Preceding Belinda and the other women I discuss in this book, there had been a long tradition of British dissenting women in England, of course. Perhaps the example most pertinent to this context is the England-born American Quaker Elizabeth Ashbridge, who published her brief spiritual autobiography in 1755.

33. See Moody, "On the Road With God," and Raboteau, "African-Americans, Exodus, and the American Israel."

34. For statistics on the numbers of nineteenth-century African American readers, see Cornelius.

35. I borrow the phrase "sensational designs" from Tompkins's 1985 title.

Chapter 1. (Im)Personal Complaints: Maria Stewart

1. Unless otherwise noted, quotations from Stewart's early works refer to the *Productions*, ed. Houchins. Cited internally hereafter.

2. Richardson notes that this statement is "a paraphrase of the words of Simeon at Jesus' circumcision (Luke 2:25–29)" (125).

3. For fuller discussion of Stewart's struggle to be compensated for her husband's military service, see Richardson, 79–85 and 91–93.

4. All quotations from the 1879 preface and "Sufferings During the War" come from *Maria W. Stewart, America's First Black Woman Political Writer,* ed. Richardson. Cited internally hereafter.

5. Stewart repeatedly faced destitution; "the distress of our heroine," she writes, often "became [so] extreme" that she was forced to turn to others for relief. Among African Americans who knew her, however, Stewart notes, "The say was, 'She belongs to white folks' church, let them take care of her'" (102). Whenever she appealed to Hall, though, he apparently assisted her.

Chapter 2. Sin-Sick Souls: Jarena Lee and Zilpha Elaw

1. According to Collier-Thomas, "at least three thousand copies of [*The Life and Religious Experience of Jarena Lee, a Coloured Lady*] were printed and distributed" between 1836 and 1849 (45).

2. The African Methodist Episcopal Church's Book Concern was assembled within the first twenty-five years of the formation of the denomination. According to Foster, "One of the first acts of the newly established African Methodist Episcopal Church was to establish a school for children and adults. In 1817, it created the AME Book Concern

to make sure that appropriate reading materials were available, and since then virtually every African American denomination has created its own publishing company" (*Minnie* xxv). Most operative here, of course, is the notion of "appropriate reading materials" since it was on the grounds of impropriety that Lee's petition was denied.

3. It would seem that in this slave state, white (or perhaps white-appearing) men were sold as slaves.

4. Here, Lee seems to suggest that Sharp's daughter had been hardened by the murders she had endured in her family.

5. As Andrews notes, the northern-born women's excursions into slave territory were extremely dangerous in the antebellum era, primarily because they were subject to incarceration or being sold into slavery if they could not certify their free status upon demand. Moreover, since the early nineteenth century, some states, including Virginia (where the two ministers frequently preached), "prohibited any slave or free Negro from conducting religious meetings. . . . Elaw's [and Lee's] punishment for breaking this law would have been a public whipping of up to thirty-nine lashes" (*Sisters* 241).

Chapter 3. Rejecting Sentimentalism: Nancy Prince

1. Thomas Pringle, original editor of Prince's *History*, recorded Prince's note that her "owners" Captain and Mrs. I—— sometimes facetiously referred to her as "Mary, Princes of Wales." "It is a common practice for the colonists to give ridiculous names to their slaves; being, in fact, one of the numberless modes of expressing the habitual contempt with which they regard the negro race" (Ferguson, *History* 84). In the *Oxford Companion to African American Literature*, Sandra Pacquet notes the importance of naming to Mary Prince by listing the various ways she indicated she was identified: Mary Prince was "also known as Molly Wood, Mary James, or Mary, Princess of Wales" (599).

2. Throughout this chapter, I use "missionary" to characterize Prince's religious activity. I have been unable to find any source that definitively certifies Prince's official membership in the interdenominational American Board of Commissioners for Foreign Missions or in the separate missionary society that Baptists had established in 1814. Nowhere in her *Narrative* does Prince apply the term to her own work.

3. See also Sánchez-Eppler, "Bodily Bonds."

4. An interesting contrast to Nancy Prince can be found in Charlotte Forten Grimké, who might be considered a secular missionary. Born in Philadelphia into an affluent and prestigious New England abolitionist family, Forten traveled to the Sea Islands of South Carolina to teach recently freed blacks during the Civil War. For more on Forten's class consciousness and travel experiences, see Brenda Stevenson's introduction to the Schomburg edition of Forten's diaries.

5. See, e.g., Sterling. On the number of extant slave documents, Andrews recently reported: "Marion Wilson Starling, one of the slave narratives' most reliable historians, has estimated that a grand total of all contributions to this genre, including separately

published texts, materials that appeared in periodicals, and oral histories and interviews, numbers approximately six thousand" ("Narrating" 15).

6. In chapter 4, I focus exclusively on the relationships between slave narrators and their amanuenses and attend more fully to representations of blackness.

7. Details of Prince's life are based on the outstanding historiography and biographical research conducted by Moira Ferguson.

8. According to a compendium of *American Religious Creeds*, "The Moravian Covenant in its original form was adopted by the Moravian Church at Herrnbut, Saxony, as the Brotherly Agreement on May 12 of the year that marked the Church's spiritual renewal, 1727." Its members "believe that Christ is present with us in Word and Sacrament" and "hold to the principles: 'In essentials, unity; in non-essentials, liberty; and in all things, charity'" (qtd. in Melton, 258).

9. For more discussion of Prince's sexuality, see Ferguson, *History*, 4–18.

10. This would have been an especially important necessity, given that Pringle maligned her in his appendix through several ambiguous statements. As Andrews notes, though Pringle praised Mary Prince's "decency," he also observed "that the former slave had 'a somewhat violent and hasty temper, and a considerable share of natural pride and self-importance.' He labels these traits 'defects' of her character, though they do not keep him from judging her 'on the whole as respectable and well-behaved a person in her station, as any domestic, white or black'" (*Six Women's* xxxiii).

11. I am grateful to John C. Caruso for making me aware of this New Testament allusion.

12. Cf. *A Room of One's Own*, in which Virginia Woolf writes about the devastation that develops from a feminist's encounters with antifeminism: "For it needs little skill in psychology to be sure that a highly gifted girl who had tried to use her gift for poetry would have been so thwarted and hindered by other people, so tortured and pulled asunder by her own contrary instincts, that she must have lost her health and sanity to a certainty" (qtd. in Eagleton 74). See also Alice Walker, *In Search of Our Mothers' Gardens*.

13. Cf. Zora Neale Hurston's 1942 memoir *Dust Tracks on a Road*. Also see Hazel Carby's excellent essay on Hurston's *Their Eyes Were Watching God*.

Chapter 4. Slavery's Sinners: Mattie J. Jackson

1. For more on the distinction between antebellum and postbellum slave narratives, see Andrews, "Representing Slavery."

2. Although Thompson's name appears on the title page as the author of *The Story of Mattie J. Jackson*, I regard Jackson and Thompson as co-authors. *The Story* forms a shared project between a preliterate woman and a formally educated one. Additional scholarship on dictated narratives and slave literacy is desperately needed in American literary studies. Exemplary contributions like Lindon Barrett's begin to address these

neglected issues, but even Barrett's very useful article in *American Literary History* does not distinguish between self-authored narratives and dictated ones.

3. The exact year of Jackson's birth is not provided, and while the autobiography denotes Jackson's age at several points, the dates given for the year of her birth conflict. From the various ones cited in *The Story*, Jackson seems to have been born between 1840 and 1846. The narrator's inability to stipulate her exact date of birth exposes one of the dehumanizing effects of slavery; as she states at the outset, "I cannot give dates, as my progenitors, being slaves, had no means of keeping them" (5).

4. Thompson's prefatory note presumably constitutes her only contribution to *The Story* in her own voice. By appending her "Note" to what seems to be Jackson's dictated preface, Thompson diverges from a racist practice common in slave narratives prepared by oft well-intentioned white amanuenses. In these, as Couser has noted, "white editors often literally had the first and last words." This meant that "the format designed to attack the most virulent form of institutional racism in America itself enacted a form of discrimination and domination" (*Altered* 120). Thompson apparently avoids this practice by providing Jackson herself with the "first words" of her autobiography in situating Jackson's preface before her own "Note."

5. A similar use of the bandwagon stratagem in dictated antebellum ex-slave narratives is described by Andrews in *To Tell a Free Story*, 113.

6. For a provocative analysis of rhetorical strategies of survival in black women's autobiographies, see Nellie Y. McKay, "The Narrative Self."

7. Tate points to the fragility of slave marriages when she writes, "Slave women had no claim on the institution of marriage at all, as the parodic ceremonies on matrimonial solemnity—'to jump the broom' or 'marry in blankets'—suggest" (25).

8. See Tompkins's essay of the same name in *Sensational Designs*.

9. "Resistant orality" is Mullen's phrase. For a thorough discussion of black women's use of sass and invective as expressions of "outraged motherhood," see Braxton.

10. For more on self-erasure in early black women's autobiography, see Moody, "Twice Other, Once Shy."

11. A similar sign appears in the autobiography of Harriet Tubman.

12. For a discussion of the fundamental differences between slave narratives by men and those by women, see Foster, "In Respect to Females." For a discussion of differences between men's autobiographies and women's autobiographies, particularly with regard to individual exploits and collective identity, see Friedman.

13. See also Mae Henderson's outstanding article on heteroglossia and dialogism in black women's writing.

14. Jackson's *Story* follows this verse of the song with three different others.

15. Although Campbell's argument offers useful insight into the differences between men's and women's discourses generally, it is also important to note that many sentimentalists lavish their texts with sarcasm. Stowe is an obvious example.

16. In this way, Jackson's autobiography anticipates the black feminist liberation the-

ology of later holy women. See especially Delores S. Williams's womanist hermeneutic as applied to the Old Testament Hagar-Sarah texts in *Sisters in the Wilderness.*

17. Andrews has argued persuasively that Brown's rhetorical apology for his trickery is similarly insincere. See *To Tell,* 148–50. See also Couser, *Altered Egos,* 131–35.

18. Thompson further reveals her intention to depict Jackson's reversal of fortune, her class evolution from slavegirl to free lady, when she reconstructs Jackson's reunion with Lewis after the Civil War. By describing the former slaveholder as "so surprised that before he was aware of it he dropped a bow" (37), Thompson implies that as a free woman, Jackson's deportment is such that she induces respect from everyone.

19. Thompson depicts herself as a prominent physician partly by having the narrator characterize her stepmother as professionally in demand: "I did not imagine she could find time to write and arrange [my story]" (36).

20. For a discussion of surface and submerged plots in women's conversion narratives, see Brereton, 28–33.

21. The phrase is borrowed from Andrews's book.

22. Cf. Couser, *Altered Egos,* 153–55.

Chapter 5. Thunderous Daughter: Julia Foote

1. Throughout her autobiography, Elaw vividly portrays a loving relationship between her own daughter and herself.

2. All citations refer to *A Brand Plucked from the Fire* as it appears in Andrews, ed., *Sisters of the Spirit.* Foote published a second edition of her autobiography in 1886, but made no changes in the text. The latter edition was reissued in 1988 in Houchins, ed., *Spiritual Narratives.*

3. For a psychoanalytic reading of Foote's relationship with her mother, especially based on the incident of the beating of her mother in bondage, see Fleischner.

4. The contrasting images of the drunken child and the sanctified child proves Sánchez-Eppler's observation that "the nineteenth century largely experienced childhood sin and sinlessness simultaneously. . . . the authors of juvenile religious fiction held an unstable double vision of children's relation to religion, at once seeing the child as naturally depraved and as naturally angelic" ("Raising Empires" 409).

5. Brereton writes, "In some cases narrators could pinpoint their conversion to a certain day or hour; the popular notion was that it took place in an identifiable instant. In other cases, however, conversion happened more slowly, over a period of days or weeks or months, during which the anxiety associated with conviction gradually abated" (8).

6. Foote's commitment to racial uplift occasions her speaking out about African American education, especially from the pulpit, rendering highly ironic Linda Kerber's observation that "skepticism was voiced with more delicacy [than suspicion about learned blacks and white women was voiced]; no minister thundered from the pulpit that the learned woman was necessarily masculine" (*Intellectual History* 256).

7. See Korobkin's discussion of the ways that the narrator's direct address to the reader functions in sentimental literature as a means of interpreting readers' lives and creating the sentimental contract between author and text.

8. I am grateful to John C. Caruso for his insight into the use of the chiasmus in slave narratives.

9. For a discussion of the history of the tradition of sanctification and holiness practices, see Collier-Thomas and Brereton. For a discussion of Foote's interpretation of sanctification, see Collier-Thomas, 57–63.

10. Cf. Brereton, who argues that white women no less than women of color used Protestant evangelicalism to defy restrictive social standards.

Conclusion. Spirit and Ecstasy

1. Cf. Brereton's chapters on such "conversion narratives" as women's feminist consciousness-raising accounts and lesbians' coming-out stories.

2. For more on Jackson's rhetorical strategies, see Sasson. For a provocative analysis of lesbian homoerotic discourses and practices in Shaker literature and religion, see McCully.

3. Cf. Hine's analysis of slave women's resistance to sexual domination. She concludes, "Therefore, when they [i.e., slavewomen] resisted sexual exploitation through such means as sexual abstinence, abortion, and infanticide, they were, at the same time, rejecting their vital economic function as breeders" (34).

4. I am deeply grateful to Carla Peterson for her suggestion that the exposé of sexual violence against black women might have appeared at least in the African American novel if not also in other literary genres like the spiritual autobiography. Pauline Hopkins's *Contending Forces* is one work in which this exposé appears.

5. Hammonds cites the "culture of dissemblance" as a term coined by Darlene Clark Hine in *Hine Sight* and the "politics of silence" as a term that comes from Evelyn Brooks Higginbotham.

6. See, e.g., Gilkes.

7. See also Trudier Harris's definitions of "Churchwoman" and "Matriarch" in *The Oxford Companion to African American Literature.*

8. I cite "nurturing" from Williams's *Sisters in the Wilderness.*

9. For a discussion of this stereotype and the ways it has been deconstructed in recent feminist scholarship, see Collins.

10. All ellipses except the last were added to this passage.

11. Lyerly offers a cogent and compellingly different response to my question. She argues that in the early eighteenth century, "proslavery whites would invent a pious, proslavery black female persona to defend the peculiar institution. The fact that she bears little resemblance to religious women in [the post-Revolutionary era], and likely to religious women of later antebellum years, should give us pause. If Jezebel was cre-

ated to assuage white guilt, perhaps Mammy was created to ease white fears of religious black women. If religious slave women were also docile, loyal, and content as slaves, there would be no reason to fear the effects of religion on bondwomen. And there would be no need to feel discomfort about religious slave women if whites could calm their fears by recounting the fable of Mammy" (211).

12. For a feminist theological discussion of the subjugation of women in early Christianity, see Buchanan, chapter 2.

13. As Andrews further notes, however, Delaney makes it clear that living for others "does not include indiscriminate self-abnegation to any and all 'others'" (238).

14. What Painter writes about Sojourner Truth is applicable as well to all manner of commodification of African American women's history: "As a work composed to raise money, Truth's *Narrative* belonged to a recognizable subgenre of black autobiography. In this regard, it resembled the tokens that recipients of charity still offer to givers. . . . Well-intentioned reformers went to hear Sojourner Truth present herself as a slave mother and bought copies of her little book to express solidarity, to contribute to her well-being, and to indicate their own relative position and status in society" (473–74).

15. Cannon, a Presbyterian minister, has also disclaimed any intention on her part "to read theo-ethical meaning into texts but [instead she seeks] to resonate with what is there. By respecting the autonomy of the novel and short story as literary art, I do not explain African American women's literature away by referencing it to Christian symbolic function nor do I dwell on thematic elements that are traditionally related to religious beliefs and moral conduct" (30).

16. In *Sisters in the Wilderness,* Williams writes: "In some African American literary history following the antebellum period, black writers infer that [a] kind of God-consciousness and God-dependence supporting black mothers is problematic. They suggest that for some black mothers, this consciousness and dependence created needs that could only be fulfilled within the limits of the black mother's religion. James Baldwin . . . demonstrated this in a scene in his novel *If Beale Street Could Talk.* Here, a black Christian woman can only make love to her husband by psychologically substituting God for the husband. Thus, the woman's pillow talk is also her god-talk, from which the husband is excluded" (41).

17. For more on the critique of Protestantism in African American literature, see Fontenot.

WORKS CITED

Allen, Beverly. *Rape Warfare: The Hidden Genocide in Bosnia-Herzegovina and Croatia.* Minneapolis: U of Minnesota P, 1996.

Allinson, Mark. "Re-Visioning the Death Wish: Donne and Suicide." *Mosaic* 24.1 (Winter 1991): 31–46.

Ammons, Elizabeth. "Stowe's Dream of the Mother-Savior: *Uncle Tom's Cabin* and American Women Writers Before the 1920s." *New Essays on Uncle Tom's Cabin.* Ed. Eric Sundquist. New York: Cambridge UP, 1986.

Andrews, William L., ed. *African American Autobiography: A Collection of Critical Essays.* Englewood Cliffs, N.J.: Prentice Hall, 1993.

———. "The Changing Moral Discourse of Nineteenth-Century African American Women's Autobiography: Harriet Jacobs and Elizabeth Keckley." *De/Colonizing the Subject: The Politics of Gender in Women's Autobiography.* Ed. Sidonie Smith and Julia Watson. Minneapolis: U of Minnesota P, 1992. 225–41.

———. Introduction. *Six Women's Slave Narratives.* Ed. Andrews. New York: Oxford UP, 1988. xxix–xli.

———. "Narrating Slavery." *Teaching African American Literature: Theory and Practice.* Ed. Maryemma Graham, et al. New York: Routledge, 1998. 12–30.

———. "The Representation of Slavery and the Rise of Afro-American Literary Realism 1865–1920." *Slavery and the Literary Imagination.* Ed. Deborah E. McDowell and Arnold Rampersad. Baltimore: Johns Hopkins UP, 1989. 62–80.

———, ed. *Sisters of the Spirit: Three Black Women's Autobiographies of the Nineteenth Century.* Bloomington: Indiana UP, 1986.

———. *To Tell a Free Story: The First Century of Afro-American Autobiography, 1760–1865.* Urbana: U of Illinois P, 1986.

———. "Toward a Poetics of Afro-American Autobiography." *Afro-American Literary Studies in the 1990s.* Ed. Houston A. Baker Jr. and Patricia Redmond. Chicago: U of Chicago P, 1989. 78–91.

Andrews, William L., et al., eds. *The Oxford Companion to African American Literature.* New York: Oxford UP, 1997.

Armstrong, Nancy. "Why Daughters Die: The Racial Logic of American Sentimentalism." *Yale Journal of Criticism* 7.2 (Fall 1994): 1–24.

Barnes, Elizabeth. "Affecting Relations: Pedagogy, Patriarchy, and the Politics of Sympathy." *American Literary History* 8.4 (Winter 1996): 597–614.

———. *States of Sympathy: Seduction and Democracy in the American Novel.* New York: Columbia UP, 1997.

Barrett, Lindon. "African-American Slave Narratives: Literacy, the Body, Authority." *ALH* 7.3 (1995): 415–42.

Belinda. "Petition of an African Slave, to the Legislature of Massachusetts." 1782? *American Women Writers to 1800.* Ed. Sharon M. Harris. New York: Oxford UP, 1996. 253–55.

Bentley, Nancy. "White Slaves: The Mulatto Hero in Antebellum Fiction." *American Literature* 65.3 (Sept. 1993): 501–22.

Beverley, John. "The Margin at the Center: On *Testimonio* (Testimonial Narrative)." Smith and Watson 91–114.

Blair, Virginia, Patricia Clements, and Isobel Grundy, eds. *The Feminist Companion to Literature in English: Women Writers from the Middle Ages to the Present.* New Haven: Yale, 1990.

Blight, David W., ed. *Narrative of the Life of Frederick Douglass, an American Slave: Written by Himself.* By Frederick Douglass. 1845. Boston: Bedford Books, 1993.

Braxton, Joanne M. *Black Women Writing Autobiography: A Tradition Within a Tradition.* Philadelphia: Temple UP, 1989.

Brereton, Virginia L. *From Sin to Salvation: Stories of Women's Conversions, 1800 to the Present.* Bloomington: Indiana UP, 1991.

Brown, Gillian. *Domestic Individualism: Imagining Self in Nineteenth-Century America.* Berkeley: U of California P, 1990.

Brown, William Wells. *From Fugitive Slave to Free Man: The Autobiographies of William Wells Brown.* Ed. William L. Andrews. New York: Mentor, 1993.

Buchanan, Constance. *Choosing to Lead: Women and the Crisis of American Values.* Boston: Beacon, 1996.

Burgett, Bruce. *Sentimental Bodies: Sex, Gender, and Citizenship in the Early Republic.* Princeton: Princeton UP, 1998.

Caldwell, Patricia. *The Puritan Conversion Narrative: The Beginnings of American Expression.* New York: Cambridge UP, 1983.

Campbell, Karlyn Kohrs. "Style and Content in the Rhetoric of Early Afro-American Feminists." *Quarterly Journal of Speech* 72 (1986): 434–45.

Campbell, Sue. "Being Dismissed: The Politics of Emotional Expression." *Hypatia* 9.3 (Summer 1994): 46–65.

Cannon, Katie. "Womanist Perspectival Discourse and Cannon Formation." *Journal of Feminist Studies in Religion* 5.2 (Fall 1989): 29–37.

Carby, Hazel. "The Multicultural Wars." *Black Popular Culture: A Project by Michelle Wallace*. Ed. Gina Dent. New York: New Press, 1998.

Carretta, Vincent, ed. *Unchained Voices: An Anthology of Black Authors in the English-Speaking World of the Eighteenth-Century*. Lexington: U of Kentucky P, 1996.

Child, Lydia Maria. "Gentleness, Patience, and Love." 1831. *Victorian Women: A Documentary Account of Women's Lives in Nineteenth-Century England, France, and the United States*. Ed. Erna Olafson Hellerstein, et al. Stanford: Stanford UP, 1981. 242–44.

Coan, Josephus R. "Redemption of Africa: The Vital Impulse of Black American Overseas Missionaries." *Journal of the Interdenominational Theological Center* 1 (Spring 1974): 27–37.

Cobb, Nancy F., et al., eds. *Root of Bitterness: Documents of the Social History of American Women*. 2nd ed. Boston: Northeastern UP, 1996.

Collier-Thomas, Bettye. *Daughters of Thunder: Black Women Preachers and Their Sermons, 1850–1979*. San Francisco: Jossey-Bass, 1998.

Collins, Patricia Hill. *Black Feminist Thought: Knowledge, Consciousness, and the Politics of Empowerment*. New York: Routledge, 1991.

Connor, Kimberly Rae. *Conversions and Visions in the Writings of African American Women*. Knoxville: U of Tennessee P, 1994.

Copeland, M. Shawn. "Wading through Many Sorrows: Toward a Theology of Suffering in Womanist Perspective." Townes 109–29.

Cornelius, Janet D. *When I Can Read My Title Clear: Literacy, Slavery, and Religion in the Antebellum South*. Columbia: U of South Carolina P, 1991.

Couser, G. Thomas. *Altered Egos: Authority in American Autobiography*. New York: Oxford UP, 1989.

———. "Autopathography: Women, Illness, and Lifewriting." *a/b: Auto/Biography Studies* 6.1 (Spring 1991): 65–75.

Croce, Ann J. "A Woman Outside of Her Time." *Women's Studies* 19: 357–69.

Davidson, Cathy N. *Revolution and the Word: The Rise of the Novel in America*. New York: Oxford UP, 1986.

De Jong, Mary. "Introduction: Protestantism and Its Discontents in the Eighteenth and Nineteenth Centuries." *Women's Studies* 19 (1991): 259–69.

Douglas, Ann. *The Feminization of American Culture*. New York: Knopf, 1977.

Douglass, Frederick. *Narrative of the Life of Frederick Douglass, An American Slave, Written by Himself*. 1845. *Frederick Douglass: The Narrative and Selected Writings*. Ed. Michael Meyer. New York: Modern Library, 1984. 3–127.

Doyle, Laura. "The Folk, the Nobles, and the Novel: The Racial Subtext of Sentimentality." *Narrative* 3.2 (May 1995): 161–87.

Elaw, Zilpha. *Memoirs of the Life, Religious Experience, Ministerial Travels and Labours of Mrs. Zilpha Elaw, An American Female of Colour*. 1846. Andrews, *Sisters* 49–160.

Ferguson, Moira. Introduction to the Revised Edition. *The History of Mary Prince, A*

West Indian Slave, Related by Herself. Ed. Ferguson. Ann Arbor: U of Michigan P, 1997. 1–51.

———. ed. *Nine Black Women: An Anthology of Nineteenth-Century Writers from the United States, Canada, Bermuda, and the Caribbean.* New York: Routledge, 1998.

Fischlin, Daniel. "'Sighes and Teares Make Life to Last': The Purgation of Grief and Death Through Trope in the English Ayre." *Criticism* 38.1 (Winter 1996): 1–25.

Fish, Cheryl. "Voices of Restless (Dis)continuity: The Significance of Travel for Free Black Women in the Antebellum Americas." *Women's Studies* 26 (1997): 475–95.

Fleischner, Jennifer. *Mastering Slavery: Memory, Family, and Identity in Women's Slave Narratives.* New York: New York UP, 1996.

Fluck, Winfried. "The Power and Failure of Representation in Harriet Beecher Stowe's *Uncle Tom's Cabin.*" *New Literary History* 23.2 (Spring 1992): 319–38.

Fontenot, Chester J. "Churches." Andrews, et al., *Oxford Companion* 143–47.

Foote, Julia A. J. *A Brand Plucked from the Fire: An Autobiographical Sketch.* 1879. Andrews, *Sisters* 161–234.

Foster, Frances Smith. "'In Respect to Females. . .': Differences in the Portrayals of Women by Male and Female Narrators." *Black American Literature Forum* 15.2 (Summer 1981): 6–70.

———. Introduction. *Minnie's Sacrifice, Sowing and Reaping, Trial and Triumph: Three Rediscovered Novels by Frances E. W. Harper.* Ed. Foster. Boston: Beacon, 1994. xi–xxxvii.

———. "Neither Auction Block nor Pedestal: 'The Life and Religious Experiences of Jarena Lee, a Coloured Lady.'" *The Female Autograph.* Ed. Domna C. Stanton. New York: New York Literary Forum, 1984. 143–69.

———. *Written by Herself: Literary Production by African American Women, 1746–1892.* Bloomington: Indiana UP, 1993.

Foster, Frances Smith, and Claudia May. "Class." Andrews, et al., *Oxford Companion* 153–56.

Frey, Sylvia, and Betty Wood. *Come Shouting to Zion: African American Protestantism in the American South and British Caribbean to 1830.* Chapel Hill: U of North Carolina P, 1998.

Friedman, Susan Stanford. "Women's Autobiographical Selves: Theory and Practice." *The Private Self: Theory and Practice in Women's Autobiographical Writings.* Ed. Shari Benstock. Chapel Hill: U of North Carolina P, 1988. 34–62.

Gates, Henry Louis, Jr. Introduction. *The Classic Slave Narratives.* Ed. Gates. New York: Penguin, 1987. ix–xviii.

———. *The Signifying Monkey: A Theory of African-American Literary Criticism.* New York: Oxford UP, 1988.

Giddings, Paula. "The Last Taboo." *Words of Fire: An Anthology of African-American Feminist Thought.* Ed. Beverly Guy-Sheftall. New York: New, 1995. 414–28.

————. *When and Where I Enter: The Impact of Black Women on Race and Sex in America.* Toronto: Bantam, 1985.

Gilbert, Sandra, and Susan Gubar. *The Madwoman in the Attic: The Woman Writer and the Nineteenth-Century Literary Imagination.* New Haven: Yale UP, 1979.

Gilkes, Cheryl T. "The Roles of Church and Community Mothers: Ambivalent Sexism or Fragmented African Familyhood?" *Journal of Feminist Studies in Religion* 2.1 (Spring 1986): 41–59.

Goodman, Paul. *Of One Blood: Abolitionism and the Origins of Racial Equality.* Berkeley: U of California P, 1998.

Graff, Harvey. *The Labyrinths of Literacy: Reflections on Literacy, Past and Present.* Pittsburgh: U of Pittsburgh P, 1995.

Grant, Jacquelyn. "The Sins of Servanthood and the Deliverance of Discipleship." Townes 199–218.

Grazel, Susan R. *Women's Identities at War: Gender, Motherhood, and Politics in Britain and France During the First World War.* Chapel Hill: U of North Carolina P, 1999.

Hammon, Briton. *Narrative of the Uncommon Sufferings, and Surprizing Deliverance of Briton Hammon, a Negro Man.* Boston: Green and Ruselle, 1760.

Hammonds, Evelynn. "Black (W)holes and the Geometry of Black Female Sexuality." *Differences* 6.2–3 (1994): 126–45.

Harding, Vincent. Foreword. *African American Christianity: Essays in History.* Ed. Paul E. Johnson. Berkeley: U of California P, 1994. vii–x.

Harris, Sharon M., ed. *American Women Writers to 1800.* New York: Oxford UP, 1996.

Harris, Trudier. "Churchwoman." Andrews, et al., *Oxford Companion* 147.

————. "Matriarch." Andrews, et al., *Oxford Companion* 484–85.

Hartman, Saidiya V. *Scenes of Subjection: Terror, Slavery, and Self-Making in Nineteenth-Century America.* New York: Oxford UP, 1997.

Henderson, Mae G. "Speaking in Tongues: Dialogism and the Black Woman Writer's Literary Tradition." *Changing Our Own Words: Essays on Criticism, Theory, and Writing by Black Women.* Ed. Cheryl Wall. New Brunswick, N.J.: Rutgers UP, 1989.

Hernton, Calvin C. *The Sexual Mountain and Black Women Writers: Adventures in Sex, Literature, and Real Life.* New York: Doubleday, 1987.

Hine, Darlene Clark. *Hine Sight: Black Women and the Re-Construction of American History.* New York: Carlson, 1994.

Hobbs, Catherine, ed. *Nineteenth-Century Women Learn to Write.* Charlottesville: U of Virginia P, 1995.

Hoganson, Nancy. *Fighting for American Manhood.* New Haven: Yale, 1998.

hooks, bell. *Black Looks: Race and Representation.* Boston: South End, 1992.

Houchins, Sue E., ed. *Spiritual Narratives.* New York: Oxford UP, 1988.

Howard-Pitney, David. *The Afro-American Jeremiad: Appeals for Justice in America.* Philadelphia: Temple UP, 1990.

Humez, Jean M. "'My Spirit Eye': Some Functions of Spiritual and Visionary Experience in the Lives of Five Black Women Preachers, 1810–1880." *Women and the Structure of Society: Selected Research from the Fifth Berkshire Conference on the History of Women.* Ed. Barbara J. Harris and JoAnn K. McNamara. Durham: Duke UP, 1984. 129–43.

Jackson, Rebecca Cox. *Gifts of Power: Rebecca Cox Jackson, Black Visionary, Shaker Eldress.* Ed. Jean M. Humez. Amherst: U of Massachusetts P, 1981.

Jacobs, Sylvia M., ed. *Black Americans and the Missionary Movement in Africa.* Westport, Conn.: Greenwood, 1982.

Johnson, Clifton, ed. *God Struck Me Dead: Voices of Ex-Slaves.* Cleveland: Pilgrim, 1993.

Jordan, June. *On Call: Political Essays.* Boston: South End, 1987.

Juster, Susan. *Disorderly Women: Sexual Politics and Evangelicalism in Revolutionary New England.* Ithaca, N.Y.: Cornell UP, 1994.

Kaplan, Sidney, and Emma Nogrady Kaplan. *The Black Presence in the Era of the American Revolution.* Rev. Ed. Amherst: U of Massachusetts P, 1989.

Kerber, Linda K. *No Constitutional Right to Be Ladies: Women and the Obligations of Citizenship.* New York: Hill and Wang, 1998.

———. *Toward an Intellectual History of Women: Essays.* Chapel Hill: U of North Carolina P, 1997.

Korobkin, Laura H. *Criminal Conversations: Sentimentalism and Nineteenth-Century Legal Stories of Adultery.* New York: Columbia, 1998.

Kupfer, Joseph. "The Sentimental Self." *Canadian Journal of Philosophy* 26.4 (December 1996): 543–60.

Landow, George P. *Elegant Jeremiahs: The Sage in Victorian and Modern Literature.* Ithaca: Cornell UP, 1986.

Lee, Jarena. *Religious Experience and Journal of Mrs. Jarena Lee, Giving an Account of Her Call to Preach the Gospel.* 1849. Houchins, 1–97.

Lerner, Gerda, ed. *Black Women in White America: A Documentary History.* New York: Vintage, 1973.

Lorde, Audre. *Sister Outsider: Essays and Speeches.* Trumansburg, N.Y.: Crossing, 1983.

Lyerly, Cynthia Lynn. "Religion, Gender, and Identity: Black Methodist Women in a Slave Society, 1770–1810." *Discovering the Women in Slavery: Emancipating Perspectives on the American Past.* Ed. Patricia Morton. Athens: U of Georgia P, 1996. 202–26.

Mancall, Peter C., ed. *Envisioning America: English Plans for the Colonization of North America, 1580–1640.* Boston: Bedford, 1995.

McCully, Susan. "Oh I Love Mother, I Love Her Power: Shaker Spirit Possession and the Performance of Desire." *Theatre Survey* 35.1 (May 1994): 88–98.

McKay, Nellie Y. "The Narrative Self: Race, Politics, and Culture in Black American Women's Autobiography." *Feminisms in the Academy.* Ed. Domna C. Stanton and Abigail J. Stewart. Ann Arbor: U of Michigan P, 1995. 74–100.

———. "Nineteenth-Century Black Women's Spiritual Autobiographies: Religious Faith and Self-Empowerment." *Interpreting Women's Lives: Feminist Theory and Personal Narratives.* Ed. The Personal Narratives Group. Bloomington: Indiana UP, 1989. 139–54.

Melton, J. Gordon, ed. *American Religious Creeds: An Essential Compendium of More than 450 Statements of Belief and Doctrine.* Vol. 1. New York: Triumph, 1991.

Metzger, Bruce M., and Roland E. Murphy. *The New Oxford Annotated Bible, with the Apocryphal/Deuterocanonical Books.* New York: Oxford UP, 1991.

Moody, Joycelyn K. "On the Road With God: Travel and Quest in Early Nineteenth-Century African American Holy Women's Narratives." *Religion and Literature* 27.1 (1995): 35–51.

———. Rev. of *Domestic Allegories of Political Desire: The Black Heroine's Text at the Turn of the Century* by Claudia Tate. *Modern Language Quarterly* 56.2 (June 1995): 241–45.

———. "Twice Other, Once Shy: Nineteenth-Century Black Women's Autobiographies and the American Literary Tradition of Self-Effacement." *a/b: Auto/Biography* (Spring 1992): 46–61.

Morrison, Toni. *Beloved.* New York: Knopf, 1994.

———. *The Bluest Eye.* New York: Washington Square, 1970.

Moses, Wilson J. *Black Messiahs and Uncle Toms: Social and Literary Manipulations of a Religious Myth.* University Park: Pennsylvania State UP, 1982.

Mullen, Harryette. "Runaway Tongue: Resistant Orality in *Uncle Tom's Cabin, Our Nig, Incidents in the Life of a Slave Girl,* and *Beloved.*" *The Culture of Sentiment: Race, Gender, and Sentimentality in Nineteenth-Century America.* Ed. Shirley Samuels. New York: Oxford UP, 1992. 244–64.

Olney, James. "'I Was Born': Slave Narratives, Their Status as Autobiography and as Literature." *The Slave's Narrative.* Ed. Charles T. Davis and Henry Louis Gates Jr. New York: Oxford UP, 148–75.

O'Neale, Sondra A. *Jupiter Hammon and the Biblical Beginnings of African-American Literature.* Metuchen, N.J.: American Theological Library Assoc. and Scarecrow, 1993.

Ostriker, Alicia. "A Word Made Flesh: The Bible and Revisionist Women's Poetry." *Reconstructing the Word: Spirituality in Women's Writing: A Special Issue of Religion and Literature* 23.3 (Autumn 1991): 9–26.

Pacinky, Diana L. *Cultural Orphans in America.* Jackson: U of Mississippi P, 1998.

Painter, Nell Irvin. "Representing Truth: Sojourner Truth's Knowing and Becoming Known." *Journal of American History* (Sept. 1994): 461–92.

Peterson, Carla L. *"Doers of the Word": African-American Speakers and Writers in the North (1830–1880).* New York: Oxford UP, 1995.

———. "'Doers of the Word': Theorizing African-American Women Writers in the Antebellum North." *The (Other) American Traditions: Nineteenth-Century Women Writers.* Ed. Joyce W. Warren. New Brunswick, N.J.: Rutgers UP, 1993. 183–202.

Posey, Thaddeus J., O. F. M., Cap. "Praying in the Shadows: The Oblate Sisters of

Providence, A Look at Nineteenth-Century Black Catholic Spirituality." *This Far by Faith: Readings in African-American Women's Religious Biography.* Ed. Judy Weisenfeld and Richard Newman. New York: Routledge, 1996.

Potkay, Adam, and Sandra Burr, eds. *Black Writers of the 18th Century: Living the New Exodus in England and the Americas.* New York: St. Martin's, 1995.

Prince, Mary. *The History of Mary Prince, a West Indian Slave.* 1831. Ed. Moira Ferguson. Ann Arbor: U of Michigan P, 1997.

Prince, Nancy. *A Narrative of the Life and Travels of Mrs. Nancy Prince, Written by Herself.* 2nd ed. 1853. *Collected Black Women's Narratives.* Ed. Anthony G. Barthelemy. New York: Oxford UP, 1998.

Raboteau, Albert. "African-Americans, Exodus, and the American Israel." *African American Christianity: Essays in History.* Ed. Paul E. Johnson. Berkeley: U of California P, 1994. 1–17.

———. *A Fire in the Bones: Reflections on African-American Religious History.* Boston: Beacon, 1995.

———. Introduction. *God Struck Me Dead: Voices of Ex-Slaves.* Ed. Clifton Johnson. Cleveland: Pilgrim, 1993. xix–xxv.

Rampersad, Arnold. "Biography, Autobiography, and Afro-American Culture." *Yale Review* 73.3 (Autumn 1993): 1–16.

Richardson, Marilyn, ed. *Maria W. Stewart, America's First Black Woman Political Writer: Essays and Speeches.* Bloomington: Indiana UP, 1987.

Romero, Lora. *Home Fronts: Domesticity and Its Critics in the Antebellum United States.* Durham, N.C.: Duke UP, 1997.

Ryals, Kay Ferguson. "America, Romance, and the Fate of the Wandering Woman: The Case of *Charlotte Temple.*" *Women, America, and Movement: Women's Narratives of Relocation.* Ed. Sharon Roberson. Columbia: U of Missouri P, 1998. 81–105.

Ryan, Judylyn S. "Spirituality and/as Ideology in Black Women's Literature: The Preaching of Maria W. Stewart and Baby Suggs, Holy." *Women Preachers and Prophets through Two Millenia of Christianity.* Ed. Beverly M. Kienzle and Pamela J. Walker. Berkeley: U of California P, 1998. 267–87.

Samuels, Shirley. *Romances of the Republic: Women, the Family, and Violence in the Literature of the Early American Nation.* New York: Oxford, 1996.

Sánchez-Eppler, Karen. "Bodily Bonds: The Intersecting Rhetorics of Feminism and Abolition." *The Culture of Sentiment: Race, Gender, and Sentimentality in Nineteenth-Century America.* Ed. Shirley Samuels. New York: Oxford UP, 1992. 92–114.

———. "Raising Empires like Children: Race, Nation, and Religious Education." *American Literary History* (1996): 399–425.

Sasson, Diane. *The Shaker Spiritual Narrative.* Knoxville: U of Tennessee P, 1983.

Schriber, Mary Suzanne, ed. *Telling Travels: Selected Writings by Nineteenth-Century American Women Abroad.* DeKalb: Northern Illinois UP, 1995.

Shange, Ntozake. *For colored girls who have considered suicide / when the rainbow is enuf: a choreopoem.* New York: Macmillan, 1977.

Sharpe, Jenny. "'Something Akin to Freedom': The Case of Mary Prince." *Differences: A Journal of Feminist Cultural Studies* 8.1 (1996): 31–56.

Shea, Daniel B., Jr. *Spiritual Autobiography in America*. 1968. Rpt. Madison: U of Wisconsin P, 1988.

Smith, Felipe. *American Body Politics: Race, Gender, and Black Literary Renaissance*. Athens: U of Georgia P, 1998.

Stepto, Robert. "Teaching Afro-American Literature: Survey or Tradition; or, The Reconstruction of Instruction." *Afro-American Literature: The Reconstruction of Instruction*. Ed. Dexter Fisher and Robert B. Stepto. New York: MLA, 1979. 8–24.

Sterling, Dorothy, ed. *We Are Your Sisters: Black Women in the Nineteenth Century*. New York: Norton, 1984.

Stern, Julia A. *The Plight of Feeling: Sympathy and Dissent in the Early American Novel*. Chicago: U of Chicago P, 1999.

Stevenson, Brenda. Introduction. *The Journals of Charlotte Forten Grimké*. Ed. Stevenson. New York: Oxford UP, 1988. 3–55.

Stewart, Maria W. *Productions of Mrs. Maria W. Stewart*. Houchins, 1–80.

Stowe, Harriet Beecher. "Children." *Uncle Sam's Emancipation; Earthly Care, A Heavenly Discipline; and Other Sketches*. Philadelphia: Willis P. Hazard, 1853. 79–83.

Tate, Claudia. *Domestic Allegories of Political Desire: The Black Heroine's Text at the Turn of the Century*. New York: Oxford UP, 1992.

Thompson, Dr. L. S. *The Story of Mattie J. Jackson*. 1866. Andrews, *Six Women's Slave Narratives*.

Tompkins, Jane. *Sensational Designs: The Cultural Work of American Fiction*. New York: Oxford, 1985.

———. "Susanna Rowson, Father of the American Novel." *The (Other) American Traditions: Nineteenth-Century Women Writers*. Ed. Joyce W. Warren. New Brunswick, N.J.: Rutgers UP, 1993. 29–38.

Torgovnick, Marianna. *Primitive Passions: Men, Women, and the Quest for Ecstasy*. Chicago: U of Chicago P, 1998.

Townes, Emilie M., ed. *A Troubling in My Soul: Womanist Perspectives on Evil and Suffering*. Maryknoll, N.Y.: Orbis, 1993.

Updike, John. "Cullen Murphy's 'The World According to Eve.'" *The New Yorker* 74.27 (Sept. 14, 1998): 93–97.

Wade-Gayles, Gloria. Introduction. *My Soul Is a Witness: African American Women's Spirituality*. Ed. Wade-Gayles. Boston: Beacon, 1996. 1–8.

Wald, Priscilla. *Constituting Americans: Cultural Anxiety and Narrative Form*. Durham, N.C.: Duke UP, 1995.

Walker, Alice. *In Search of Our Mothers' Gardens*. New York: Harcourt, 1983.

Walker, Clarence E. *A Rock in a Weary Land: The African Methodist Episcopal Church During the Civil War and Reconstruction*. Baton Rouge: Louisiana State UP, 1982.

Watson, Julia, and Sidonie Smith. "De/Colonization and the Politics of Discourse in Women's Autobiographical Practices." Ed. Smith and Watson, xiii–xxxi.

White, Deborah Gray. *Ar'n't I a Woman? Female Slaves in the Plantation South.* New York: Norton, 1985.

White, E. Frances. "Africa on My Mind: Gender, Counter Discourse and African American Nationalism." *Words of Fire: An Anthology of African-American Feminist Thought.* Ed. Beverly Guy-Sheftall. New York: New, 1995. 503–24.

White, Isabelle. "Sentimentality and the Uses of Death." *The Stowe Debate: Rhetorical Strategies in Uncle Tom's Cabin.* Ed. Mason I. Lowance, Jr., et al. Amherst: U of Massachusetts P, 1994. 99–115.

Williams, Delores S. *Sisters in the Wilderness: The Challenge of Womanist God-Talk.* Maryknoll, N.Y.: Orbis, 1993.

———. "Women's Oppression and Lifeline Politics in Black Women's Religious Narratives." *Journal of Feminist Studies in Religion* 1.2 (Fall 1985): 59–71.

INDEX